Make Your Mark!

Make Your Mark!

INFLUENCING ACROSS YOUR
ORGANIZATION

Sue Craig

THE McGRAW-HILL COMPANIES

London · New York · St Louis · San Francisco · Auckland
Bogotá · Caracas · Lisbon · Madrid · Mexico · Milan
Montreal · New Delhi · Panama · Paris · San Juan
São Paulo · Singapore · Sydney · Tokyo · Toronto

Published by
McGRAW-HILL Publishing Company Europe
Shoppenhangers Road, Maidenhead, Berkshire, SL6 2QL, England
Telephone 01628 23432
Facsimile 01628 770224

British Library Cataloguing in Publication Data

The CIP data for this book has been applied for and may be obtained from the British
Library, London.

Library of Congress Cataloging-in-Publication Data

The LOC data for this book has been applied for and may be obtained from the Library
of Congress, Washington, D.C.

ISBN   0 07 709159 0

2345 CUP 21098

McGraw-Hill

A Division of The McGraw-Hill Companies

Typeset by Mackreth Media Services, Hemel Hempstead

Printed and bound in Great Britain at the University Press, Cambridge

Contents

Acknowledgements

The following people were kind enough to help me with ideas, stories and/or interview contacts. I am very grateful to all of them.

John Stubbs contributed to and reviewed Part II at a time when he was himself very busy. I have learned a lot from him about achieving results in large organizations. Other managers and consultants from Shell who were generous with their time are Margaret Neal, David Black, Terry Haskins, Gary Steel, Mac MacDonald, Andy Johns, Charles Gent and Pieter Kapteijn. Thanks also to Hans Janssen, Janny Spilsbury, Rick van Motman and the other course participants who shared their experiences.

Gerry Buckley and Michael Staunton from Management Centre Europe reviewed and contributed to Chapter 9. Gerry also introduced me to other experienced influencers who were very helpful, including Roger Rémy, Tony Taylor, Ruth Ann Lake and Chris Parker. Win Nyström shared much of his networking experience with me. Thanks also to Kim Lafferty, and to Jacek Beldowski, Janis Blum, Ivan Ševčík and Lev Yelin.

My clients and colleagues from Logica supplied a large number of stories and ideas, especially Johan Tasche, Jim McKenna, Trisha Robinson, Mario Anid, Sa'ad Al-Hilli, Iain Fisher, Donald MacRae, Tom de Neef, Klaas van der Poel, Wim Kardux and Herma Volwater. I am also very grateful to Dr Martin Read for introducing me to Joseph de Feo of Barclays Bank, who made time to share his thoughts on managing change and in turn put me in touch with Kathryn Vagneur of the London Business School.

The Erasmus University, Rotterdam has also been a source of inspiration. I am grateful to Ria Visser, Dr Rinus van Schendelen, his colleague Roger Pedler of the European Centre for Public Affairs, and to Ronald Morcus and Roosmarie Aelmans.

Friends and colleagues Jenny Gent, Hank Williams, Gill Cottray, David and Eva Coleman, Patrick Lybaert, Margaret and Clive Purrett and Peter Callender have all helped with ideas and also introductions to John Haigh, Rachel Spooncer, Bernard Midgley, Peter Argent, Judy Moody-Stuart, Jennie Hawks, and Alan Jelly and his team, all of whom have given me valuable material.

Judy Larkin, Roger Hayes of the British Nuclear Industry Forum and Paul Reeves all contributed to the networking chapter. Peter van Zunderd and Aad van Rijswijk made time to share their experiences of influencing in the public sector. David Cormack was generous as always with his time and his material.

Sylvia Tóth of Content NV, Hadi Jassim of the Dutch PTT and Umberto Quilici of Data Management all gave me important insights into organizational cultures. Thanks also to Julia Scott and Victoria Baker of McGraw-Hill for their suggestions and friendly encouragement, and to Paul Sitkowski for his constructive criticism.

Finally, thanks as always to my very supportive family, Duncan, James and Katherine.

Introduction

The purpose of this book

This is a book about organizational influencing, for managers and consultants working in the private and public sectors. If you are in the kind of job, at any level, where you have to get active support from a number of people in order to achieve results, and where you cannot always use the power of the line to do so, then this book is for you. You can read here about:

- How to plan an effective influencing strategy
- How to navigate the maze of organizational politics (without becoming a 'politician' in the negative sense)
- How to build support for your ideas through coalitions
- How to set up a professional network of contacts who can give you information and advice (and whom you will help in return)
- How to deal constructively with resistance from your staff and your colleagues
- How to set up co-operative relationships with your key stakeholders
- How to lead a team through periods of change.

If you are a middle manager or a technical specialist trying to get agreement for a proposal from senior management, or trying to get staff and colleagues to implement your ideas, you will find guidelines in this book to help you. If you are an internal or external consultant, having to manage the politics of the organization in addition to your client relationships, you will find suggestions contributed by professionals who have dealt successfully with problems which may be similar to yours. If you are a senior manager wanting to get active support for a strategic change from your team and your organization, I hope you will be able to recognize some of your challenges in the cases contributed by senior staff, together with models and guidelines to make your task easier.

All these guidelines and techniques are intended to make your work more rewarding, and to reduce some of the stress and frustration of organizational life.

Influencing is a complex process

Influencing is often more complex than managers realize. Kathryn Vagneur of the London Business School points out that influencing is a process, not an event—you cannot just 'influence someone' in a five-minute encounter and think your task is finished. She likens a good influencer to a master mechanic. The master mechanic understands the interactions between the components of an engine, and knows that making even a minor intervention can have far-reaching consequences elsewhere in the system. Consequently the master mechanic monitors the performance of the machine as a whole. Similarly, in coalition-building a chance remark to a senior manager in a corridor can have consequences—good or bad—which you may not have anticipated. Experience enables you to seize opportunities, as well as anticipate risks. You have to manage a large and complex system over a period of time, and you are dependent on the actions of others, just as the master mechanic is on the skill and performance of the driver. You cannot control everything, but you can systematically influence the majority of outcomes.

How this book can help you

The guidelines and techniques in this book are based largely on advice from the 'master mechanics' of effective influencing, the practitioners and the researchers who have studied the subject in depth. I consulted the literature, added my own experiences of working for a broad range of organizations and interviewed over 60 managers and consultants who had a reputation for achieving results. Their recommendations highlight the priority areas for planning your own influencing case. I hope you will also find it useful to hear how some of them have learned from their mistakes. If they can point out the pitfalls for us, we may be able to avoid some of the same painful errors. Because many of the stories in this book are inevitably sensitive, I have changed the names and some of the details in the cases, except where contributors have been acknowledged in full.

I have aimed throughout the book to give general principles and guidelines, backed up with a wide range of options. The idea is for you to select the techniques which will fit best with your own personality. You will also need to adjust your approach according to the national and corporate culture in which you are working, and I have given examples of the kinds of variations in influencing style that you can expect to find in different countries and organizations. You will find cases throughout the book to illustrate the choices open to you.

The interpersonal side of influencing is not described in detail in this book, because it has been covered by other authors. You will find reminders, however, of interpersonal and communication skills throughout the text. I am assuming that you have already studied interpersonal skills and are now interested in addressing the organizational aspects of influencing.

The increasing need for good influencing skills

A number of changes in the working environment have resulted in an increased need for good influencing skills. You may recognize some of them in your own organization.

The need to take more responsibility

Staff in many organizations are being urged to take active responsibility for processes from start to finish, rather than working with the old 'departmental mentality' that 'I do my part, you do yours, and if anything goes wrong we blame each other'. The transition from the 'departmental mentality' is not an easy one for people to make. It can feel as if your responsibilities have increased way out of line with your salary and your power base. People are suddenly confronted with the requirement to influence their colleagues in a different unit, without the backing of any line authority. It is a whole new set of skills.

The need to 'do more with less'

Increased competition in the marketplace and reduced budgets for overhead costs have meant that many managers are having to achieve better results with fewer resources. Since one of the most flexible resources in any organization is the people, this has resulted in increasing demands on managers' delegation and motivation capabilities. Organizational influencing skills include the ability to work with resistance and to build high-performing teams in the context of continuous change and uncertainty. Busy managers often have to meet these demands with a larger number of reports, and sometimes with staff who may be scattered over different locations. You need an excellent understanding of the influencing process in order to get results in these circumstances.

Having to make do with what you have

Not all organizations are changing so dramatically. Many of the managers I meet come from large, stable organizations, such as banks, and government ministries. They may be working in countries such as

Italy, where it is virtually impossible to get rid of staff. It is not so much the constant change that is the problem for them—more the problems of working in rigid hierarchies, with a boss who could be there until he or she retires. They have to make the most of what they have, and that requires good influencing skills as well as patience and pragmatism.

Changes in organizational structures and the power of the line

The trend towards flatter organizations has altered the ways in which people function in the line. The old direction of communication was strictly 'top-down'. When people in different departments wanted to communicate, they had to go up their own line, across at the top to the other department, and down the line to their 'opposite number'—with all the accompanying inefficiencies and delays. Since the advent of matrices and flatter structures, staff have been encouraged to work laterally, building relationships across departments as well as up and down the line.

Diagonal lines of communication are also becoming more common, so that some managers now talk directly to the staff reporting to their peers, for instance. Diagonal lines only work effectively if the managers trust each other, and are confident that their colleagues will not misuse these relationships in any way.

Some managers welcome these changes because of the increased speed of response and efficiency which can result. Others perceive lateral and diagonal communication as a threat to their territory. Many organizations have mixtures of styles of communication, depending on the preferences of the individual managers. You have to understand the preferences and manage the increasing number of work contacts with the necessary tact and diplomacy—not an easy task. Good networking and stakeholder management are essential.

All these trends have made work more interesting, but also more demanding. A knowledge of organizational influencing can help you to manage these challenges with more confidence and more success.

A word on ethics and influencing

Some readers may be concerned about the ethics of influencing. The people I interviewed stressed that effective influencing is based on trust, honesty and integrity, combined with a good dose of realism. I hope the techniques recommended in this book reflect that view. They are, however, like any set of tools, and can be used for good purposes or bad, depending on the intentions of the person using them. My aim is to help those people in organizations who work conscientiously and ethically to achieve their goals in line with their principles.

The structure of the book

Part I of the book describes the different approaches and strategies you can choose when you want to influence a person or a group of people. At the end of Part I there is a questionnaire to help you assess your own influencing style and the skills which you would like to develop. Part II explores the key influencing skills and strategies in more depth, in the fields of coalition building, networking and working with resistance. You will find models, examples and guidelines to help you cope with a wide range of situations. Part III describes specific cases where you need to apply your influencing skills, with key individuals and with leading groups. It includes examples of advanced influencing approaches, to show how you can deal with more difficult challenges.

Note

One famous influencer who has become notorious as a manipulator is Niccolò Macchiavelli, whose slim volume *The Prince*, Oxford University Press, World Classics, 1984 is still worth reading today. In between the more bloodcurdling recommendations there is a lot of sound, non-manipulative advice.

Part I
CHOOSING YOUR STRATEGY

2 Your basic choice: a participative (BUILD) or a directive (PUSH) strategy

Choosing a strategy

If you ask managers which influencing strategies they use, they will often look quite puzzled at first, because they are not used to thinking about influencing quite so formally. In reality, of course, most will be using a wider range of strategies and techniques than they realize. The purpose of this chapter is to help you become more aware of the choices you make when you set out to sell an idea. Here is an example of a situation where you would have to choose which influencing strategy to take.

CASE STUDY 2.1   HOW WILL YOU 'SELL' THE NEW PROCEDURE?

Suppose you have designed a new procedure which will make one of the key processes for your organization run more smoothly. You work in the head office of your organization. Your manager is enthusiastic about your idea, so he suggests you should now sell it to the other affiliate organizations. If you could persuade all the affiliates to move over to using your idea, you would also be able to collate information which would be very useful for head office.

You call a suitable contact in one of your affiliates located in Paris. You have not met him before. He agrees to schedule a meeting for you with himself and some of his staff in two weeks' time, but he stresses that he is very busy, so you will only have 40 minutes for the meeting. Your contact has considerable influence in his affiliate, so you are pleased to have made this appointment.

How will you use the 40 minutes? How will you prepare for the meeting?

Here are two possible ways to handle the situation, selected by two managers with very different influencing styles.

CARLA CHOOSES THE DIRECTIVE, *PUSH* APPROACH

Carla decides that a clear, professional presentation would be the best way to use the 40 minutes. She plans for the meeting by having some top-quality overhead slides produced, and by checking that the benefits of the new system are explicit. She is a lively presenter, but she practises her talk anyway with her team to ensure she is really well prepared.

Carla arrives in Paris in time to check the conference room where the meeting will be held. She introduces herself briskly to her Paris colleagues at the start of the meeting, then gets straight down to work with her presentation, which is planned to last for 25 minutes. She gives an overview of the need for the change, the way the new procedure will operate, and a time scale for implementing the change. When one of the Paris colleagues raises a minor objection, she answers him clearly and confidently, then asks for further questions to be held until the end of her presentation, so that she can complete her story. There is still time for a few questions before the meeting is ended. She leaves the meeting feeling pleased that she has been able to cover so much material in such a short time.

JAMES CHOOSES A PARTICIPATIVE, *BUILD* STRATEGY

James thinks that he should use the short time frame primarily to get to know the Paris colleagues and to have an idea of their needs and their operation. He prepares for the meeting by asking around about the business performance of the French affiliate, and about the personalities of the people whom he will be meeting. He tries to talk on the phone to the people who will be coming, but when he cannot get hold of them he chats to some of their junior staff instead and gets up to date with the gossip.

In the meeting he starts by asking the Paris managers about the procedures they are currently using, and whether they are satisfied with their current system. After about 15 minutes, he explains why he thinks a change in the procedures might be helpful to them, and checks if they agree. He uses the last ten minutes to run through the key points from his proposal. As he is walking down the corridor with the manager who organized the meeting, James agrees to send him a draft of his new proposal, with some revisions based on the discussion in the meeting. He leaves the meeting feeling pleased that he has been able to get a feel for the Paris operation in such a short time.

Which approach do you think would be more successful? Who makes more progress in the 40 minutes? The answer depends, of course, on the circumstances surrounding the situation. Either approach could work very well, but either could be a complete disaster. We will look first in more detail at the characteristics of the two strategies.

Characteristics of the two strategies

The two basic strategies are represented in Fig. 2.1 as two ends of a continuum. At one end is the BUILD approach, used by James. At the other end is the PUSH strategy, used by Carla. You can choose a starting point at any point along the continuum, as you will see from

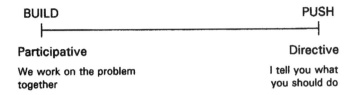

Fig. 2.1 The range of influencing strategies (based on Tannenbaum and Schmidt)

later cases. First, however, it is helpful to understand the key differences between the two extremes.

Carla's directive PUSH strategy is based on:

- More talking than listening
- Emphasis on rational arguments—facts, not feelings
- The influencer works primarily alone
- The focus is on quick results.

The aim is to get the other parties to follow a specific course of action—fast. James's participative BUILD strategy is based on:

- Listening and asking, then some talking
- Emphasis on understanding needs and getting to know the people
- The influencer works together with others, using networks and coalitions
- The focus is on long-term co-operation.

The aim is to get the commitment of all the parties involved to implement a jointly decided outcome.

How should you choose your strategy?

Most people choose the strategy which fits best with their personality. For some the directive PUSH style is virtually the only influencing approach they ever use. For others the BUILD approach will be much more natural. There are also many variations and combinations of the two basic strategies. The principle behind effective influencing is to choose the approach which is most appropriate for the context you are working in—what one senior manager called 'situational influencing'. We will explore the concept of situational influencing in the chapters that follow, but here is a brief overview of the benefits and pitfalls of each strategy and the main criteria for choosing one approach or the other.

Criteria for choosing a directive, PUSH strategy

- *The problem must be acknowledged and defined—and the definition must be agreed* by the people you are trying to influence. For Carla to be successful with her approach, the colleagues in Paris must recognize the need for a change in procedures before she gives her presentation, and their problem definition must match hers.
- *You must have high personal credibility.* Ideally there would be an obvious match between the problem definition and your reputation for solving this kind of problem. If Carla has a reputation in Paris for designing and implementing new procedures, then the colleagues in France will take her suggestions seriously. They will not want to be consulted: they will simply want to hear her advice as to what they should do. Credibility also depends on other factors, including your power base, and you can read more on this in the next chapter.
- *You must be working in an emotionally neutral environment.* Your proposal ideally should not threaten the job, status or territory of the people you are trying to influence. A directive approach works best in a context where people are not worried about any negative implications for their own jobs. Centralized change tends to trigger resistance, so Carla could encounter problems, depending on how much the Paris staff feel they need to change their way of working.
- *Your approach must fit in with the expectations of the culture in which you are working.* This is becoming increasingly important for staff who work internationally, or who work in different organizations where the corporate culture varies. The rule is 'if in doubt, ask a local colleague'. Carla's formal approach could be just right in large institutions in southern Europe, for instance, but colleagues in flatter, customer-driven businesses in, say, Holland or Denmark may not take so kindly to being told what to do. Her long (25-minute) presentation is risky in any culture—you need a lot of personal credibility to carry that off successfully. The French colleagues might well appreciate her clarity and her confidence, but she could be making heavy demands on their patience by asking them to keep their questions to the end. Cultural flexibility is essential for good influencing.

The benefits of the directive approach

The directive (PUSH) strategy represents the high-profile side of influencing. If you get the 'fit' right, the PUSH approach really will get fast results and your authority will be enhanced. The ability to present a clear, convincing and coherent case in presentations and meetings is essential for anyone who wants to work effectively in or with organizations. The large number of presentation skills courses and books available on the market reflects the demand for mastery of the directive approach, though increasingly staff start by learning PUSH approaches then progress to developing their BUILD skills as they move further in their careers. PUSH strategies include reports and written proposals, because these are also one-way forms of communication where the writer assumes the authority to express his or her views.

Directive strategies, used appropriately, can be immensely rewarding. You are in full control, your authority is recognized, and your proposals are listened to attentively. Many people will describe a 'buzz' during a good presentation. The audience is alert, the debate may be lively but your extra adrenaline enables you to think fast. For the audience, the experience is stimulating, and they are so busy working on the details of your proposal that they are entirely unaware of the strategy you have skilfully chosen.

The pitfalls of using the directive approach inappropriately

Unfortunately, for every successful presentation there are far more that go wrong. You will see some examples in the following chapters. The problem with PUSH strategies is that it is not enough to walk onto the stage: the audience has to be willing to let you take the floor.

One-way communication entails risks. The audience can switch off, the reader can file your carefully worded report in the bin, and your colleagues' polite silence in that meeting could mean resistance, not support for your proposal.

Inappropriate use of directive strategies can cause others to resent you. PUSH can be a self-centred strategy, and a failure to listen means a failure to pick up clues. If you are chairing a meeting very directively and talking a lot, the other members could be trying to send you signals that they are tired, confused or bored. If you continue to talk, they will give up listening to you. Your influence will fade much faster than their memory of the bad meeting.

What are Carla's chances of success?

So how would Carla get on? If she is a recognized expert, and if procedures are not too controversial, she might indeed have used her time wisely, and she may impress her new colleagues very favourably.

She cannot afford to be too complacent, however, because she will need to invest a lot of time in follow-up work to ensure that her idea really gets implemented.

If the Paris staff do not recognize Carla's expertise, or if they do not like the idea of head office telling them how to run their business, then Carla's prospects are much less favourable. She is unlikely to be invited back, her reputation personally will suffer and her new procedures will be ignored. The short time for discussion at the end of the meeting means that she has had little immediate feedback. The negative consequences of choosing an inappropriate PUSH may become apparent only in the longer term.

Criteria for choosing the participative, BUILD strategy

Let us think now about James's approach. He has invested his effort quite differently, and he has focused more on the relationships than on selling the product. Is this a 'weak' approach, a waste of time in comparison with Carla's more dynamic attack? Again it depends on the context. The BUILD approach is a more appropriate choice if you want to get results in the following circumstances:

- *BUILD is better if the problem you are tackling is complex,* and if the people you are influencing interpret the problem in different ways. This is a situation which is becoming increasingly common, as the complexity of organizations increases. The well-defined problems tend to be more strictly technical, rather than organizational. With organizational problems, you need more time to agree what the problem is before you try to solve it. If, like James, you consult a number of different people, rather than trying to solve the problem on your own, you may get a better perspective on the problem and a better long-term solution. In James's case, the different affiliate companies may have different local needs which could also affect the choice of procedures.
- *Your credibility may not be high.* A number of factors may cause you to be working with lower credibility than you would normally have. Perhaps the people you are influencing do not know you, as was the case in our example, and you have not yet had the time to prove your worth. Or you may have been asked to take on responsibilities which were not in your original area of expertise, so you cannot (yet) establish a reputation as an expert. With job rotation, you may have posts during your career where you have to build new relationships and develop new skills and knowledge at

the same time. Wherever you work, there are bound to be situations where you may have a good idea, but you do not have high credibility. Your personal credibility will also be affected by the part of the organization you represent. Head office staff like Carla and James tend to have a hard time selling ideas outside their home base. Your credibility may also depend on how well you demonstrate an understanding of local problems. The staff in the Paris affiliate may feel that their needs are quite different from those of staff in other parts of the organization, and if you do not recognize those differences no-one will listen to your presentation or read your report. When your credibility is not high, you have to use the BUILD approach and move slowly and steadily.

- *People may be worried about the implications of a change—you could be dealing with emotional resistance.* Working with resistance is one of the most difficult aspects of influencing. If the managers in Carla's audience are anxious about the implications of her proposals, they will not be swayed by rational arguments, carefully collated facts or her smart overhead slides. Trying to impress an audience with logic will just make the resistance worse. If staff are feeling worried or suspicious about a change, they will feel more reassured if they can contribute their own ideas, and a patient BUILD approach will give you time to survey the situation. By taking a gentler pace at the start of the meeting, James may be able to pick up signs of trouble at an early stage, giving himself space to choose his next step with care.

- *BUILD is best if you want high commitment to a course of action*—especially if your proposal has an important impact on the people you are influencing. Key decisions deserve the BUILD treatment. Even senior managers with high credibility will use a BUILD approach to check that their teams really support a way forward, as you will see in later stories. Coalitions, described in depth in Chapter 6, are a very effective way of testing and refining proposals in order to ensure a high level of commitment from all the key players who need to implement them. If James suspects that his Paris colleagues will be sceptical about his new procedures, the best way of getting their full support is to involve them in the process from the start. Carla runs the risk that they may agree on the surface to her suggestions, but ignore them as soon as her back is turned and she has returned home.

The benefits of the participative BUILD strategy

The BUILD approach requires patience, but brings with it a number of long-term benefits for you and your organization. By working together on a problem you may come up with a solution which is not only more appropriate but also better quality than the one you had first identified.

Collaborative working also fosters strategic networking, both inside and outside your organization. Your network is an investment which can help you to solve subsequent problems, by providing you with access to resources, information and ideas. Networking will also enable you to manage risks, solve conflicts, build business and extend your power base.

Decisions that have been made with the participative approach are nearly always easier to implement. Few staff like to have decisions imposed on them. The BUILD approach results in much higher commitment, better motivation and a pool of goodwill which you will be able to use for subsequent projects.

The BUILD approach brings you personal rewards. Although you will not get the instant recognition which a successful 'push' style presentation can bring, over the long term you can establish trust, build your credibility and earn a reputation for solving the more challenging problems associated with your role. Ironically, the more you use the BUILD approach successfully, the more power you gain to use a PUSH approach effectively as well.

The pitfalls of using BUILD inappropriately

The BUILD approach requires a much bigger investment of energy and effort. Situations requiring the BUILD approach tend to be complex, and if you make a mistake you may lose control of the influencing process and waste a great deal of time. You can also waste the time of a lot of other people. A related problem is that some managers will use participative strategies not just for key decisions but also for less important ones, and these managers can appear indecisive as a result. Excessive BUILD can lead to a culture where consultation serves as a way of avoiding individual accountability.

Some managers and consultants fail to recognize that their credibility is actually quite high, and that a directive PUSH approach would be more appropriate. This can cause frustration in the people they are trying to influence, as in the following case.

CASE STUDY 2.2   INAPPROPRIATE USE OF *BUILD*—
THE CONSULTANT WHO WOULD NOT GIVE ADVICE
'We asked a consultant to help us develop new business in Eastern Europe. The man we had chosen came highly recommended and had years of experience. At the time we hired him, we knew very little about East European culture. We wanted to get going quickly on a marketing strategy, and we were really

looking forward to his first set of recommendations. I was very disappointed when a large, unstructured report landed on my desk. It was full of information, but had no clear advice. The consultant was obviously nervous about giving us direction. He said he wanted to talk the situation through with us, but I was rushed off my feet. I didn't want to be consulted—I wanted him to show me what to do!'

Over-use of BUILD irritates people and lowers your personal credibility.

The major challenge with the BUILD approach is the amount of skill, flexibility and perseverance that it requires. You need to be good at working with others, and at the same time you need to keep your eye fixed on the goal ahead. It is not an easy combination. You also have to be generous about recognition, as Gary Steel of Shell describes. One of his aims is to encourage progress towards collaboration and providing service for internal customers, and he says "It's about the power and the glory. If we want to increase our power to influence, we have to let our customers have the glory." That takes some getting used to, although in the long run, as you achieve successes, you will get more glory too.

How would James get on with his BUILD approach?

James has made a good start with collecting information and getting to know the staff in the Paris affiliate, so he has avoided the pitfall of antagonizing his new colleagues. His next step should be to demonstrate his added value, otherwise he could be dismissed as 'friendly, but ineffectual'. He could build his credibility by tailoring the new procedures to the needs of the Paris office, by working closely with a few of their staff to design an appropriate solution, and perhaps by identifying other problems in Paris where he can offer practical help.

The different approaches used by James and Carla both entail risks. Carla has proposed a clear solution, but her directive approach means that her solution could be rejected or sabotaged. James has established a good relationship with the Paris colleagues, but if he fails to follow through and implement the change then he will not be taken seriously and his preparatory work will be a waste of time. Managers who use the BUILD approach must deliver results, and they often need to combine their interpersonal skills with sound management to gain respect inside and outside their organization. We can sum up the different strategies in Fig. 2.2.

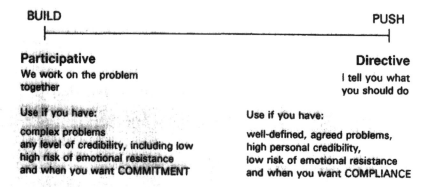

Fig. 2.2   Using the range of influencing strategies (adapted from Fiedler and Vroom)

If in doubt, lobby!

Figure 2.2 shows the two extremes of the strategies. Real life is more subtle. The critical point in choosing a strategy is often where to begin. A useful rule of thumb is 'If in doubt, lobby' (Fig. 2.3). Try your idea on someone whom you trust, to get an early view of the level of acceptability. If your ally thinks your idea has a high chance of succeeding, you can move towards the PUSH end of the continuum and start proposing it. If your ally hesitates, and raises objections, then take the hint and move back towards the BUILD end, to explore the resistance and redesign your proposal with the help of your colleagues.

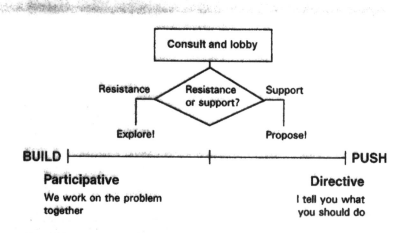

Fig. 2.3   If in doubt, consult and lobby!

Combining the approaches for optimum results

Influencing is a dynamic process, and most managers use combinations of the two approaches, adjusted to match their style and situation. Often you will notice that your choice of strategy also varies over time. When you start in a new job and your credibility is low, you may decide to use a BUILD approach to give you time to establish a power base. Once your track record is known, you may be able to save time and use a PUSH approach very effectively to get fast results.

There are a lot of examples of combined approaches throughout this book, but here is the story of a senior civil servant who learned to adjust his style to the situation, and who used a combination of influencing strategies to excellent effect.

CASE STUDY 2.3   THE SENIOR CIVIL SERVANT—
USING A COMBINATION OF STRATEGIES

'Some years ago I took over a new department which required some major reorganization. I'd always seen myself as a democratic manager, so I started by consulting my staff to find out their views. I set up a working party, and arranged to hear their findings in a large meeting. Unfortunately I didn't structure my consultative approach adequately, so the meeting turned out to be a disaster. The staff were critical and unconstructive—I felt I was receiving all the blame for decisions which had been made long before I arrived. And their proposals were simply unrealistic, so I couldn't accept most of them. I went ahead and made my own changes, to the resentment of some of the more vocal members of the staff. They said behind my back that my consultation exercise was nothing more than play acting, so that didn't do my reputation any good.

Getting it right
This year, in my new job, I've tackled the consultation exercise quite differently. Again, I had to reorganize the department—this time we were merging two departments into one. The level of confusion and demotivation was high. I chose the co-ordinator for the working party, very carefully—she is an experienced manager, respected by her colleagues and by senior staff. I made it quite clear to her that the suggestions from the working party should be constructive and practical, and that she should exercise her judgement in deciding which proposals to work through in detail. I also told her that I would make my own decision about which suggestions to adopt. Beyond that, she was free to manage the process as she wanted.

The meeting—making the ground rules clear
A month later, the co-ordinator showed me a draft of the report. I was impressed. There were a few points which I disagreed with, but there were also some excellent ideas. Again the results from the working party were presented and discussed in a large meeting, but this time I managed it differently. I stated at

the start that I appreciated the efforts of the working party, and would take their suggestions very seriously. I also said that I would make my own decisions, and would tell them immediately if there were suggestions which I intended to reject. We would start to implement the successful suggestions within the next month, and my management team would keep them all informed about progress.

We had a lively, open discussion, and have now implemented two thirds of the initial suggestions. The working party is still operating, although in a reduced form, and the morale inside the department is steadily improving. I was very pleased with the outcome—and so were the staff.'

Learning points

- *Think through the process.* Try to anticipate the main risks—such as what you will do if you cannot accept most of the suggestions raised by your staff. Identify other measures to help you manage the risks, such as choosing someone to head up the working party who is trusted both by you and by your staff.
- *Make your constraints and boundary conditions clear.* Failure to provide an adequate structure is a common weakness of managers who tend to over-use BUILD strategies, and it can cause a lot of frustration. BUILD approaches are not a 'free for all'—your staff will expect to be working within limits.
- *Be prepared to learn from your mistakes.* This senior official was able to recognize and acknowledge the weaknesses in his previous approach, and adjusted his strategy.

Developing your influencing skills

Most of us would find it difficult to be completely flexible and to use any approach along the continuum with equal skill and ease. You will always retain a personal bias. In many cases this will not matter—after all, your own corporate culture will also have a large effect on the influencing strategy you use. There are organizations which expect more of a directive approach and there are those that prefer a more participative approach, and you will be expected, on the whole, to fit in with your organizational norms. As long as you have chosen your job in such a way that the culture fits your personality, a modest broadening of your skills should be enough to improve your chances of success.

Sometimes your job changes, and suddenly you have to become more flexible. You may be placed in some kind of liaison role, where you need to work with outside parties, or you may be given a posting to another culture, with dramatically different expectations. Here is an example from a Dutch manager.

CASE STUDY 2.4 'WHAT I LEARNED FROM WORKING WITH THE JAPANESE'

'My influencing style had always been very directive—the Dutch have a reputation for saying what they think. When I moved to a company run by Japanese managers I was very puzzled at first by the way they made decisions. Instead of the noisy debates I was used to, they lobbied quietly in the evenings after the formal working day was ended. This process seemed to me very lengthy—often it would take two weeks before a simple decision was agreed. However, once they had all decided to support a course of action, there were no more problems or arguments in the implementation stage. It often saves time in the end. I'm still not absolutely comfortable with this process, to be honest—but I can see it works for them, so I've adjusted.'

The manager above was able to extend his natural skills with just a few BUILD techniques when he could see that they were really needed. We will be focusing mainly on the techniques associated with the BUILD strategies in this book, because they require a lot of thought and skill in order to be effective.

Summary of choosing a strategy

By selecting your influencing strategy carefully you can increase significantly your chances of success. Think of influencing strategies as *a range of options* open to you:

- *Directive (PUSH) strategies—if used appropriately—give fast results and personal recognition.* If used inappropriately, the directive strategy can appear overconfident and domineering, and your credibility will drop as a result.
- *Participative (BUILD) strategies—if used appropriately—enable you to establish a network of co-operative relationships.* They also engender more commitment to the course of action chosen, making the solution easier to implement effectively. If used inappropriately, the participative strategy can result in 'committee cultures'.
- *If in doubt, lobby!* Start by consulting your allies. If you meet with resistance, you should back off and explore the other person's objections. If you meet with more enthusiasm, move to a more directive approach and 'sell' your idea energetically.
- *Often you'll use combinations of approaches.* In a new job, for instance, you may start with a careful BUILD approach and then move on to using a PUSH approach as your credibility increases. Aim to broaden your natural range with new techniques.

Notes

The concept of a range of influencing and leadership styles dates from the 1950s, from an article by R. Tannenbaum and W. H. Schmidt entitled 'How to choose a leadership pattern' in the *Harvard Business Review*, 1957, **3**, 95–101.

The guidelines on using leadership styles are adapted from Fred Fiedler's contingency theory of leadership, and from the contingency model developed by Victor Vroom and Philip Yetten. Further references and an overview of the work of these researchers can be found in *Management of Organizational Behaviour—utilizing human resources* by Paul Hersey and Ken Blanchard, Prentice Hall International, 1988.

The advantages of using the participative approach in complex situations where you need commitment have been described by a number of authors, including Rosabeth Moss Kanter in *The Change Masters—Innovation for Productivity in the American Corporation*, Simon & Schuster, 1983. She refers to participative techniques again in a later work, *The Challenge of Organisational Change—how companies experience it and leaders guide it*, by Rosabeth Moss Kanter, Barry A. Stein and Todd D. Jick, The Free Press, Macmillan, 1992.

I have used the terms 'build' and 'push' as a shorthand for the participative and directive strategies. (Tannenbaum and Schmidt originally called these the democratic and authoritarian patterns.) Some readers will be familiar with the terms 'push' and 'pull' styles of influencing, described briefly, for instance, by Jonathan Coates in his book *Managing Upwards*, Gower, 1994. 'Pull' refers to an approach based on listening and questioning. I chose the term 'build' to describe the broader activities of networking and coalition building, and to represent a slow, patient, and skilled process of getting support.

This book focuses on developing your 'build' skills, but if you would like to extend your 'push' skills you could read *The Complete Spokesperson—a workbook for managers who meet the media* by Peter Bartram and Colin Coulson-Thomas, Kogan Page, 1991. Good presentation skills courses will also help you to develop your clarity and confidence.

The literature on cultural differences is fast expanding, but one of the best books is still *Riding the Waves of Culture*, by Fons Trompenaars, The Economist Books, 1993. A very readable introduction to culture is *The New International Manager—an action guide for cross-cultural business*, by Vincent Guy and John Mattock, Kogan Page, 1993. For more on organizational cultures, see Chapter 16 of *Inside Organizations* by Charles Handy, BBC Books, 1990. For an in-depth treatment of the subject you could read *The Character of Organizations* by William Bridges, CPP Books, 1992.

Assessing your credibility, and selecting the best approach

Credibility is about perceptions

The previous chapter described why your level of credibility is one of the key factors to bear in mind when you choose an influencing strategy. This chapter explores the concept of credibility in more depth.

Credibility is about perceptions. It is not about how you feel about yourself and about your proposals—it is about how others assess you and your contribution. Your credibility is also dependent on the context in which you are working. Right now, there will be contexts in which you have high credibility: with your own team, for instance, or perhaps with your manager, or with some colleagues inside or outside your organization whom you have helped in the past. At the same time, there could be people sitting in an office in a different part of your organization with whom you have low credibility. They may not know you very well, or they may have an unfortunately long memory of a mistake you made in the past, or they may simply associate you with a part of the organization which they do not particularly respect. You remain the same person, with the same talents, but your credibility rating changes according to who is assessing you.

Do not take low credibility too personally

High credibility is no problem—it is the low-credibility situations that managers understandably get anxious about. The important point about low credibility is not to take it too personally. If you get angry, you may behave subsequently in a way which lowers your credibility even further. You have probably met people like this. They fail to recognize that they have to build up their credibility at the start of a relationship, and instead they use a directive approach right from the beginning. When their good ideas are ignored, they complain about the injustice of it all, rather than reviewing their approach. Next time they make the same mistake all over again, and this lowers their credibility even further.

If your credibility is low you must acknowledge it as a potential problem, then select an appropriate BUILD strategy and get going on your action plan. You will find a wide range of examples and techniques to help you throughout this book.

Your credibility rating can change quite quickly

In the early stages of a relationship, your credibility can rise or fall, sometimes within a very short space of time. Here is an example from a new task force which had just been set up inside a flat organization. The task force had a chairman, but had not yet elected a formal leader.

> CASE STUDY 3.1 WATCHING YOUR CREDIBILITY RISE (OR FALL)
>
> The team was busy agreeing the objectives of the task force. One of the members, Bart, was having great difficulty getting the group to accept his views. He was talking a lot, interrupting the others and repeating his views with increasing volume. He was a friendly man and well liked, but the more he talked, the less the group listened to him. He was quite unaware that his credibility was falling.
>
> This noisy meeting was being chaired by Carel, an older man from a different part of the business. Carel said very little about his own views to start with, but he intervened regularly to summarize the progress of the group, to clarify key points and generally to keep the group on track. The meeting gradually became more orderly. Carel started to tuck in an idea of his own at the end of his summaries—and nine times out of ten, the group would follow his suggestion. As Bart's credibility was dwindling, so Carel's influence was increasing.
>
> After the meeting the group reviewed the way they had worked together. Bart was cheerfully open-minded in the face of considerable criticism. What really impressed him, however, was a revelation from Carel. The group had assumed that Carel was a 'natural chairman', but he assured them that this was not so. 'I started out just like Bart,' he admitted. 'But then I realized that I couldn't just shout others down, so I changed my behaviour. I learned to hold back until I'd established my position in the group. At that point you can say what you think, and people will follow you.' Food for thought for the group.

The more you can monitor fluctuations in the way you are perceived, the better you will be at adjusting your approach. Later in a relationship your credibility rating will be harder to change.

Factors which influence your credibility rating

How do other people measure your credibility? The factors to take into account vary in importance according to the corporate and national culture in which you are working. We will address two sets of factors: personal and organizational.

Personal factors

Relevant technical expertise

Are you acknowledged as an expert by the people you want to influence? Many managers commented in interviews that their technical background contributed considerably to their credibility rating with their staff. One scientist who is a modest man but highly regarded by his colleagues commented that 'Having a reputation is quite a responsibility. People tend to take what I say very literally—if I'm not careful, they assume I have thought the whole problem through, and rush off to follow my so-called advice, when really I have just been thinking out loud. It is all very flattering but a little worrying.' Many of us would find that quite a luxury.

Some people have the uncomfortable task of managing specialists who are working in areas where the manager himself or herself has very little knowledge. The secret here is not to try to compete in the area where your credibility is low. Enlisting the help of a colleague who has the necessary expertise is one option. Sometimes a better approach is to stress the areas which are actually most relevant to your managerial position, such as your knowledge of the organization, your project and its goals.

What if you do have expertise, but no more than the people with whom you are working? In these circumstances you would do best to use a BUILD approach and work on the problem as a team.

Proven track record

How much have you been able to demonstrate your 'added value' to the people you are trying to influence? Track record qualities are not just technical. They could include your ability to solve problems, to navigate organizational politics, to be diplomatic, reliable, trustworthy, decisive, supportive or whatever other qualities are relevant to the people who are assessing you. Here is how one senior consultant described his track record as perceived by his major clients.

CASE STUDY 3.2   'THEY KNOW I'M OBJECTIVE'

'There are two things clients recognize about me. First, I'm objective. If I recommend a certain course of action to them—like bringing in staff from my own organization, for example—they know that I'm doing it because I genuinely feel it's right, not because I want artificially to generate more business for my unit. Second, they know I'm not out to get a place on the board or to promote my career. I enjoy my current job, and if I didn't I could easily find another job elsewhere. Working in Holland—a Calvinistic environment—

people believe you more if they can see that you won't profit directly or personally from your recommended course of action.'

Another manager said that 'Once you're known as a problem solver, people look at you differently—they know they can count on your help. And trust is vital. People watch you closely to see if what you say in the corridor is the same as what you say in the meeting with your manager present.'

You may want to think about how you can present your experience to people who do not know you, so that you can highlight past projects and successes which are relevant to them.

Interpersonal skills, quality of relationships

How much do people like you and relate to you? How approachable do they find you? Another factor affecting your credibility could be your ability to put people at their ease. If people feel you are being overbearing you could get a reputation for being 'difficult to work with'. Emma, who works in the public sector, soon discovered the importance of building harmonious relationships.

CASE STUDY 3.3   EMMA LEARNS FROM EXPERIENCE

Emma has worked for the last ten years in the Commission of the European Union. Much of her work consists of liaison with outside parties, and some of those contacts are considerably more efficient in their working styles than others. On one occasion she was very frustrated by the late responses of one group to her requests for the documents and numbers needed as preparation for an important meeting. In exasperation she decided to teach them a lesson and cancel the meeting. When she checked with her boss if that was all right, he hesitated, wiped his glasses and said she must do what she thought was right.

'Rashly, I went ahead and cancelled the meeting—only to feel the quiet shock waves of disapproval through my unit. I'd broken an unwritten rule: to be pleasant and reasonable at all times. No lasting harm was done, but I learned my lesson. Those lateral relationships both with outside parties and inside the Commission are extremely important.'

Emma changes her approach

'I now handle things differently, by sending carefully worded reminders well in advance and making personal visits and phone calls. I also prepare very carefully for the meetings myself, so that my contacts know that if they fail to supply me with necessary information I will notice that and remind them—very nicely—to send it after the meeting. My Head of Unit commented recently that I have built a reputation with my own colleagues and with external contacts for being firm but friendly. As he said: We must always be polite.'

Emma's technical credibility was already high. By the time she had adjusted her approach to her external contacts, her personal credibility had risen also.

Often your colleagues may be prepared to overlook gaps in technical expertise if your interpersonal qualities are what they need. One senior engineer said 'in the current business climate, I'd rather have a group of team players, even if their technical record wasn't outstanding, than one or two prima donnas who wouldn't co-operate. I could achieve more with the team than with the individuals.'

Different cultures measure personal qualities in different ways

Colleagues from different national cultures will attach quite different values to different personal qualities. One example is the preference of most Scandinavians for a more consensus-based, BUILD approach. A British engineer who is seen as decisive in his own culture could be criticized as aggressive in Norway.

Expression of emotions is another sensitive area. A show of anger in the Far East could meet with total incomprehension from your colleagues, who would be embarrassed for you at your lack of self-control. Colleagues in South America might welcome your display of feeling as a sign of your authenticity. Your character stays the same, but your behaviour will be interpreted differently according to where in the world you are working. And you cannot assume that a frank and open discussion will clear the air after a misunderstanding—in cultures where saving face is essential, open discussion will be frowned upon. Cultural differences are invariably more subtle and profound than most of us initially realize, and the best approach is to seek advice from colleagues who understand the local protocols.

How about charisma and confidence?

Is charisma part of personal skills? Certainly a confident, authoritative image can improve your delivery style in a presentation, but if people do not trust you then an impressive appearance will not win you credibility. One danger with focusing on charisma, rather than on the added value you can offer, is that it can be interpreted as egocentric. According to recent research on leadership, people accord charisma to leaders whom they perceive as providing a genuine service, so searching to develop your own charisma may well be a lost cause.

Developing your presentation and delivery skills is sensible for everyone, as long as you also have a useful message to deliver. Working on your non-verbal behaviour—your way of talking and moving—can certainly increase your authority. Appearance also influences the way in which you are perceived, and is worth taking seriously.

Organizational factors which contribute to your credibility

Your position in the organization

Credibility is not only about who you are—it is also about where you work. In more traditional, formal organizations, the higher you are up the ladder, the more weight your opinions will hold. In flatter organizations, your status may not command as much respect—people will be more interested in how directly you contribute to the successful performance of your organization. If you are working on a key project which has high visibility and a lot of attention from management, you will automatically have high credibility.

Occasionally, skilful managers can turn a position which looks initially unpromising into quite a power base. A good example is a position in the training department. At worst, this can be a real backwater. If the training manager is a dynamic influencer, however, he or she can use the opportunity to become a 'spider in the web' at the centre of a highly influential network with staff at all levels.

Even in more hierarchical organizations, you will observe that not every senior person has high credibility. Some middle managers have less formal status, but more informal influence, and we will come back to this theme in later chapters. The position someone has in an organization is best assessed in relation to his or her power base.

Your power base

The concepts of credibility and power are closely linked. Credibility is about your personal reputation: power is about your ability to make things happen. Some managers will be able to achieve more than you would anticipate from their formal position in the organization. Others will be able to achieve less than you might expect. Organograms and organization charts will not be much help in understanding the power politics of an organization, because the truth is inevitably more complex. Here are some questions based on material by Rosabeth Moss Kanter to help you analyse the power base of any individual. You could start with yourself.

Questions for assessing your power base

- Can you get access to additional resources when you need them, such as budget, equipment or staff?
- Are you able to influence the career progression of your staff? Can you secure promotions? Can you block a subordinate's career path if you feel the person is incompetent?

- Are you able to attract high-quality staff to your unit? Do they ask of their own volition to join your team?
- Are you consulted regularly by more powerful colleagues when they have to make an important decision?
- Will senior managers make time available for you promptly when you want to consult them?
- Do you have demonstrable influence on the key decisions made in your organization?
- Are you always fully informed—at an early stage—of important developments in your organization?

Managers who can answer a confident 'yes' to most of the questions above will be the 'Movers and Shakers'—the people who can achieve more inside and outside the organization than you would expect from their formal role. Ideally you would be a Mover and Shaker yourself, but the next best thing in terms of developing your power base is to build relationships with Movers and Shakers through your coalitions and networking.

The quality of your network

How good are your relationships with the influential individuals inside and outside your organization? Networks are a valuable source of help and information for any manager. As far as your credibility is concerned, you will also need contacts to give you technical information, and to keep you up to date with trends. And you will need some allies, to give you moral support and advice.

An effective network stretches across departments and includes both senior and junior staff. One Mover and Shaker who is very well connected with senior staff said that it was often his contacts at more junior levels who gave him the most valuable information about the problems in the organization itself. As he put it, 'Don't just look up the ladder—you've got to look around.' Networking is becoming a key skill for all managers, and you can audit your own network in more depth in Chapter 7.

Certain national and organizational cultures value networking particularly highly as an indicator of power and credibility. One Italian manager, who is working very successfully in a joint Anglo-Italian venture, pointed out that in Italy a good network was regarded as absolutely essential. 'We manage by relationships,' was his comment.

The credibility of your unit, and your manager

Your manager's reputation may have a direct impact on your credibility. The degree to which this applies will depend on the kind of organization you work in, but your credibility score could double if your manager has high credibility, and unfortunately it could halve if you have a low-credibility boss. Does this hold true for where you work? Certainly the credibility of your unit will have a major influence on your choice of influencing strategies inside your organization.

> **CASE STUDY 3.4** HOW CREDIBLE IS YOUR MANAGER?
>
> One young engineer who had worked for his organization for six years was telling a training group how rewarding it was to work in his current department. He had a boss with high credibility, and he had never seen so many results achieved in such a short time. He did not have to worry about organizational politics, because his manager dealt with that. 'We can just get down to the technical work—what we're good at,' he said. And, of course, he could use a lot of PUSH style influencing.
>
> Another course member provided a telling contrast. Where she worked, her manager was more of a liability than a help. She had had to develop her network, very cautiously, in order to get the help she needed with any new initiatives. 'The only good thing that's come out of the experience is that I've learned about the value of coalitions,' she said. 'In circumstances like these, if you try to do something on your own it feels like banging your head against a wall.' A skilful BUILD approach was the only way forward—a frustrating fact of organizational life for this young woman whose natural style was more directive.

Choosing the best strategy for different levels of credibility—some suggestions

You have seen in Chapter 2 that the credibility principle behind choosing an appropriate strategy is as shown in Fig. 3.1.

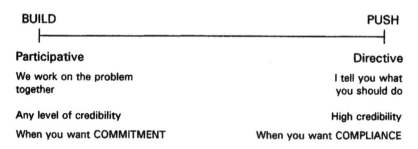

Fig. 3.1 Credibility and your choice of strategy

Adjusting your PUSH strategy to variations in credibility ratings

Using a PUSH strategy when your credibility is low means that you will be heading for disappointment. Once you accept this fact, you can often trust your 'gut feel' or intuition to warn you when your credibility level is at risk. A medium-credibility rating may still be adequate for a presentation, but you would be well advised to adjust your approach. If you have put yourself on the agenda rather than being invited, for example, and you are feeling a little nervous at the prospect of speaking to a particular audience, then your nerves may be a signal that you should convert the presentation to a more informal discussion, or at least shorten it. Try consulting some key members of the audience, talking through your main points in advance to get agreement and doing some BUILD style influencing before you take up your position by the overhead projector.

Medium credibility? Check you are 'on the same wavelength'

Credibility may drop during a PUSH-style presentation if you fail to demonstrate that you are on the same wavelength as your audience. Even high credibility can dwindle dangerously fast if you are not well prepared about the concerns and the interests of your audience. Andy Johns offers the following advice:

CASE STUDY 3.5 AVOID THE 'DATADUMP', IF YOU WANT TO STAY CREDIBLE

'Too many managers when they give a presentation do a "datadump". They assume that if they provide the information and the arguments, the audience will be able to sort it out and know how to move forwards. This is simply not true.

You have to remember what a pitiably low influence you have in any presentation. People assume they're going to occupy 100 per cent of the audience's bandwidth. In reality, even if you're highly regarded, the best you can hope for is that you will get 20 per cent. That means you've got to make your presentation really good.

Start with a message and a simple purpose in mind, then work backwards. Identify the three or four thoughts you want to leave in people's minds. Identify three or four key questions that you must answer—ask yourself what are the issues that you've got to get out of the way, in order for people to listen to you. Above all, answer the key question: "What have they got to go out of the room believing?" If you want to stay credible, you've got to be on the same wavelength.'

An alternative way of dealing with low credibility—get someone else to PUSH for you

Your usual choice if you know you have low credibility, and if the problem you are trying to sell is an important one, is to slow down and switch to a participative BUILD approach. This is a safe strategy which brings with it a number of other benefits. Sometimes, however, you genuinely do not have the time to come to a gradual consensus. Another way of coping with low credibility is to find someone with higher credibility to present your proposal for you. Here is an example.

CASE STUDY 3.6 FINDING SOMEONE WITH HIGH
CREDIBILITY TO PRESENT OUR CASE—THE TELEVISION
PRESENTER

'We had reduced the number of staff in one of our older plants from 2800 to 1200, and now we needed to make further cuts. The choice was to contract down to 500 staff, or to close the plant altogether. We needed to get the union's support for the "survival plan" of 500.

Many companies make the mistake of assuming that the best people to sell this sort of difficult proposal are the senior staff. Unfortunately, in situations such as this with all the accompanying anxiety and tension, senior staff may not have the credibility and the influence to deal with the staff effectively. Our management were deeply committed to saving the plant, but the staff were understandably suspicious.

We recognized this problem and decided to present our case instead with the help of an outsider, a television presenter who had a detailed knowledge of the chemical industry. This knowledge gave him the starting point for his interviews with the MD and the plant manager. We discussed the arguments with him, and made a video which was shown to all our staff and their families.

The key to the presenter's credibility was that he asked the questions which staff would have posed to management if they had been in the interview. A video is a one-way medium. You feel when you're watching the television that you want to tap on the screen and ask your own questions, but you cannot, so the interviewer must do it for you. The presenter asked the right questions and didn't let the managers off the hook, and that gave him (and us) the necessary credibility. The video was a success, and the survival plan was voted in.'

Learning points

- *The managers in this case were realistic.* Many senior managers are unable to detach themselves from the problem in this way—they make the mistake of assuming that status and credibility are the same.
- *The choice of the television presenter was imaginative.* The presenter had credibility because of his technical knowledge and because he was prepared to ask genuinely searching questions.

The only pitfall with this approach is that you because you are using a variation of a PUSH strategy, you must ensure that the person you choose to present your message really does have high credibility. Inside large organizations it can be difficult to assess how some staff are perceived. Sometimes well-meaning colleagues will advise you to get the support of a senior manager who turns out later to have less credibility than you had hoped. This is where a good network is so useful. You can consult other contacts, including junior colleagues, who are politically aware and who can give you an accurate 'grass roots' reading of the way the senior manager is perceived.

We will finish with a story of a manager who is a skilled influencer, and who used a high-credibility PUSH approach combined with a careful use of BUILD.

When it all goes right—using and building your credibility to achieve outstanding results

Pieter is a senior engineer in a multinational organization. He has just completed managing a technically complex and innovative project, which has made a major profit for his organization and was completed in record time.

CASE STUDY 3.7 MANAGING A CHALLENGING PROJECT

'I was lucky first of all with my team. The project I was managing was a new technology trial, and it attracted people who were really committed to making the project a success. I didn't have to do much convincing—we all wanted it to work.

We wanted to shorten the time scales of the project generally, so we dispensed with a lot of the standard procedures such as feasibility reports and pilot studies. Because of the novel technology, I persuaded my managers that there was little point in writing a complete project plan. Instead we wrote an outline, and updated it as we went. We had a clear goal, and an agreed course of action, but few formal controls. There was a steering group, which I kept informed of our progress, but they were prepared to trust me when I said we were making good progress.

Sorting out problems

Once we had decided where we wanted to go, my role was primarily to sort out problems so that the team could get on with their work. For instance, we needed a modification to be made in the field within six weeks. Engineering told us it would take between four and six months if we went the usual route. I contacted the manager in the field, and found that the bottleneck was the work scope document. I asked him if he needed it for control purposes—was it useful? He replied that it was useful for complex projects, but that on small projects like this it just slowed things up. Getting the document would take as long as doing the work itself.

So I used my network to find a way round the paperwork. What we needed, to by-pass the usual procedure, was some extra budget. I found a colleague who was interested in my project and asked for his help. He'd underspent his budget, and was prepared to give me some of his budget for the modification I needed. Armed with a budget number, we had the modification built in six weeks, not six months.

Keeping team motivation high

We all shared and celebrated the successes—I think this is very important. I made sure no-one "hijacked" the results. If a senior manager wanted to find out about the project, he talked directly to the person doing the work—and the result was that the team worked all the harder. Once the good results started coming in, the team motivated itself. I had T-shirts made for the project, and organized a big party for the team after we'd got approval for full field implementation.

The results

My boss was very supportive throughout the project. He trusted me to work round the system in a way which was appropriate but which didn't upset anybody. The interesting thing with a project like this is that you build a reputation as a team for getting things done. Just recently, we needed another process speeded up for business purposes. We got in touch with the same contacts, and got their help once again—only this time their response was even faster! The pay-off for the organization of a project approach like this is potentially huge, as we proved. This informal approach may not be right for bigger projects, but it gave us the flexibility we needed. A little trust is often enough to achieve extraordinary results.'

Learning points

- *Pieter led primarily with a participative style.* Once he was convinced that his team were fully committed to the project goals, and they had sorted out where they wanted to go, he left them as much freedom as possible. Pieter identified his own role as that of problem solver, and emphasized that the success of the project was due to the efforts and talents of the team. On projects which are technically complex and where the team are highly experienced, this approach is becoming increasingly common. It leaves the manager free to deal with some of the more critical interfaces with the rest of the organization—to clear away the obstacles, as Pieter put it.
- *He used his network to access additional resources.* Pieter is a typical Mover and Shaker, who understands how his organization functions and can find creative ways round the bureaucracy. Your

network will only work for you if you invest in it. The colleague who helped Pieter with the budget had had help from Pieter before.

- *When Pieter talked to the manager in the field, he was careful to ask him about his needs.* He did not make the common mistake of complaining about the long delivery time and the procedures. Instead he worked with him to find a solution which would meet both their needs.
- *Success breeds success.* The project and the people associated with it gained in credibility, so that when Pieter wanted help again he got it—faster. And he is quick to point out that this is an example of the organization learning and benefiting as a whole.

Summary of assessing your credibility

- *Credibility is about other people's perceptions of you.* We each have contexts in which we have high credibility, and other contexts where our credibility is only medium or low.
- *Credibility is affected by personal factors,* such as relevant technical expertise, track record and the quality of your interpersonal relationships.
- *Credibility is also affected by organizational factors,* such as your position in the organization, your power base, your network, and the credibility of your manager and your unit.

    All these factors are interrelated. Different national and organizational cultures will give different weightings to the various factors.
- *Do not take low credibility too personally*—adjust your influencing strategy instead.

Notes

The concepts of power and credibility have been explored by a number of authors, and my list of factors which influence your credibility rating is based on work by John P. Kotter in *Power and Influence: beyond formal authority*, Free Press, 1985, and Jeffrey Pfeffer in his book *Managing with Power—politics and influence in organizations*, Harvard Business School Press, 1994. Both books make fascinating reading if you are interested in American organizations and politics.

A comprehensive overview of the current literature on power and credibility can be found in *Developing Management Skills for Europe* by David A. Whetton, Kim S. Cameron and Mike Woods, HarperCollins, 1994. I have drawn on the authors' reference to Rosabeth Moss Kanter's early article, 'Power failure in Management Circuits,' *Harvard Business Review*, July-August 1979, for my list of questions for assessing your power base, and for some of the material on organizational factors affecting credibility.

For literature on culture, see Trompenaars (1993) and Guy and Mattock (1993).

Complex problems: the case for BUILD strategies

The importance of assessing the problem

The previous chapter focused on you: your credibility and your power base. In this chapter we will address the type of problem you may be aiming to solve, and the different strategies you can use to tackle it. Some managers use the same strategy whatever the type of problem. The result is then 'hit or miss', and often people justify their failures by blaming the other individuals involved. There is a clear relationship between the nature of the problem and the type of approach which tends to work best.

Directive strategies work best when problems are clearly defined

Here is an example of classic use of a PUSH approach, where a credible manager presents his solution to a problem which had been well defined and agreed in his management team.

CASE STUDY 4.1 THE FINANCE MANAGER AND THE NEW ACCOUNTING SYSTEM

The finance manager was presenting the case for a new accounting system. His colleagues were listening attentively. Everyone had become aware of the problems with the existing system—it generated data but little information, and was a source of irritation across the organization. For years there had been complaints, but no-one had the right combination of financial expertise linked with a sound understanding of how the company ran its business to come up with a valid alternative. The finance manager was a relative newcomer to the management group, but he had already demonstrated his added value, so the audience was optimistic.

The presentation lived up to their expectations. The finance manager had anticipated objections about the investment costs, and pointed out that the implementation of the new system would pay for itself within 18 months. He had the data to support his arguments and he spoke confidently and to the point. The benefits were in the new pieces of key management information which could be generated within months. A good presentation is a pleasure to experience: by the end, the solution to the problem seems so obvious. 'What's the verdict?' he asked. 'Go ahead,' was the unanimous response.

The finance manager had met all the criteria for successful PUSH: high personal credibility, a well-defined, agreed problem, and an emotionally neutral atmosphere.

Directive approaches fail if the problem is not agreed and defined

The more senior you become, the more the complexity of the problems you have to tackle increases. One senior consultant who works a lot with management teams said that 'It's the problem definition that's the hard part. If you can articulate the problem you don't need particularly smart people to solve it.' You must also check that the people you want to influence agree with your problem definition. If this is not the case, and you use a PUSH approach, you can get into a very uncomfortable position, as Mike in the following case soon discovered.

CASE STUDY 4.2   THE PROBLEM WITH THE PROBLEM—WHEN *PUSH* GOES WRONG

Mike was standing in the centre of the conference room, looking fed up and red-faced. Each time he suggested a sensible solution to the problem he had been shot down by one or other member of the group. They had started out at the beginning of the change workshop as a friendly, mature set of managers, embarking on an interesting new phase in the reorganization of their company. Whatever had made them all so obstructive?

At first sight the problem was simple enough. The group had been told by the management consultants who were facilitating the change process that they should sort themselves into task forces, to study the different business challenges currently facing their organization. They should think carefully about the composition of the task forces. Some of the managers came from different parts of the company and had not met each other before the reorganization, so this was an opportunity to network.

Mike had missed the first day of the workshop because he had been abroad on a client visit. He had been accompanied on the second day by two other latecomers. By the time they'd heard about the task forces, all the other managers had sorted themselves out and Mike and his two colleagues were out in the cold. A group of three was too small for a task force, so the latecomers could not work together. When Mike had raised the problem over coffee, the colleagues from the existing task forces had been sympathetic but non-committal.

Mike had agreed with the consultants that he should raise the issue after lunch with the whole group. As he did not want to take up too much time, he had prepared three possible solutions for shuffling all the task forces, and he presented these in the meeting. But each solution was countered with objections—the new composition meant that too many people from the same sector would be together, or there would be problems for colleagues coming from different locations, or whatever.

'Look, we'll never be able to get a perfect solution,' Mike said to the group. 'I appeal to your sense of collective responsibility.' But the meeting dragged on, the atmosphere became tense and small groups of individuals began to drift off together. Mike was wondering what he had committed himself to with this change process.

Learning points: what had gone wrong?

- *The problem was not agreed and defined.* Mike had assumed that the group would help, but as one manager put it ' I'm sorry that they're floating around, but they should have attended the first day like the rest of us'. Until his colleagues owned the problem, Mike's plan was doomed to failure.
- *Mike's credibility had dropped during the meeting.* His intentions were to help his fellow latecomers as much as himself, but the group soon saw him as a self-appointed chairman using the situation to achieve his own ends. Although the group liked him, after the first ten minutes they were feeling irritated and his credibility had dropped.
- *The climate was not emotionally neutral.* Those friendly groupings concealed some important hidden agendas. People are particularly sensitive about being accepted by their peers in the early days of any programme, and once they had bonded, several groups were not prepared to change. One manager expressed this explicitly during the meeting: 'I'm in a good group now—and I don't want to move.' Mike's proposals were threatening those fragile new relationships, and the individuals concerned counterattacked with a raft of objections.

Mike's story had a happy ending. The group was able to analyse and learn from the meeting, he eventually got support for his problem, and a pragmatic solution was reached. The point here is that you should consider in advance whether you may meet resistance, and if that is the case you avoid using a directive 'push' strategy.

Complex problems and resistance often go together

Complex problems often threaten people's sense of security in one way or another, and so complexity and emotional resistance often go hand in hand. As one manager put it, 'I like change when it's my idea—I don't like it if someone else is pushing me.' Resistance is both human and understandable, and a good influencer has to anticipate it and deal with it sensitively. Because resistance is such a minefield for influencers you can find a whole chapter devoted to the subject in Part II of the book, but here are some points based on Mike's story.

Sometimes symptoms of resistance can emerge even if your meeting starts off well, so you should be on the lookout for clues. People who are showing signs of resistance are unhappy or uncomfortable with the subject under discussion. Enthusiastic presenters tend to miss the clues and ignore the signs. Resistance may be expressed in any of the following ways:

- Openly—in personal attacks and aggressive behaviour in public
- Covertly—when people sit silently through a presentation, or leave the meeting early, or later withhold active co-operation
- Indirectly—when people zoom in on details, for instance, and take up your energy and attention in trivial debates.

If you spot resistance, you must BUILD

Mike realized later that he would have done better to have sat down after the first ten minutes, to have a quiet think and to choose an alternative approach. This is a lesson that most managers only learn by experience. Most of us tend, like Mike, to respond to resistance with more PUSH, because we think that if we try once again to make our point clear to our dense colleagues they might finally capitulate.

In Mike's group, some of his colleagues had a lot of trouble accepting that a directive approach really would not solve the problem of the sub-groups. While the consultants were reviewing the meeting and discussing the problem of emotional resistance, a number of managers jumped in at intervals to propose 'the final solution that would cut out all the talk and solve the problem once and for all'. All that happened as they interrupted the review was that the level of resistance grew yet again, and their proposal was inevitably rejected. One colleague persisted in trying his 'solutions' until the whole group shouted for him to shut up. The importance of adjusting to a BUILD approach is a very difficult lesson for some managers to learn!

The limitations of logic—when rational argument just will not work

Many managers with a technical or scientific background have been brought up to feel that all problems should have a logical solution.

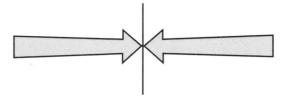

Fig. 4.1   Stalemate: both parties using a directive approach

Anyone arguing against the logic is, they believe, stupid, irrational or both. The difficulty with complex problems is that by their very nature they do not have one right answer—indeed, they may not have an 'answer' at all. Rational arguments can then hinder rather than help. The problem with piling on the logic is that if the person you are trying to convince feels uncomfortable with your proposal, he or she will argue back just as forcefully. Try as you might, you will not find the definitive answer. The result is a stalemate—with both parties feeling annoyed (see Fig. 4.1).

Some people instinctively mistrust logical arguments and prefer to follow their personal values. One sales supervisor said when he heard that his organization was cutting back on staff numbers 'I don't want to understand the rationale. In a company like ours, it's just wrong.' A secondary school teacher talking about proposals for a performance appraisal system said 'It's the values of our school that matter. Logic is like statistics—you can twist it any way you want.' Logic will not work with colleagues who put their principles first. Even if you do not agree with their views, you have to respect and acknowledge the integrity of their intentions.

If the problem you are tackling is important for your organization, you must use some form of BUILD approach. A belief in rational argument often leads to over-use of PUSH strategies, with a consequent loss of credibility and failure to achieve results.

Get agreement on the problem first: lobby and consult

Your first step with any complex problem is therefore to get agreement that there really is a problem, and then to agree on the problem definition itself. Often this means that you have to do some careful lobbying and consultation, particularly if you anticipate some emotional resistance and you want to deal with it early. Mike should have invested more effort in talking informally to his fellow participants and the consultants, to raise awareness in the group that this was 'their' problem as well as 'his' problem. People will always talk more openly to you in one-to-one meetings than in larger gatherings where their colleagues will be observing them. Much of BUILD influencing is about empathy—being able to put yourself in someone else's place and guess how they feel. Once you have an idea of the person's worries, you may be able to suggest an elegant problem definition that does not upset your key players and which enables you to move forward with a solution.

CASE STUDY 4.3 BERNARD *BUILDS*—TO GET AGREEMENT ON A PROBLEM DEFINITION

Bernard was called in by a client to help identify what was going wrong in a huge Information Technology project. A sensitive man, Bernard was respected for his 'people skills' as much as for his technical expertise. The managers in the client organization were getting desperate. The suppliers of the system had been working hard, but they were now two years into the project with no real results to show. The suppliers themselves seemed as stuck with the problem as everyone else. The software was complex but not intrinsically difficult, and the hardware delivery had been slow but not impossible to manage. The problem, Bernard suspected, was much more to do with the people than with the technology.

He found a possible way out of the mess when he examined the documentation. The fact that it was all so sketchy provided him with a potential problem definition. He talked his approach through in his business manager's office. 'If we talk about the inadequacies of the documentation, we can explain the problem in a way that doesn't criticize any one person directly,' Bernard explained. 'It may not be the whole story, but it could provide us with an acceptable way forward. I'm going to try the idea out in a one-to-one meeting, just to check I won't be stepping on anyone's toes. I'll start with the client project manager—if I can win him over, he'll persuade his colleagues.'

Bernard put his diagnosis forward tentatively in the project manager's office. 'You've never had a clear specification of the functionality of the system,' he explained. 'That means you have nothing to plan, produce or test against. Does that sound reasonable?' The project manager thought for a moment. 'Yes, it does—but what should we do next?' Now Bernard had to move carefully. 'My team can write a specification for you, and help you get back on track,' Bernard continued. 'But that idea won't be popular with your supplier. We'll need to find a way forward which takes account of the work they've been doing for the past two years.' The project manager reached for his diary. 'We'll talk to the supplier—you think your solution through and present it to us next Wednesday,' he said.

Learning points

- ■ *The problem definition you choose is part of your influencing strategy. You can choose to broaden the problem definition or to* narrow it. Bernard opted to narrow the problem definition and to focus—at least initially—on the documentation.

How should you decide whether to broaden or narrow your problem definition? Broader definitions are often better for tackling the causes of a problem, rather than just the symptoms, but only if your client has both the will and the means to achieve a solution. Bernard took a pragmatic approach. He could have spent weeks trying to get to the bottom of what had gone wrong, and he may never have found out the whole story. He settled therefore on one aspect—the documentation—where the gaps and ambiguities were evident to everyone. Experienced consultants recommend choosing the problem definition that:

- Enables you to work within your capabilities
- Is within the power of your client to handle
- Will produce an outcome that is genuinely useful to the organization
- Fits in—within reason—with your client's own agenda and needs.

- *Some face-saving was necessary.* Rightly or wrongly, if the client project manager had felt exposed, he would not have gone further with Bernard's help—and the client's organization would have suffered further from the delay. By focusing on the problems with the documentation, Bernard was able to find an acceptable way forward.
- *Bernard talked his approach through with his business manager.* In situations which are complex, it is sensible to consult your allies first, to make sure your solution makes sense.
- *Bernard then consulted the client project manager* in a one-to-one meeting to check that he was comfortable with the problem definition.
- *The supplier was obviously going to be unhappy* with Bernard taking over. Bernard anticipated this in the meeting with the client project manager and checked that the project manager would address the problem urgently.
- *Bernard only went ahead with the presentation at the invitation of the client project manager*—he knew then that his credibility had risen (see Fig. 4.2).

People with a more technical background sometimes feel uncomfortable at the idea of lobbying, because they feel there is something secretive about working one to one. As long as you feel that your solution is genuinely in the interests of the organization (and not just in the interests of advancing your career) one-to-one meetings are a

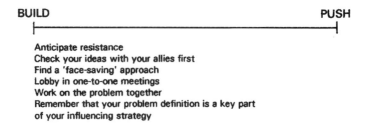

Fig. 4.2   Using a BUILD approach to work with complex problems and resistance

sensible and professional use of your time. Failure to lobby and consult can mean failure to get acceptance for your good idea—and your organization suffers accordingly.

Many cultures are well aware of the value of this informal lobbying process. One manager who had worked extensively in France said that his colleagues graded the seriousness of organizational problems by referring to them as 'four-lunch' or 'five-lunch' problems. Talking outside the office in a more relaxed atmosphere often promotes communication and creativity.

More BUILD strategies for dealing with resistance

BUILD strategies are based on the assumption that you want to get active co-operation from the people you are trying to influence, and that there is not just one way forward. This holds true both for managers working from a small power base and for those with much greater credibility. Here is an example of a problem which looks straightforward enough in retrospect, but which, if Rita had not handled it properly, could have caused delays and inconvenience.

CASE STUDY 4.4   RITA GETS CO-OPERATION FROM A NEW COLLEAGUE

Rita was working with a number of European universities to put together some joint programmes. She had good relationships with most of the professors, so she had set up some meetings to bring them all together. The problem was the logistics—and in particular, the interface with the co-ordinator in Italy was causing problems. 'For him, the result was more important than the process,' she said, 'and that was tough to work with.'

She flew over to meet him. He was pleased that she had made the effort to see him personally. 'It's the human contact that's so important,' she said, 'Once I was in Milan, he was almost obliged to listen to me. It's the same as with videoconferencing or electronic mail—they are wonderful, but not with problems like these. E-mail is a statement. What you need is a discussion.'

In the meeting she checked that he agreed with her description of the problem. He did. She then asked him what he advised. Later she explained her approach as follows. 'If you tell someone the solution you will get resistance. You have to open up a dialogue. Also, the solution I had in my head might have been wrong—he could have had a better idea. In meetings like this you must show the person that you value his time and his opinion.' The last stage was the emphasis on action. Rita asked him what they should do next, and they agreed an action plan. 'Never leave until you know what you're going to do next,' she said. 'Goodwill on its own won't get results.' The relationship between Rita and her Italian colleague has run much more smoothly since.

Learning points

- *Rita set up the interview very carefully*—she flew to Italy to meet her colleague face to face on his home ground.
- *She checked explicitly for agreement on the nature of the problem.*
- *She consulted the other person,* rather than imposing her own solution, and she was genuinely open to his ideas.
- *She ensured that she had commitment to an action plan* before leaving.

In Rita's case she only had to get the support of her manager (who trusted her judgement) and of her colleague in Italy. If you are dealing with problems which affect other people in your organization, who also feel strongly about the solution chosen, you have to take other factors into account when planning your BUILD strategy.

Understanding the politics of your organization

To understand the politics of your organization you must identify all the people who will be involved in the decision-making process, and the different roles they play. Inexperienced influencers often focus all their efforts on the person who will make the final decision, and ignore all those who will be offering him or her advice and opinions.

The 'shadow organization'

If you are working in large and medium-size organizations, you should identify the influential members of the 'shadow organization' (see Fig. 4.3). The shadow organization is composed of all the people who assist the middle and senior line managers. These can include assistants, secretaries, advisors, people in quality assurance, legal departments,

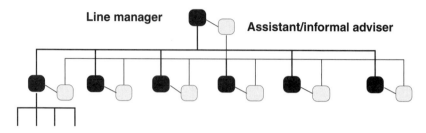

Fig. 4.3   The shadow organization

accounting and organizational development. People in staff functions often have the in-depth technical knowledge needed for assessing technical documents, together in some cases with an excellent understanding of how the organization functions. This gives the shadow organization considerable informal power. A headmaster of a large independent school, for instance, freely admitted that he relied on the advice of 'our excellent PR manager' before making any major decision. At the very least, staff functions will be consulted by their manager. They may be fully responsible in practice for making decisions, which are then simply signed off by the formal decision-maker.

Every organization has its own form of the informal network, or shadow organization. You ignore it at your peril.

Understanding the history

The historical context is another dimension to consider when you are tackling complex influencing cases. One senior manager said that 'Corporate memory is very important. It enables you to position a problem. If you know who owes whom, and what the scores are, you may be able to sort out problems discreetly and save face.' The historical perspective enables you to understand some of the hidden agendas which are blocking progress, as in the following example.

CASE STUDY 4.5   USING THE HISTORICAL CONTEXT
TO FIND A WAY FORWARD
'I was working in the Head Office of a large corporation based in Continental Europe. I'd been asked to assess a potential acquisition in Spain. This was an initiative sponsored by my Director, who wanted to develop outsourcing in Southern Europe. I agreed with him that the acquisition could enable our business to expand substantially.

The problem lay with the reporting structure. The Chief Exec of the acquisition wanted to report direct to Head Office—and my Director wanted that too. However, in order for the acquisition to succeed, we needed the Chief Exec of our own Spanish company to agree to work closely with the Chief Exec of the acquisition, and to commit to making the partnership work. Our Chief Exec was not keen. He said he couldn't accept any real responsibility for the profit and loss of the acquisition unless it reported directly to him. We had a stalemate. Both the Chief Executives were talented executives, and we couldn't afford to lose either of them. Above all, we needed the commitment from our man.

I turned my attention to the corporate history. I'd only been in the organization for a short time, but by asking around on my network I heard that our executive in Spain had some problems with inter-company trading—he'd co-operated closely with one of the Directors in the Far East, but then felt subsequently that the Director was taking all the credit (and most of the profit) from the partnership.

'I look on problems like that as opportunities. I checked out the situation in the Far East, and found a solution that was more acceptable to both parties. Once he saw that I would help him, he agreed to co-operate with the Chief Exec of the acquisition. This sort of approach is good for the business. I see myself as a 'corporate agent', there to ensure that the shareholders get maximum value. Everyone was happy with the solution.'

Learning points

This manager had recognized resistance from the Chief Executive in Spain, and rather than focusing all his efforts on trying to convince him, which could have made the resistance worse, he sought for a solution to the deadlock elsewhere. The corporate history offered a clue to the underlying problem. Having a good network is very important for successful BUILD approaches. Other colleagues can often offer information which can shed light on problems and point the way forward to a creative solution. Here is a different example of how a historical perspective can help.

CASE STUDY 4.6   THE SENIOR CONSULTANT SIFTS THROUGH THE PAST

A senior consultant was explaining to me why he thought an overview of the past was so important for understanding the present. 'If you are brought in to help an organization which is in a certain state, you can't just take a snapshot and expect to understand it. You have to take the past into account. It's like a doctor who asks for your medical history, or an architect rebuilding an old city—you have to appreciate the previous infrastructure. Organizations grow in a particular way—they have roots, and the roots give you the clue to the cause of the problems they are suffering. Try to find out the main events which have had an impact—the arrival of a new Chief Executive, for instance, or the passing of a particular piece of legislation.'

As our interview drew to a close, he pulled out of his briefcase a file containing three organograms. 'Here's an example of how history can help,' he said. 'The organograms are all from the same large organization—my current client. They span the last five years. I have been comparing them—checking who's been present throughout in the senior management, who dropped out, and trying to figure out why. Only 20 per cent of the names in the second organogram have remained in the third one.' Like an organizational archaeologist he was sifting patiently through the dust, looking for clues.

Organograms and the 'wave effect'

Organograms are always reflections of the organization's past. At best, they describe the recent past. In large, fast-changing organizations in particular, organograms are frequently distorted by the 'wave effect', which works as follows. The corporation reorganizes, starting with the top management, and a new organogram is duly issued to staff. The new organogram is an accurate description of the top level of the organization, but while you are reading it at your desk, the senior managers are busy reorganizing the level below them. By the time you have filed the organogram, the middle level of management is changing, and the wave effect is in motion. When the changes in middle management are captured in the next version of the organogram, the top and the middle levels may be accurate, but, of course, the middle managers are now reorganizing their staff. When the bottom level of the organogram is accurate, of course, the top team is ready for another change, and so on.

Occasionally you encounter something more like a geological fault, when one of the new directors, for instance, has been particularly quick in restructuring a division. Your organogram may now be more or less accurate for four of the five divisions, but the fifth division, with the dynamic new director, actually looks nothing like the diagram. The message is always to consider organograms as historical data, and never to expect them to be accurate reflections of the current reality.

Managing your stakeholders—and using your network

Stakeholders are the people who have an influence on your organization, and are influenced by it. They have an interest in how your organization performs its business and how it goes about achieving its goals.

The more complex the problem you are dealing with, the more stakeholders will be involved. The increasing demand for inter-departmental and inter-organizational co-operation has drawn attention to the need for stakeholder management and professional networking, as a crucial part of your BUILD strategy. Here is an example of a senior manager who co-ordinated the agendas and interests of a large number of stakeholders very successfully.

CASE STUDY 4.7   MANAGING YOUR STAKEHOLDERS— THE WORLD CUP FOOTBALL MATCH

Peter van Zunderd, a District Chief of Police in Rotterdam, was in charge of the police response to the World Cup football match between Holland and England in October 1993. The operation was a success, with a minimal number of incidents. When he had started planning for it in December 1992, however, there was considerable concern about the behaviour of the English hooligans, and city-centre shopkeepers were already getting anxious. The dilemma for the police was to maintain the friendly climate needed for an enjoyable match, while at the same time to maintain public order. Peter started off with a careful BUILD approach, based on consultation of all key stakeholders to get agreement on the problem.

Getting agreement on the problem and the purpose
He started ten months before the match by placing it on the agenda of the meetings attended by himself, the mayor of Rotterdam and the general prosecutor. He then talked to the advisors of the mayor, trying to find an approach which would be acceptable to all the parties involved. Together with the mayor and the general prosecutor, he formulated a policy statement which represented his purpose: 'To guarantee the public order before, during and after the match and prevent riots and damage'. In parallel, he brainstormed with his own team and set up initial contacts and exchange of information with the English Football Association and the British police.

Managing the stakeholders
Peter described the next steps as follows. 'We held extensive consultation talks with all our strategic partners, including the Ministry of Justice, the Immigration Office, the British consulate, the Dutch railways, the railway police, the Dutch and English Football Associations and national criminal intelligence services, the stadium management and the union of shopkeepers. Later we were able to use these contacts to communicate police policy and to keep them up to date with developments. When we started to put a number of measures in place, to control the ticket sale for example, we knew we could rely on the support of the parties concerned. By the time we were coming up to the match, we had organized a massive presence, an extensive infrastructure and a three-phase policy, and had gained the agreement from the mayor that he would make emergency legislation operational if necessary to enable us to make early arrests. We were feeling cautiously optimistic.

Managing the cross-disciplinary teams
Meanwhile we set up cross-disciplinary teams—for processing information, for instance. We ensured that they had a clear shared purpose, and a very clear

understanding of the role of each individual. We also held a press conference in London to make it clear that we wouldn't allow hooligans to riot in Rotterdam. The cross-disciplinary teams worked really well, and made a vital contribution to preventing violence. And throughout this period we kept our key stakeholders—such as the mayor, for instance—informed at each step. The outcome of the match was really very rewarding—particularly as our Dutch team won! And I'd recommend a strategy based on extensive consultation to anyone who needs the same degree of active support.'

Learning points

- *Identify all your major stakeholders.* Peter estimated that he talked to as many as 200 key individuals in the months leading up to the match. With his own team he wrote a 'storyboard' to plan all the contacts he needed to make. 'Each match is a project,' he explained. The Dutch and British Football Associations, British colleagues in the police, and the stadium management were priority stakeholders. Contacts with the ministries and transport organizations were also very important.
- *Get agreement on the problem definition.* The District Chief of Police first worked closely with the mayor's advisors (the 'shadow organization') to try out some drafts. Once the policy had been defined and agreed by the mayor and the general prosecutor he could move faster on implementation, knowing he was working from a sound base.
- *Aim for an escalating consensus.* Peter worked towards a 'snowball effect', getting agreement initially from the mayor and the general prosecutor and then building commitment with the other stakeholders involved. The policy for this match was an unusual one, with some original measures—he made sure he had all the commitment needed to support it, well in advance.
- *Work selectively.* Peter knew from experience who could be most helpful to him, and who could supply him with high-quality information.
- *Have your network already in place.* You need an established web of relationships to create consensus on this scale and within a tight time frame. Peter invests time and effort in building these relationships and establishing mutual trust well in advance.
- *Move from a participative to a directive approach.* Once Peter had established support for the policy, he changed to a more directive approach. With the cross-disciplinary teams, for instance, he set clear goals and defined the roles of each of the members. By now the problem was agreed and defined, and the teams were under time pressure, so the PUSH approach was the appropriate choice.

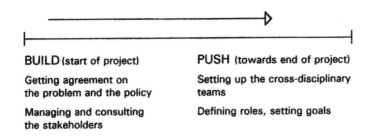

BUILD (start of project)

Getting agreement on
the problem and the policy

Managing and consulting
the stakeholders

PUSH (towards end of project)

Setting up the cross-disciplinary
teams

Defining roles, setting goals

Fig. 4.4   Moving from BUILD to PUSH as the context changes

The team members needed a clear structure within which to accomplish their tasks. Good influencers are able to spot changes in the context and to adjust their approach accordingly (see Fig. 4.4).

Managing stakeholders to prevent conflicts and promote co-operation

A BUILD approach based on consultation of key stakeholders is also effective in contexts such as setting up contracting strategies, as many large organizations are discovering. The old view of the negotiation process was largely based on directive influencing, and relied heavily on arguments, energy and willpower. The contract was just the starting point for further conflicts and yet more negotiations. One manager described how he uses the BUILD strategy with his contractors as follows.

CASE STUDY 4.8   USING A *BUILD* APPROACH TO MANAGE CONTRACTORS
'The participative approach works particularly well in parts of the world where, as a European, you are obliged to deal with a small group of contractors. Rather than fighting this, we plan for it. We involve the contractor right from the start—trying to agree with him an accurate estimate of his base costs, then a reasonable profit margin. We extend our boundaries in effect to include him, not to exclude him. We plan and schedule together, and agree that if we come in under budget and ahead of time, we share the profits. Equally, if we run over time and/or over budget, we share the costs.

This approach enables you at an early stage to spot any weaknesses the contractor may have in his organization. You can then decide if additional resources will be required. In situations where the contractor base is small and the overall capability is low, the BUILD approach enables you to pre-empt problems and to avoid having to use confrontation with the contractor later.

You can minimize the risks to your project. In more mature areas, where substantial contracting capabilities are available, you can adopt a more 'hands-off ' approach to contracting out work. The potential financial benefits for both organizations are huge.'

Many large organizations are following this path, to address complex problems not only with their contractors but also with works councils, trades unions, 'citizens' juries', environmental bodies, community organizations and other key stakeholders.

Summary of complex problems—the case for BUILD strategies

- *Use a directive PUSH strategy with well-defined problems.* If the problem is not well defined and agreed you can get into difficulties.
- *Complex problems and emotional resistance often go hand in hand*—use a BUILD approach to explore the needs.
- *Logic does not always work.* Piling on rational arguments can make people feel pressurized—they then attack back. More logic usually makes resistance worse.
- *If you encounter resistance, lobby and consult.* Find out what the objections are, and work on a joint problem definition with the people you are trying to influence.
- *Understand the politics.* Do not focus solely on the decision makers—identify the shadow organization and the hidden influencers as well.
- *Understand the history.* This can often give you clues to hidden agendas.
- *Manage your stakeholders.* Use a BUILD approach to work with them, and to prevent conflicts and promote co-operation in sensitive commercial situations.

Notes

The concept that complex problems are best addressed using a BUILD approach is based on the work by Fiedler, Vroom and Yetten (see Hersey and Blanchard, 1988). See also Pfeffer (1994) Kotter (1985) and Moss Kanter (1983).

Peter Block's *Flawless Consulting—a guide to getting your expertise used'* Pfeiffer and Company, 1981, is a classic for consultants and contains an excellent section on recognizing and dealing with resistance.

For more on the concept of logic versus values, read *Gifts Differing* by Isabel Briggs Myers with Peter B. Myers, Consulting Psychologists Press, 1980, 1990.

5 Assessing your style: selecting the skills you want to develop

Identifying your own style—some cases for you to try

In the 15 situations described below, select the action which you think would be most effective. In all these situations, the correct way forward depends on the assumptions you make about the environment in which you are operating, so in some cases you may want to select more than one action. At the end of the questionnaire are some answers. The learning points from these situations are explored in greater detail in subsequent chapters of this book.

The situations

1 Feedback for the team member

One of your team members has handled a client meeting badly. He talked too much, and he interrupted the client several times. When you give him the feedback back in the office, he instantly goes on the defensive and starts to argue. He has reacted like this before and you feel quite irritated with him. What do you do?

(a) Repeat the feedback, clarifying further, and talking over him if necessary. ☐
(b) Sit back, listen and observe for a few minutes. ☐
(c) Shrug and give up—if he is not prepared to learn, that is his problem. ☐

2 Proposing the new standard

You are working for quality assurance in a large matrix organization. Your task is to propose a new standard which will affect almost everyone in your corporation. You have worked out a draft which has been approved by your line manager, and are now planning your next step. What should it be?

(a) Start selling the concept through your organization, even before you have worked out the details. ☐

(b) Concentrate on refining the standard further on your own. ☐

(c) Expect your boss to do the selling—that is his job. ☐

3   The divisional meeting

You are in a meeting convened by the director of your division to discuss a major organizational change. The director is fair-minded and genuinely interested in the views of the staff. You are a senior consultant, and your preference is to avoid company politics and to concentrate on producing high-quality work. Your track record in the organization is good. At one point in the meeting, another participant puts forward a suggestion which, if it were adopted by management, would have very serious negative consequences for the Division. This participant is a forceful personality and politically astute. When you tentatively express your concerns about his proposal, he dismisses your objections. What do you do?

(a) Stress that you feel strongly about this, and that you want to put forward your case. ☐

(b) Wait until the coffee break to find out if other colleagues share your concerns. ☐

(c) Give up and save your energy—he has the ear of the director. The best you can do is to hope that the director has the sense to reject the proposal. ☐

4   The new colleagues

Your division has been expanded and reorganized. Two new managers have joined you at your level. One of them, Diane, is friendly and co-operative, and you've talked together over lunch. The other, Rolf, is more quiet and distant. Diane is from the USA, but Rolf is German and his English is not yet fluent. The working language of your organization is English. What do you do?

(a) Wait—make no contact with Rolf as yet, but observe his movements from a distance. ☐

(b) Make an appointment with him to hear about his role and his objectives. ☐

(c) Concentrate on developing your relationship with Diane, since she is easier to work with and the two of you should be able to get a lot done together. ☐

5   The posting in the Far East

You have been posted to a subsidiary of your organization in Malaysia. On your arrival you notice a number of matters which are not being handled efficiently. Your new manager is a local man in his early fifties—charming and courteous. You feel it is your duty to point out the inefficiencies to him. What do you do?

(a) Tell him frankly that these matters must be changed—after all, you are both adults and this situation must not be allowed to continue. ☐

(b) Shut up. You know that this is a culture which is sensitive to saving face, and you do not want to offend him—he will find out the problems eventually for himself. ☐

(c) Consult one of his local colleagues over a game of golf, and ask him if he thinks your manager has had the opportunity to consider a couple of ideas. Then explain your proposals. ☐

6   The lack of clear objectives from your manager

You are a team leader in a large organization. Your own objectives have not been well defined by your manager, partly because of impending changes, but also because your manager tends to be rather vague about objective setting in general. You do not have a lot of respect for her, and you are feeling increasingly frustrated. In a team meeting, one of your more vocal team members complains that because of the lack of clear objectives, he cannot prioritize his workload. What do you do?

(a) Tell the team that you have tried your best with your manager, but that she has not given you a satisfactory answer. ☐

(b) Agree with the team a temporary set of objectives and priorities, so that at least they can get on with their work. ☐

(c) Go back to your manager and tell her firmly that unless she sets clearer objectives, you will talk to her manager. ☐

(d) Plan your meeting with your manager—think about what is causing her problems with setting objectives, and how you can resolve the problem together. ☐

7   The problem with the office manager

Your office manager is a warm, sensitive, older woman, whose team has consistently provided good service over the ten years she has worked for your company. Just recently, however, there have been a number of complaints about the work of her team, and you need to find out what is going wrong. You go to her office. When you confront her with the problems, she looks upset and anxious, and her answers are evasive. You are under pressure from your boss to improve her team's service—fast. What do you do?

(a) Explain to her clearly that this is a serious situation. ☐
(b) Ask her directly what is wrong—and if she is still evasive, say to her that you will not leave her office until you know what is going on. ☐
(c) Sit back, reassure her, remind her of her past successes, get her a cup of coffee and start again more slowly. ☐
(d) Ask her staff what is going on. ☐

8   The presentation to the committee

You are a university lecturer, and you have been assigned the task of setting up a part-time course for adults in your area of expertise. You have designed the outline, and have spent some time addressing the economics and marketing. Now you must present your findings and recommendations to the senior staff on a university committee. You want to raise a number of issues about the content of the course, and the target group. You are particularly uneasy about the fee that was initially proposed, which you think may be too low. Your presentation has been scheduled to take 30 minutes. You have got a good reputation in the university, but you dislike giving presentations to management—they make you nervous. How will you organize your time?

(a) Concentrate on the content of the new course—after all, that is your main area of expertise. Take about 25 minutes to present, with 5 minutes for questions. You will mention the fee problem in passing—they will pick it up if they think it is important. ☐
(b) Give a detailed overview of all the problems, using the full 25 minutes to present—you will need that time to cover all the information. ☐
(c) Think about the outcome you want, and give a 15-minute overview of the main issues, with the fee issue right up front. The remaining time can be used for discussion. ☐

9   The new job in head office

You have been transferred from a line position to a functional position in head office. You are not very happy about your new role—you fear you will have to deal with a lot of organizational politics, and that has never been one of your strong points. Which of the following options would be your top priority now?

(a) Immerse yourself in the documentation—find out what this
     job is actually about. ☐
(b) Make a list of the key contacts in your organization, and set
     up some meetings. ☐
(c) Concentrate on your own team and your own targets. ☐

10 The unenthusiastic client

You are an external consultant working on a management project for a client. You have been asked to design a number of workshops to support a change process. You have worked hard on this project and are proud of your proposal. You talked it through with the client and he seemed positive. When you present your design for formal approval, however, the client is not as enthusiastic as you had expected. What do you do?

(a) Go through the key points again—more slowly and clearly.   ☐
(b) Remind him politely but firmly that your proposal is absolutely
     in line with the specification of needs which he had given you. ☐
(c) Stop your presentation, and ask him to explain his concerns. ☐

11 Getting help from your colleagues

You need some help on one of your projects from three colleagues in other departments. The project is interesting, but will involve a considerable commitment of effort from everyone. Your manager is optimistic that the colleagues will co-operate, but he is leaving it up to you to persuade them. How will you handle this situation?

(a) Draft a standard note explaining the project to all of them, and
     send it by e-mail. ☐
(b) Talk to their managers and ask for their approval. ☐
(c) Work out what each of the colleagues stands to gain from
     helping you, and make an honest estimate of the effort needed
     —then approach them individually. ☐

12 The cross-disciplinary task force

You have to set up a cross-disciplinary task force for an important project. None of you knows each other very well, and everyone is very busy. You need to get going on the planning phase as quickly as possible. What do you do?

(a) Use the first meeting to agree the objectives and discuss the plan with the new team. □

(b) Write the project plan yourself, to save time. Distribute copies in the first meeting. □

(c) Use the first meeting just to get to know each other. □

13   Your idea for helping the section

Your section has not been working very efficiently. You have thought of an idea for managing the interfaces between you more effectively. You present your idea in a weekly meeting of the section. It meets with a mixed response—some colleagues are tentatively enthusiastic, while others seem doubtful of your motives. What do you do?

(a) Explain your idea again—you are sure it represents an improvement. □

(b) Take the tentative support as a starting point, and explore other options. □

(c) Drop the idea—this looks like too much hard work. □

14   The manager who refuses to change

You have recently joined a large bureaucratic organization. Your reputation is good, and your task is to accelerate the change process to a more business-oriented approach. Only a week after you joined you encountered heavy opposition to one of your key proposals from a middle manager who reports to you. His contribution to your team is important but not vital. He says your proposal will not work, and that senior management will not back you. You check with your manager and he assures you that you have his support, though you sense he has some doubts. The other members of your team are fairly positive. You are under intense time pressure. What do you do?

(a) Take time with the hostile middle manager to explore the causes of his opposition to your proposal. Only move forward when you have his support and when the whole team is behind you. □

(b) Have a series of meetings with the other team members to check they are fully behind you, and try to persuade them to convince the middle manager. □

(c) Take a risk and go ahead with your proposal anyway, telling the middle manager that you understand his objections but hope he will give your proposal a fair chance. □

15   Managing company politics

You want to change some of the procedures in your organization, but you are only a middle manager with a limited power base and with an older, very conservative boss. You are disappointed with his lack of proactive support. The decision maker is the general manager, with whom you have had little personal contact. You are wondering how to build support for your idea. Your manager's boss is a vice president who has considerable influence with the general manager. You have met him twice and he seemed to like you. You also play squash with the general manager's personal assistant, who is experienced in the workings of the company. What do you do?

(a) Make an appointment with the general manager. ☐
(b) Ask the assistant how he thinks you should handle this. ☐
(c) Talk directly to the vice president, and ask for his support. ☐

Some Answers

1   Feedback for the team member—deal with resistance by listening

This is a situation about dealing with resistance on a one-to-one level. These cases are particularly difficult if you do not like the team member much—it is so hard to be patient. Unfortunately, it is then all the more vital that you give him the space to express himself.

(a) *Repeat the feedback:* this is asking for an argument. Interestingly, you are also modelling to him the very behaviour you want him to change with the client. Whatever you might feel about him personally, and however eager you are that he should recognize that you are right and he is wrong, this is unlikely to work.
(b) *Sit back and listen:* this is the best option, although it requires self-control and flexibility. This BUILD approach is counter-intuitive to many managers, who fear that they are 'giving in' to the team member by listening. However, the purpose here is to pick up the clues to his resistance, so that you can find other ways to persuade him to change his behaviour. By choosing this approach you will have given your team member the best chance of learning and changing, and that is your job as a manager.
(c) *Shrug and give up:* do not give up on him before you have tried option (b) first. I would argue that you should also say to him in the meeting that he should think about the implications of his behaviour overnight. If you cannot resolve the problem, you will still have the difficult decision about what to do with him. These

sorts of interpersonal problems come back in appraisals and in feedback from other colleagues. It is best to invest effort in dealing patiently with the resistance as soon as it appears, in order to get the team member thinking about how he can adjust his behaviour.

Scoring: if you like scoring systems, and if you agree with my reasoning, give yourself 5 points for choosing option (b) and 0 points if you chose (a) or (c).

2   Proposing the new standard—the person who has the idea should sell the idea

Your new standard is going to affect everybody, so there is a high risk that you could encounter opposition and complaints from all sides if you were unlucky. I have not said anything about your personal credibility in this situation, but how many quality assurance departments do you know whose word is law? Because of the high impact I think you have little choice but to BUILD. The good QA managers I know are very careful about getting early support.

(a) *Start selling the concept:* this is the preferred option. You could get some feedback and some ideas for improvements, if necessary. And people always feel more positive about adjusting to change and dealing with its accompanying inconveniences if they feel they have been consulted.

(b) *Concentrate on refining the standard on your own:* this is an understandable choice, because many managers are inherent perfectionists who feel more secure burrowing into the details and assuring themselves that the standard is fully coherent. The trouble with this approach is that you could develop a beautiful product which nobody wants—and then you have wasted your time. Most of us have done this at some stage in our career. You must be brave and get out selling.

(c) *Expect your boss to do the selling:* fine, if he or she is good at selling and has the time and interest to do so. Most bosses these days would have their own priorities to manage, and will expect you to take responsibility for your initiative, including getting the organization to 'buy in' to it. Above all, do not *expect* the boss to do the selling—if you have a manager who is prepared to do so, then you are exceptionally lucky. (Or as one reader commented, 'if your boss is prepared to do the selling, then he probably hasn't enough of his own work to get on with'). On the whole, the person who has the idea should sell it. It is part of your job.

Scoring: 5 points for option (a), 0 points for (b) and a token 1 point for option (c) if you can say with your hand on your heart that you know a boss who really is prepared to do that selling for you.

3 The divisional meeting: 'The right message at the wrong moment is the wrong message'

Three things are significant in this case: the issue is important to you, you have good credibility, and the timing is right for you to express your opinion—you have been genuinely invited to discuss the change. It is a situation where you should use a directive, PUSH approach and put forward your views clearly and with conviction.

(a) *Stress you feel strongly:* this is the preferred option. This is sometimes difficult for quieter technical experts, but it is vital here to speak out at the right time. The consultants from Personnel Decisions Inc. express this well in the slogan 'The right message at the wrong time is the wrong message'. People who prefer to think first, and speak later, are often at a disadvantage in meetings such as these. Experienced managers recognize this and plan some time for people to reflect and come back later, but often the pressures of workloads are such that they cannot wait too long. Another disadvantage of waiting before you speak is that your astute colleague will be able to exploit your delay. Even if you cannot articulate your views perfectly on the spot, you should convey your concern and do so promptly.

(b) *Wait and talk to colleagues:* lobbying is a BUILD approach and usually a safe option, but if you delay here you might find you have missed your moment. And do you really need to wait to get your colleagues' support before you speak out? If they agree with your concerns they can say so in the meeting. If your director were less open-minded, and you felt politically vulnerable, then building a coalition with your colleagues would be the wise option, though you would still have to move fast. In this case, I suggest you are being too cautious. You can always use this option and talk to your colleagues *after* you have made your point in the meeting.

(c) *Give up*—already? What a pity. If you have a good reputation and a fair director, then you will also have a fair chance of being listened to. It does require courage to speak out in a public arena, but making the effort will increase your self-respect and the respect which others feel towards you. You will not be the only person in that room who feels awkward about speaking out in a meeting. Some staff bear the bruises of political confrontations in the past, and this can make them withdrawn and cynical. They then operate inside a vicious circle: 'no-one in this organization pays attention to my views, so I won't bother to express them, so no-one pays attention, etc.' This can have serious consequences inside the organization. Even if this is not one of your patterns, you may recognize the same attitude in some of your colleagues or your staff. Good managers will explicitly encourage staff to express their views in meetings by inviting them by name, or consulting them informally during the coffee break.

Scoring: 5 points for option (a), 1 point for option (b) and no points for option (c).

4   The new colleagues—make an effort with other nationalities/personalities

If people have a very different communication style from yours, and a different native language, you have to make more effort to communicate with them. This is common sense, but in reality we often delay making that extra effort. The chance of making errors of judgement with other nationalities is also much higher. Each culture calibrates non-verbal behaviour differently, and first impressions can easily turn out to be wrong. You can only find this out if you give the relationship a try. There is another vicious circle here—we do not like the look of Rolf, so we do not talk to him or give him a chance, so we do not like the look of him. Make an active effort to make contact.

(a) *Wait and observe*: the problem with this option is that the longer you wait, the harder it will be to build a co-operative relationship. The most logical moment for making contact with a new colleague is when he or she arrives in your department. If you delay, Rolf could justifiably draw the conclusion that you are not very friendly yourself. Waiting games work well with colleagues whom you have good reason not to trust—because a friend has warned you of the person's manipulative behaviour in the past, for instance. Rolf's only crimes could be that he is shy and that his English is not very good.

(b) *Make an appointment*: this is the preferred option, for the reasons given above. The chances are that you will both feel that the meeting has been useful. If not, you will not have lost anything by trying, and you can still implement options (c) and (a).

(c) *Concentrate on Diane*: this is the easy option, but the more you develop the relationship solely with her, the more excluded Rolf will be. Of course, it also depends on the interfaces between you—if you have to co-operate structurally more with Diane, it would make sense to spend more time with her than with Rolf.

Scoring: 5 points for option (b), no points for (a) or (c). Give Rolf a chance.

5   The posting in the Far East: ask advice about cultural differences

Here is culture again, but in a context where the differences are much more marked, and the relationship—with a new boss—is potentially much more sensitive. My answer is based on advice from colleagues with a lot of experience as expatriates. The main point here is to try out some ideas in an informal environment, where there is no risk of anyone losing face. Ideally, you would build up a good relationship with someone from the community who could give you sound advice.

(a) *Tell him frankly:* this option is very risky, because it causes loss of face for the manager. The logic and norms of one culture— northern European, for instance—can be much more different than you realize from the logic and norms of the Far East. Be careful too with issues such as age, which can be associated with low status in one culture and high status in another.

(b) *Shut up:* this could be a good option, depending on what the inefficiencies are, and the extent of your network. At first sight, however, it seems we are jumping from one extreme in option (a) to another extreme—doing nothing—in option (b).

(c) *Consult a local colleague:* this is the best option, assuming the colleague is experienced and sensible. Your golf partner can draw his own conclusions about the value of your suggestions and the wisdom of passing them on discreetly to your boss. The indirect approach enables you to get a hearing for your ideas while at the same time saving face. And if you are successful, you will have the satisfaction of hearing your manager propose those same ideas a little later to you himself.

Scoring: 5 points for option (c), 1 point for option (b), no points at all for option (a).

6   The lack of clear objectives from your manager—be prepared to 'influence up'

This is a common problem—the boss who fails to live up to expectations. It can feel both frustrating and unfair. You have to form a realistic assessment of the situation, and you must take your corporate culture into account. If you work in a results-oriented, fast-changing organization, your best move would be to put the task before the relationship and to set your own objectives. Option (b) would then be your choice. If you are working in a more stable environment, then any kind of autonomous action on your part might be risky, and option (d) would be a safer way forward. I think you could do both, depending on the extent of your patience and perseverance. Expending some effort in influencing your manager is always worth a try, and this theme is covered in Chapter 9.

(a) *Tell the team that you have tried your best*: blaming your boss will not help you. Your team may be sympathetic, but they may also feel that you are just as ineffectual as she is.

(b) *Agree a temporary set of objectives*: this is a pragmatic way forward, which at least offers your team a structure in which they can work. It is a useful solution when your organization is undergoing change, and you want to reduce some of the stress resulting from confusion.

(c) *Go back and say you might talk to her manager*: you are threatening her, and going over your manager's head is rarely wise. Few managers appreciate being criticized to their boss, so your relationship with her would almost certainly be damaged. You would also put her own manager in an awkward position, because you are indirectly criticizing his management of your boss. This is a very risky option.

(d) *Plan your meeting with your manager*: this is the other possible option. You may find it helpful to talk this through with a friend or ally, so you can 'unload' your feelings and step back from the problem. It is a classic BUILD approach for a complex problem where you have a limited power base.

Scoring: two right answers: 5 points for (b), 5 points for (d), 0 points for (a) or (c).

7 The problem with the office manager—flexibility gets results
This case is about adjusting your approach in order to meet the office manager's needs, and at the same time to gain accurate information. People who are sensitive, as she is, will respond better to a more supportive approach than to a confrontational one.

(a) *Explain the situation is serious*: she probably realizes this already, so you have not offered any added value with this remark.

(b) *Ask directly, and say you will not leave until you find out*: asking directly is legitimate, but the threat is a reflection of your frustration and is very unlikely to help.

(c) *Start again more slowly*: the best option. She may be being evasive because she is protecting her staff. You want to persuade her that she can protect them more effectively if she gets help from you now, rather than letting the situation deteriorate further. If you can convince her that you are there to help her, she may well open up. Once you have defined the problem you can start working with her on the solution.

(d) *Talk to her staff*: here you are ignoring her and undermining her authority, so although it looks like a possible shortcut it could cause big problems in the long run. If her staff are as loyal to her as she is to them, they will feel very embarrassed and you will not be any the wiser.

Scoring: 5 points for (c), 1 point for (a), no points for (b) or (d).

8   The presentation to the committee—be clear and concise

This is a situation in which you are going to use a directive, PUSH approach, and the question is which variation of the directive approach to use. The presenter has a well-defined problem, and is credible, but dislikes giving presentations to this audience. Presenters who feel nervous often talk at length, and do not give a clear, crisp message. This defeats the purpose of a directive approach. As a presenter, ask yourself: What do I want the audience to *do* at the end of my presentation? If you want them to discuss the fees issue, you must raise this point clearly and up front.

(a) *Concentrate on course content, mention fees in passing*: this is a weak option, because the audience may well miss your reference to the fees altogether. Talking at length about the content is probably unnecessary—if it is your expert area, a brief overview of content will be all they need.

(b) *The 25-minute overview*: the audience will find it hard to listen actively to all that material, and you have almost no time for questions. The chances are that the presentation will overrun so that you will either have no feedback from the audience, or you will have to take up time scheduled for something else on the agenda, and that is impolite. You are not using your influencing resources effectively here.

(c) *The short overview, with the fees up front*: this is by far the best option. You make it clear here what you need from the audience, with time for discussion so you can get their advice or approval. When you use a directive approach you must invest the planning and the practice time. Rehearsing in front of a helpful colleague is often the best way to check that your message really does come across effectively.

Scoring: 5 points for option (c), no points for (a) or (b).

9 The new job in head office—plan your network

Many large organizations use job rotation as a way of making staff more aware of the perspectives and agendas from different parts of the business, so that they gain a good understanding of the organization as a whole. It is also an opportunity to establish an informal network, so the solution is not to duck this opportunity but to plan it.

(a) *Immerse yourself in the documentation:* for many staff this is a familiar process which they feel comfortable with, but it is the least effective of the three options. Make the contacts first, and do the reading later.

(b) *Make a list of contacts and set up meetings:* working methodically is a helpful start, and this approach will enable you to make the most of your stay in head office. This is the best of the three options.

(c) *Concentrate on your own team and targets:* this is better than option (a), but the scope is too narrow. You need to build relationships with a broader range of stakeholders.

Scoring: 5 points for (b), 1 point for (c) and no points for (a).

10 The unenthusiastic client—when you meet resistance, stop and explore

The lack of enthusiasm is an indication of underlying resistance. You need to recognize this and find out the causes.

(a) *Go through the key points again:* it is unlikely that the client's lack of enthusiasm is due to hearing difficulties or to problems with understanding, but I suppose this option would at least buy you thinking time. It is tempting to try to sell a proposal by repeating the arguments. Occasionally it works—the client might have missed a step in your thinking process first time round—but usually the resistance is due to hidden worries which you need to investigate with patience.

(b) *Remind him that your proposal is in line with his specification:* I doubt whether this sort of pressure would be helpful. He has a right to change his specification anyway, particularly in the middle of a change process where the situation is bound to be fluid. You will come across as rigid and unhelpful with this PUSH approach.

(c) *Stop and ask him to explain:* this is the best option, and classic BUILD. He may not tell you straightaway about his concerns, but you are moving in the right direction.

Scoring: 5 points for (c), 1 point for (a), no points for (b).

11   Getting help from your colleagues—identify the benefits for each individual

This case is about building and using co-operative relationships with colleagues across your organization. Mutual trust is the essential element here—ideally, you would have helped these colleagues with some of their problems in the past. Either way, you must tailor your approach to their individual needs, and be honest.

(a) *Send a note by e-mail:* some managers would like to trade most of their interpersonal contact for e-mail messages, but standardized requests for favours rarely work. We need to be treated as individuals. You can use e-mail to support your influencing initiatives, but never to replace them.

(b) *Talk to their managers:* now you are going over the heads of your colleagues, and they are unlikely to appreciate that. If you want their full co-operation, they must have a genuine choice as to whether to work with you or not.

(c) *Work out what each person stands to gain, and be honest about the effort:* this is the best BUILD approach. Honesty, together with some thought about each person's agenda, will increase trust. You can read more about this approach in Chapter 7.

Scoring: 5 points for (c), no points for (a) or (b).

12   The cross-disciplinary task force—involve your team in key decisions

This is about choosing your decision-making procedure at a critical point in an important project. You need the full commitment of your team, so whatever your credibility and power base you should actively involve them with a BUILD approach.

(a) *Use the meeting to agree the objectives:* this is the preferred option, because you can get the team to 'buy in' to the project.

(b) *Write the plan yourself:* whatever time you save by writing the plan yourself, you lose later if you find out that the team members are not fully committed to it. Even if they seem reasonably happy with the copies you distribute, you will have missed a critical opportunity to align the team at the start.

(c) *Use the meeting to get to know each other:* I would find this a rather 'woolly' start to the project and would prefer to get going on the plan, particularly if everyone is busy. The team could then socialize in the evening or over lunch. You could make a case for this option, however, if you are working in a corporate culture where personal relationships are very important to staff, and where they find it normal to get to know each other properly before settling down to the task.

Scoring: 5 points for option (a), 1 point for (c) if you are working in a very social corporate environment, no points for (b).

13   Your idea for the section—be flexible in the early stages of coalition building

Your idea will affect a lot of your colleagues, and you have mixed credibility, so it makes sense to be open to your colleagues' suggestions. Some 'give and take' is always necessary at this stage of coalition building. Try to get the colleagues to put forward suggestions for improving your proposal.

(a) *Explain your idea again:* repetition will not help, and suppose they have some good suggestions? If you work on the idea together it will be much easier to implement it.

(b) *Take the tentative support as a starting point:* some flexibility is always helpful. This is the classic BUILD and the best option.

(c) *Drop the idea:* do not give up too soon—influencing requires stamina! If you cannot get a ' critical mass' of support behind you then you may have to back down gracefully, but you are not at that stage yet.

Scoring: 5 points for (b), no points for (a) or (c).

14   The manager who refuses to change—if your credibility is good, take a risk

Here you are dealing with resistance, but your credibility is good and you have reasonable support from your boss and the other members of your team. The manager's contribution is important but not vital. In these circumstances you can afford to take a risk and to go ahead with the change anyway, using a directive approach rather than a BUILD approach. The other two options for this case have their merits also—a lot would depend on just how pushed you were for time.

(a) *Take time with the hostile manager:* if you could get him behind you that would be ideal, but with your high credibility I do not think this is essential for moving forward. In most cases managers who see their colleagues going with the change will eventually co-operate also. A different reason for choosing this option could be if the hostile manager is particularly popular with his colleagues, or is very much respected by them, and/or if your corporate culture sets great store by friendly teamwork and you think confrontation would be frowned upon.

(b) *Have a series of meetings with the other managers:* the success of this option would depend on their relationship with the hostile manager, and on how much he trusted them. If he can see you holding the meetings, and realizes what you are doing, he may become a lot more suspicious of you personally, so this option could be risky. The managers could also feel in an awkward position—they may feel you are manipulating them.

(c) *Take a risk and go ahead anyway:* this is my preferred option, but you would need a fallback plan—the opportunity to spend time trying to win the hostile manager over, or of transferring him if the worst comes to the worst. We are assuming, of course, that you are right, and that the hostile manager is wrong about your proposal.

Scoring: 5 points for (c) because I think it is worth the risk, 3 points for (a) if you are working in a culture which sets great store by friendly relationships, and 1 point for (b)—there is a chance (b) could work, but you would have to consider the trust angle.

15 Managing company politics—consult the 'hidden advisers'
This is about analysing organizational decision making, and about building support when you have a limited power base.

(a) *Make an appointment with the general manager:* talking direct to the main decision maker is always risky if you have no track record with him. You need to be more patient and build up support with the other managers whom he will consult.

(b) *Ask the assistant how to handle this:* this is a safe and sensible option. The assistant is a 'hidden adviser' and will be well placed to advise you. I am assuming you have a friendly relationship with the assistant, otherwise he would not play squash with you.

(c) *Talk directly to the vice president:* this is risky, because you are going over your boss's head, and most organizations strongly discourage this because it sabotages the line structure. You would need at the very least to consult and inform your boss first.

Scoring: 5 points for option (b), no points for (a) or (c).

Scoring your responses—an overview

In Table 5.1 circle the answers which you have chosen. A letter (B) behind the score indicates correct use of BUILD. A letter (P) indicates correct use of PUSH.

If you have scored between 55 and 91, you obviously have both an interest in influencing and an aptitude for it—at least on paper! You are also ready to tackle the more complex influencing cases coming up in later chapters.

If you have scored between 35 and 54, you have made a good start but you might need to check out any in-built bias in your style. You

Table 5.1

Question no.	Option (a)	Option (b)	Option (c)	Option (d)
1	0	5 (B)	0	
2	5 (B)	0	1	
3	5 (P)	1	0	
4	0	5 (B)	0	
5	0	1	5 (B)	
6	0	5 (B)	0	5 (B)
7	1	0	5 (B)	0
8	0	0	5 (P)	
9	0	5 (B)	1	
10	1	0	5 (B)	
11	0	0	5 (B)	
12	5 (B)	0	1	
13	0	5 (B)	0	
14	3	1	5 (P)	
15	0	5 (B)	0	

may have a tendency to over-use the directive style, for instance, or you may be giving up on some situations too quickly. The next section helps you to analyse your style more closely, so you can identify any underlying patterns and plan which skills to develop.

If you have scored below 35, you may be unusually honest. Most people who have tested this questionnaire have said that they could work out quite easily what the 'right' answers should be, but admitted that in reality they might react rather differently in some of the situations. Another explanation for a lower score could be that you are in a job where you work primarily on your own, and that you have not had an opportunity to develop your influencing skills. If you think that the options you have chosen really do reflect your behaviour, then you probably have an underlying bias either towards excess PUSH, or to avoiding the influencing opportunities. Reviewing your influencing style could be a first step towards becoming more effective at work.

Analysing your answers to assess your own style

Look back at the answers you have selected. If you chose six or more of the inappropriate PUSH answers, you may also be over-using the directive style at work. If you selected two or more of the inappropriate BUILD answers, you could be a good influencer who is a little too cautious. I would argue that you are missing some opportunities for the directive approach, and that over-use of BUILD could cost you and others unnecessary time and effort. This depends on the corporate and national culture in which you are working—some organizations expect more use of BUILD.

You can also analyse your answers according to the type of BUILD activity. Situations which require appropriate *networking*, for instance, are 2, 4, 9, and 11. If you missed two or more of those, it might be worth reviewing the value of networking to you in your current job. Answers which reflect appropriate ways of *dealing with resistance* are 1, 7 and 10. If you missed all those you may need to work on your listening skills!

Doing no influencing at all—giving up too early, thinking it is not your job, blaming others, etc.

Doing nothing is a valid and sensible option if the timing for an idea is wrong, if you missed the opportunity to do some necessary lobbying, or if your credibility and power base are too limited for you to have any effect. In all the following situations I would argue that this is *not* the case: 1, 2, 3, 4, 9 and 13. If you chose five or more of the 'wrong' options in those situations, you may need to reconsider the amount of influencing power available to you. With a better understanding of the influencing process and of influencing techniques, you may be able to have more impact at work.

The blocks to developing your BUILD influencing skills

Certain beliefs and attitudes may prevent managers from developing their skills. Here are some examples, followed by counter-arguments for you to consider:

1. 'Consultation is a waste of time—it takes too long'
2. 'If I don't get things going, no-one else will take the initiative'
3. 'Honestly, I'm not convinced the others have anything to contribute'
4. 'If I listen to other people, they'll just ignore me'
5. 'Look, I know I'm right—they should listen to me'
6. 'I hate politics, and I don't believe in lobbying—it's underhand.'

1   Does the BUILD approach waste time?

Yes, if you use the approach inappropriately, with trivial decisions, for instance. However, over-use of the directive approach also wastes time and resources. If you are for ever telling people what to do, you will demotivate your team and alienate your colleagues. That is inefficient too.

2   If you do not lead the group, will there be a leaderless vacuum?

Some inveterate PUSHers will ask at the beginning of a discussion 'Does anyone want to lead the group?' or state 'I think we need a chairman'. They wait about three seconds, then leap in with 'In that case I'll do it'. Give others the chance to develop their skills and confidence, and often they will do a good job. Share the power and share the work.

3   Do the others really have anything to contribute?

This is a doubt which is rarely expressed openly, but you can see from the dismissive behaviour which some managers display in meetings that it is running through their minds. If you do not give people a chance to contribute, you will never discover what they have to offer.

Cross-disciplinary, cross-functional and cross-cultural teams are particularly vulnerable to insensitive behaviour from one or more team members. If you are responsible for a mixed team, take time in the first meeting to explain the function of the team and what the individuals and the organization stand to gain from it. If it turns out that someone really has little to contribute to the team then there should be no obligation on either side for the person to attend more meetings.

If you are chairing a new team with mixed membership, the following suggestions can promote co-operation between members:

- *Make it clear at the start of a meeting **why** each person has been invited,* and what his or her particular contribution could be, so that the other members of the team are aware of each person's qualifications for being there.
- *Invite people explicitly—by name—to contribute,* and give them time to formulate their thoughts, especially if they are not working in their native language.
- *Acknowledge the contribution individuals have made,* including the work done outside the meeting, so that the noisier members of the group, for instance, appreciate what the quieter members have been doing in the background.
- *Be very careful about any criticism,* even if it is only implicit, which is given in any public arena—even a hint may discourage less confident members of the group.

CASE STUDY 5.1   THE SUPPORTIVE WORK GROUP LEADER

Years ago I assisted a leader of a multinational work group. The task of the work group was to make recommendations for a forthcoming reorganization, and the membership was very mixed—a nervous young typist found herself sitting next to a highly articulate senior manager. The work group leader was sensitive, supportive and firm. He made it clear from the start that in this normally hierarchical organization, for this project every individual's opinion was equally important. In the first meeting he invited everyone to introduce themselves, and encouraged the more junior members explicitly to contribute their views. Inevitably there were moments of tension, but he followed up after the meeting by sending a note to the braver members of the junior staff, thanking them for their frankness. The result was that nearly all the initial members of the group worked hard right the way through the project, and the work group was a success. That was a manager who had no trouble motivating his staff.

4   If you listen to others, will they take advantage of your goodwill?

If you are working in a very hostile environment then I suppose this could be a risk, but most people would not exploit good listening. You may need to develop your communication techniques so that you can manage your re-entry into a discussion, staying courteous but also making your point.

Suggestions for listening—and being listened to in turn

- *Try to put your own opinions to one side* before you start listening, so you can concentrate on the other person.
- *Listen right the way through to the end* of the other person's sentences—do not cut them off.
- In sensitive situations, *try to wait 3 seconds at the end of the other person's sentence* before you jump in with your views.
- *If you ask an open question, allow the other person time to think.* Recent research suggests you should *wait up to 7 seconds* before you give up (7 seconds can seem an age to talkative extroverts, but waiting really does work!).
- *Avoid the 'Yes, but . . .' opener* as you put forward your opposing point of view. 'Yes, buts . . .' are a real give-away—they show you have not really been listening, just waiting for the other person to draw breath so that you can leap in. Try the following tips instead:
- *Discipline yourself to summarize*—this shows you have listened and is a much more powerful intervention than a contradiction. A useful sequence is the following:
  - *Summarize:* say, for instance, 'If I understand you right, you're saying that . . . Is that right?'
    Check that you have understood correctly—otherwise listen again and then correct your summary.
  - *Link and make your point:* Start by linking in to what the person has said, then state your view clearly, using a question to invite a response:

  'I take your point about the costs, but couldn't we solve that by . . . ?'

  This protocol proves to the group that you really have listened to their views, and enables you in turn to get a fair hearing.

People who get regular feedback that they are impatient are often simply bad listeners. Listening is a skill, not a personality trait, so you can improve it with practice.

5   But what if you are certain you are right? Surely the others should then listen to you?

Unfortunately not. One young manager said that 'Hell is knowing you're right, and not being able to convince the others'. Good influencers recognize that other colleagues have agendas, needs, priorities and values which could be very different from theirs, and that they have to make an effort to bridge the gap. You cannot *expect* others to listen to you unless you have high credibility. Usually you have to rely on your influencing skills to create interest and support.

Some managers make almost every argument an issue of principle, and they can be very tiring to work with. All organizations require a certain amount of 'give and take.' The cry 'I'm doing what I believe is right' can be used to imply that other colleagues are being cowardly—in attempting to co-operate with difficult clients, for instance, instead of refusing to work with them. We need to be honest with ourselves about whether something really is an issue of principle or not.

6   What if you hate politics, and think that lobbying is 'underhand'?

If you are clear in your own mind that you are working in the interests of your unit and of your organization, then an influencing technique like lobbying is often the best way forward. Much of lobbying is actually about sensible planning, to enable you to contact the right person at the right time, as you will see from Chapter 6. If you are in a very political organization you will have to be particularly careful about the sequence in which you lobby, but the process itself should not be secretive in any way.

We move into the grey areas of ethics when a particular proposal is likely to promote your own career as well as the reputation of your unit. Who really stands to gain the most? Are you deceiving yourself when you declare that you are working in the interests of the organization? Only you can tell. Realistically, most managers will put most effort into proposals which promote both the unit's interests and their own. Occasionally, however, managers may be prepared to sacrifice their own interests in order to help their organization.

Examples of behaviours which are important for ethical influencing are:

- Being honest about the 'downside' of proposals
- Ensuring in networking that you give at least as much as you take
- Keeping your manager informed of your actions
- Giving credit where credit is due
- Genuinely aiming for ways forward which take other people's needs into account
- Giving your staff, your colleagues and your own manager a fair chance to put forward their views and to have those views understood.

Trust is such an essential component of effective influencing that ethical influencers have an advantage in most organizations over their more manipulative counterparts.

A dislike of politics is sometimes a cover for the feelings of uncertainty that many managers feel when dealing with 'soft issues'. The solution is not to avoid organizational politics but to invest effort into understanding and dealing with them effectively, and that is what this book is largely about.

Blocks to using the directive PUSH style appropriately

Here are some of the beliefs that prevent people from using the directive style as much as they could:

1. 'I think you should always be prepared to compromise'
2. 'I don't like telling people what to do—I think group decisions are better'
3. 'People need a lot of time to adjust to change.'

1   Should you always be prepared to compromise?

Compromise can become a way of life in large organizations, and some managers forget they have the right and responsibility to assert their views. In situations where you have valuable expertise and experience in particular, your colleagues need you to give clear advice and directions. Sometimes standing up for your opinions is a question of courage, as well as judgement. Assertiveness training and literature can help, and I have included books on assertiveness in the chapter notes. Under-use of PUSH can mean that you do not get the respect and recognition that you deserve.

2   What if you dislike making decisions yourself, and prefer to make decisions in the group?

The consensus approach is very valuable with key decisions which affect everyone in the group. Examples of such decisions are agreeing objectives, roles and responsibilities, important procedures and methodologies—anything where you genuinely need the full commitment of your team. Consensus is *not* an appropriate decision-making procedure for issues which are not so important and which affect only part of the team, or for decisions which depend on the manager's own broader understanding of organizational objectives.

Consensus is also not appropriate in situations where your team needs you to take responsibility for a difficult or painful decision which is necessary for your organization.

3   Do people always need a lot of time to adjust to change?
This is a rather different kind of block and a complex question. On the one hand, change does require time. On the other, some of the endless discussions planned by senior managers to ensure 'buy-in' of change can be stressful for staff who wish 'they'd just get on with it and tell us what to do'. Generally, if the change process is inevitable it is better if you tell that clearly to your staff, and then give them the time to process the consequences. The rate at which people adjust to change depends on individual needs, and your team members will adjust at different speeds. If you wait until the last person has adjusted, some of your other staff may already have left for jobs elsewhere. In a recent meeting, one civil servant said that a business process re-engineering initiative would take at least six years in his department to complete. His neighbour, a manager in the building industry, laughed and said that his business would be bankrupt by then. You need to use your judgement with your own staff, and be prepared to take the occasional risk. The techniques and models in this book should assist you in deciding at which point you can 'PUSH' an initiative.

Suggestions for developing your directive style

- Identify those issues which you feel strongly about, and prepare your arguments—that way you will be ready in a meeting to present your views with confidence.
- Check when you have to make a decision whether you really need the support and contribution of all your group, or whether it would be quicker and more efficient to make the decision on your own.
- Check your credibility ratings in the different contexts in which you work—remember that in high-credibility contexts you should use a more directive style.
- Practise assertive behaviour in low-risk situations inside and outside work. Tell trusted friends and colleagues that you are working on your influencing style, and ask for their support.
- Identify some managers who have an influencing style which you admire, and who have the skill to make a point forcefully without overpowering others. Observe how they behave—ideally, ask for their advice and coaching.

- Do not assume that you always have to be cautious with change situations—assess them on a case-by-case basis.

Summary of assessing your own style

- Your personal influencing style is based on your skills, experience and personality. Some aspects will be more difficult to change than others—either way, you should use a style with which you feel comfortable.
- Most of us tend to over-use one style at the expense of the other, and it is useful to compare your choices in a given situation with someone else's. Often you find that a small adjustment could enable you to reap good results in a wider range of contexts.
- You may also need to think about some of the blocks which prevent you from developing your skills in a particular direction— are you working on the basis of some unfounded or out-of-date assumptions?

Using this book further

You have now completed Part I of this book, which has given an overview of the main criteria for selecting a particular influencing strategy, together with some of the pitfalls to avoid. Part II describes the core BUILD skills in more depth, with examples and step-by-step approaches to help you tackle the more difficult influencing situations (see Fig. 5.1). Part III describes applications of BUILD techniques, with key stakeholders who are important to your success at work, and with groups and teams when you are leading change initiatives.

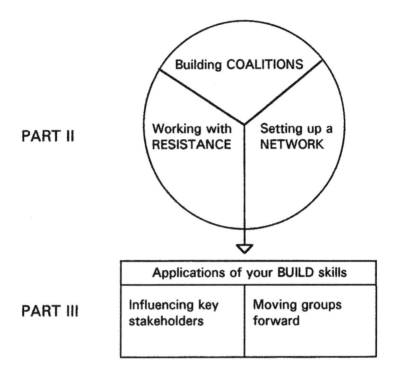

PART II

PART III

Fig. 5.1 BUILD skills

Notes

For an accessible overview of competencies for managers, see *Successful Manager's Handbook—Development Suggestions for Today's Managers* written by Brian L. Davis, Lowell W. Hellervik, James L. Sheard, Carol J. Skube and Susan H. Gebelein, published by Personnel Decisions. Inc., 1992.

For literature on culture, see Trompenaars (1993) and Guy and Mattock (1993). For literature on assertiveness for PUSH influencing, read the classic on assertiveness, *Assertiveness at work* by Ken and Kate Back, McGraw-Hill, 1982. You can also find a readable, updated view in *Positive Management— assertiveness for managers* by Paddy O'Brien, Nicholas Brealey, 1992.

Part II
DEVELOPING YOUR
BUILD SKILLS

6 SPLASH: how to build coalitions and get your change implemented

The need for coalitions

Much of management is about solving problems, and it is easy to think that the answer to problem solving lies simply in finding a good idea. Actually your idea is only the start—not the end—of what can be a long and complex journey. Here is an example of someone who is just embarking on the influencing process.

CASE STUDY 6.1 PETER AND THE NEW
RECRUITMENT PROCEDURE: INSPIRATION DAWNS!

Peter was sitting one fine Sunday afternoon at his kitchen table, scribbling furiously. As HR manager for a midsize engineering company he had been struggling with the problem of how to improve the quality of staff being recruited. Some of his older colleagues in particular were convinced they could assess the quality of applicants on 'gut feel' and in five minutes flat. The results in some cases had been disastrous and costly. Now inspiration had dawned and he reckoned he had cracked the problem. His action plan for the new recruitment scheme read as follows:

- Agree statement of problem
- Produce list of key competencies and job profiles for all technical positions
- Set up training course with help from external consultants to train all senior and middle-level staff in interviewing techniques
- Design interviewing forms that can be used by all managers to structure their interviews
- Get all interviewers to produce detailed interview reports
- Persuade all managers in the company to contribute and adhere to new guidelines—get their buy-in.

Now what?

Peter paused after reading the last line. 'That's the tricky bit,' he thought. 'Who do I need to talk to first?' He made another list:

- The HR director—Peter's boss, well meaning but usually dashing all over the world, talking to people in the other subsidiaries

- The other divisional directors—who would have mixed responses to the change. The technical director would resist the new system at all costs, seeing it as a waste of time and an invasion of his territory
- The chief executive himself? He had never been seen on a training course, but Peter would have to get him on this one if his plan were to succeed.

Peter filed his notes carefully. He could work out the next steps on Monday.

Ideas do not sell themselves—you have to sell them. Peter realizes that he will have to expend time and effort to get his plan implemented. Often managers wrestle for a long time with a problem and feel exhausted by the time they come up with an answer. It can then seem very unfair if your colleagues do not embrace your solution immediately with gratitude and enthusiasm. This is one senior manager's experience:

CASE STUDY 6.2   CHANGING THE SALES COMMISSION SCHEME: WHERE WE WENT WRONG

'We'd had a reorganization in our products company. A working party was set up to see how we could change the sales commission scheme for our senior sales staff, to encourage them to spend more time selling into key international accounts. We had to do this at zero cost—not easy. We worked together for weeks to try to find a mechanism that would be fair, that wouldn't distort our accounting practices and that would be relatively straightforward to implement. In the working party we felt pleased with the solution. Our mistake was to assume that everyone else would be as pleased with our efforts as we were.

With hindsight we realize now that we omitted some important steps. Because we were still busy with the reorganization, two of our key managers were not actively involved in our project, and we never really got their full support and commitment. Similarly, we didn't invest enough time in convincing all the top management. We've made respectable progress, but we haven't achieved all the changes we were aiming for. We're now having to go back over some of the steps, to make sure people really understand why the mechanism is designed as it is, and how it actually works. We'd have got much better results if we'd built more solid support at the time.'

Selling the solution across your organization often takes more time and effort than devising the solution in the first place. Unless you are prepared to invest the effort, your idea will never be fully implemented. Even if you are a senior manager with plenty of credibility and power, you still have to go through the process of selling your ideas to your staff if they are to feel committed and if you want to see results.

Don't give up! Use the SPLASH approach

'It all looks like too much hard work,' said one manager when confronted with the realization that he had a long way to go before his

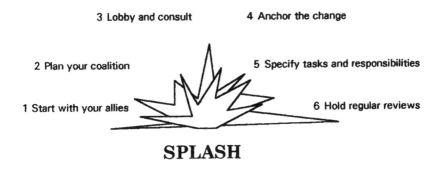

3 Lobby and consult   4 Anchor the change

2 Plan your coalition   5 Specify tasks and responsibilities

1 Start with your allies   6 Hold regular reviews

SPLASH

Fig. 6.1 SPLASH—a model for building coalitions and implementing change. © Sue Craig

proposal would be accepted. However, coalition building is easier—and faster—if you keep an overview of the main stages in your head. The *SPLASH* model (Fig. 6.1) gives you a step-by-step approach for building coalitions and getting support for your idea, right the way through to the implementation stage.

SPLASH—Stage 1: *Start with your allies*

Try your idea out with trusted colleagues first. This enables you to speak freely in a safe environment, where you will not make a fool of yourself if your idea does not stand up to the light of day. Assuming yours is a good idea, you can use this opportunity to work on it further. Typically your allies will be:

- Experienced members of your own team
- Colleagues at your own level in the organization who will give you constructive criticism and genuine support, and with whom you have a track record
- Your manager, and/or any other senior staff with whom you have a relationship based on trust and mutual respect.

The emphasis in Stage 1 is on *validating your proposal*—what Rosabeth Moss Kanter calls a 'sanity check' (Fig. 6.2). By talking through your idea with people you trust you will be able to do the following:

1. *Get agreement that there really is a problem.* Be prepared to discuss what is wrong with the current system, and what the consequences are. Check your perceptions of the current situation

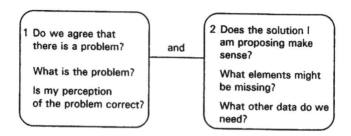

Fig. 6.2 Validate your proposal

against those of your colleagues. If you cannot prove the need for change, your initiative will not get off the ground. You may need to collect hard data (via benchmarking for instance) to prove that a problem exists and has to be solved. Do your allies agree the current system is unsatisfactory? Have you, as one manager put it, ' struck a chord'?

2. *Check your idea makes sense.* Is your solution coherent? Realistic? Are your assumptions correct? How does your idea fit into the business objectives or wider mission of your organization? What's the link? What are the implications for the future? How exactly will your proposal improve the performance of your organization? How will that improved performance be measured? How can we quantify the gains and the benefits?

Your answers to these questions will determine whether or not you should go ahead with your proposal. If your allies disagree with your problem definition, there will be little point in your continuing with your proposal in its current form. If they cannot support your outline solution, you should either give up or go back and think again.

Think also about the timing generally for your proposition. You may be able to save yourself a lot of work by waiting until one of your senior managers is interested in the idea you are proposing. If your allies do broadly support your idea, then you can go ahead to the next stage and start asking for their help in refining and improving it (see Fig. 6.3).

3. *Refine your idea with your allies' suggestions.* Get their help in clarifying your views and anticipating objections. What are the possible advantages and disadvantages of your proposal? What are the potential risks—and how will you manage them? Ask them to find ways of making your proposal more robust and more attractive. If you take your allies' ideas on board, they will share ownership for your proposal.

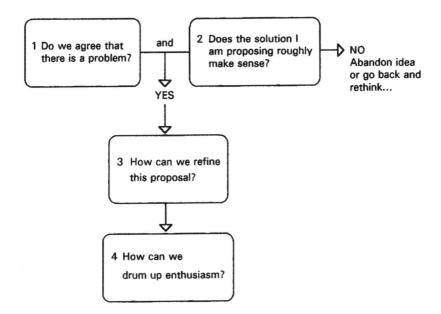

Fig. 6.3   Go ahead or not?

4. *Drum up some enthusiasm.* If you cannot inspire your allies you
   will not convince your enemies. Try to develop a 'vision' of the
   solution that will appeal to people's imagination and which will
   be easy to communicate.

CASE STUDY 6.3   THE NEW RECRUITMENT
PROCEDURE: PETER TESTS HIS IDEA WITH A FRIEND
Peter went for lunch with Martin, an old friend and colleague who worked in
accounts. Martin had been with the company for years, and was liked and
respected by many of his colleagues including his boss, the finance director. He
had never been particularly interested in promoting his own career, and so was
regarded as an unbiased adviser. Peter outlined what he saw as the problem and
how he proposed to resolve it. 'There's a clear business reason for changing the
system,' he said. 'The general manager's been talking about growing the
company by 25 per cent over the next two years. In itself that's going to be a
headache, but if we don't have a proper approach to recruitment it could be a
disaster in the longer term.'

Martin refines Peter's idea
'I can see what you mean,' Martin said, 'but what have you got in the way of
hard data to support your arguments? How much does it actually cost to
recruit, say, a graduate and train him up? How much money do we lose if a

graduate leaves, or if we've over-estimated someone's potential and have to persuade them to go? If you want me to talk to my manager for you, then you will have to give me some numbers—that's what he'll be interested in. And you'll have to work out the costs and the return on investment roughly of your new scheme.' Peter hated numbers—and his face said it all. Martin chuckled. 'Get one of your team to come over to our department,' he said. 'We'll show them where to start.'

'Do you think my proposal makes sense, though?' Peter asked. 'Sure,' Martin replied. 'But you have a lot of work to do before you can convince the directors.'

The principle behind coalitions is to achieve escalating agreement—a snowball effect. Armed with Martin's suggestions and some new data, Peter can now talk to his own manager, the HR director.

CASE STUDY 6.4   PETER TALKS TO HIS MANAGER—THE IDEA CHANGES SHAPE

Back in the office Peter talked on the phone to the HR director. He was in Hong Kong. 'Great idea, Pete,' he said, 'but I think you're being a touch ambitious. All those competency profiles will take too long. You'll have to be more pragmatic. And that firm of consultants you wanted for the courses—too pricey. See if you can sort out some deal for training on an in-house basis. Fax me your thoughts and I'll see what I can do.' 'Terrific,' thought Peter. 'If this turns out to be a success he'll be saying it was his idea. And if the management team doesn't like it, I'll take the rap.'

His team member, Diana, brought him a cup of coffee. 'That's the way it goes,' she said. 'We'll just have to make it a success and then we'll all get the credit. I wonder whether some kind of pilot scheme might be worth considering? You know, start the scheme in one division, then expand it when we can show it works... Worth thinking about?'

Key points for Stage 1: Start with your allies

- *Expect your idea to change shape.* An early pitfall in Stage 1 is being too rigid and too protective of your initial proposal. One manager said 'I don't like to share my ideas with colleagues—I'm always worried that they'll change them.' The whole purpose of talking your idea through is that other people will want to influence your idea if they are to own it and implement it. Robin Pedler is Executive Director of the European Centre for Public Affairs, and he helps organizations to lobby European Union institutions. He says you should 'work out your prime objectives, but be realistic. You're going to have to trade if you want your idea to be accepted. Limit yourself to what you think you can get agreed, and be prepared to compromise on the rest.'

- *Be an 'opportunistic influencer'.* Much of successful influencing consists of grasping the chance opportunities which come your way. Diana's idea of a pilot scheme is an example.
- *Be prepared to share the credit.* Yes, of course it *was* your idea really, but 'our idea' will sound so much more appealing to your colleagues. You will need active support from a number of people if your idea is to survive through to the implementation stage. Be generous with sharing recognition if you want your proposal to succeed. Peter will have to involve and acknowledge help from a number of people, including:

  – Martin, who has offered suggestions and advice
  – His team—Diana is already making a helpful contribution
  – His own manager—the HR director will expect to have a stake in Peter's success, and will quite reasonably expect him to come up with good ideas which will strengthen the reputation of the whole HR division.

- *Let other people propose your idea if necessary*—sometimes this is politically wise. If you stand to gain personally from the proposal, you may evoke scepticism and resistance elsewhere in the organization because others mistrust your motives—however unfounded this mistrust may be. Getting other people to present your idea could then promote your chances of success, especially if they are not automatically seen to be your allies. Robin Pedler advises Finns and Swedes, for instance, that if they have a proposition for the European Parliament, getting support from the Danes may not be enough to ensure success. Instead they should try to find a Greek or Portuguese group to agree with them, so that the idea is not labelled as 'Northern'. In Peter's case, Martin's support is all the more useful because Martin works for another division and is perceived as neutral.
- *Think before you speak!* This is a warning above all for enthusiasts. Do not expose your ideas too soon to colleagues who could be hostile to you. Your critics in the organization may be quick to point out flaws which you have not had time to think about. If this happens in public you could lose support and credibility.

CASE STUDY 6.5   PETER ALMOST MAKES A MISTAKE
The technical director came into the office to put something in the HR in-tray. For once, he looked in a good mood—he actually greeted Peter. A small faint ray of hope passed through Peter's mind—suppose the TD turned out to like the

idea? Suppose for once he did not say something critical about HR? Should Peter seize the moment and fly the idea past him? Diana saw him hesitate. 'Don't even think about it,' she said. 'He'll tear our proposal to bits. Better work more on it first—he hasn't agreed there's a problem yet. I have got some time free tomorrow so I'll go over to the accounts department and get started on those numbers.'

Summary of Stage 1: Start with your allies

- Validate your idea with people you trust, before you take any further steps.
- Be prepared to abandon your proposal if you cannot get early support for it, or if the timing for your idea is unfavourable.
- Be flexible and pragmatic—expect your idea to evolve.
- Share the credit.
- Think who should present your proposal.
- Think before you speak, especially to critics.

The output from Stage 1 is *a proposal which is coherent, realistic and robust*, and which is already *generating enthusiasm and support.*

SPLASH—Stage 2: Plan your coalition

Stage 1 was about *refining the content* of your idea: Stage 2 is about *planning the process* you will use in order to get support for it. To plan your coalition you must decide:

- *Who to contact*: identify your strategic targets—the stakeholders who can influence, support or veto your idea, at any level in the organization.
- *What sequence* you will use when you contact them. Start with the people who are most likely to be open to your idea. Once you have built up a basis of support you can tackle the people who will have objections. Be careful not to back anyone into a corner—people like to feel they have choices, so make sure you have left them a way out if they are not prepared to support you actively.
- *Who can help you* in the lobbying process. Aim to get advice and active help in the coalition-building stage, both from your allies and from the strategic contacts who agree to support you and who could in turn lobby others for you. Other colleagues may have more credibility with senior staff than you do, for instance, and they may have easier access to some of your key contacts.

Influencing is a highly dynamic process. Dr Rinus van Schendelen of the Erasmus University in Holland says that coalition building is not an orderly game of chess, where you plan and make your moves. It is more like an 'Alice in Wonderland' game where the pieces stand up of their own accord and walk around, and other invisible hands hover over the board. If you walk away from the game you do not know quite what you will find when you return. The emphasis in Stage 2 is therefore on setting up a flexible, co-ordinated approach, preferably in discussion with your allies.

Identify the decision maker(s)

A logical starting point is to think about the major decision makers you need to influence. Peter begins by thinking about the management team in his organization. The general manager is the key decision maker, but Peter does not have enough credibility or power to lobby him directly. The general manager will consult his management team about any proposal which has a broad impact on his organization. Some directors in the team will have more influence than others, and Peter needs to know who these are. The influential directors will in turn consult their advisers among their own staff to hear their opinions on Peter's scheme. Peter must persuade these advisers to back his scheme.

Identify the Movers and Shakers

The Movers and Shakers are the people at any level in an organization who make things happen. One senior British engineer in a mid-sized Norwegian company made this point to an expatriate friend who had recently been posted to join him. 'This company is run by 14 people,' he said. 'And they're not all the senior managers.'

Many organizations are the same. They are driven by a small number of people at the middle and senior levels who have the energy, vision and political skills to initiate and implement change. Movers and Shakers are involved in all major initiatives, and you will notice that they are often consulted by senior staff. Sometimes they include staff functions or administrative posts which have little formal status but a surprising amount of informal influence. If you want to get things done in your own organization you need to identify your Movers and Shakers and build a relationship with them.

One consultant who is politically very skilled said that the best way to identify the influential people is to observe who decides the outcome on important decisions, and whose name is mentioned most often by those around you. This is particularly important in organizations where people may be reporting to two different managers—one in the local organization, for instance, and another in head office. Which manager is more powerful? The consultant's advice was simple: 'Watch and learn.'

Here is a story from a manager about a Mover and Shaker in a large bank in the Benelux:

CASE STUDY 6.6 A MOVER AND SHAKER: MR SCHMIDT WOULD SEE IT THROUGH

'Four years ago we replaced the traditional departments in our bank with an organization based on account management. A special Change Management Section (CMS) was set up to implement the change. The section itself was small and had limited authority, but the head, Mr Schmidt, was very close to the divisional director, and we quickly realized that he wielded enormous influence. If he thought you had a good idea, he would see it through—even if it had nothing to do directly with his section's responsibilities. I noticed this when I made budget requests. In theory I had to get the permission of the much larger administration department, which on paper had all the power to grant or refuse my request. In practice, I just talked it through with Mr Schmidt, and if he agreed then I'd get it. The head of the administration department had nothing like the influence of Mr Schmidt.

Two years later Mr Schmidt was promoted to a more senior post in a different part of the organization. He went on from strength to strength, but the section lost all its power and was disbanded shortly afterwards.'

We will now have a look at some of the Movers and Shakers where Peter works. The directors who are truly influential are indicated in italics in Fig. 6.4. Each of these directors has a number of subordinates, but the figure includes only those who are Movers and Shakers.

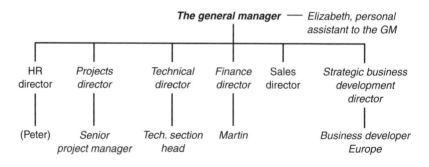

Fig. 6.4   Coalition planning: the Movers and Shakers

What if your line manager is not a Mover and Shaker?

Figure 6.4 depicts a common dilemma. Many managers have been taught to respect and work through the line—in Peter's case, through the HR director. Unfortunately, you may find that your own manager, like Peter's, does not have the influence to help you. Sometimes the manager has influence, but little time. Either way, you have to find another route to sell your idea—usually by working laterally across your network. You should, of course, keep your manager informed and consult him or her regularly, especially in areas where your manager has the expertise and resources to help. Peter has done this.

Working outside the line always involves some risk and a lot of tact. Some organizations will encourage this approach because they recognize it as effective and efficient. One manager said that working in this way was often 'the basis for re-engineering a change of culture'. Other, more traditional organizations will discourage it. Many organizations will be quite happy for you to work this way as long as (1) you do not upset anybody and (2) you are successful. If you share the credit then, of course, your boss, your unit, your career and your organization will all benefit.

Who influences whom? Sketching the informal network

Movers and Shakers can influence not only up their own line but also across other lines. They are experts at getting the commitment of others to a particular course of action, and this is crucial information if you want to lobby successfully. You can often represent this lateral, informal influence better with a sketch, showing the key decision maker(s), the Movers and Shakers and the people who advise them, and finally putting your own name into the picture.

Here is a story of a fairly simple coalition, where this technique was particularly helpful.

CASE STUDY 6.7   BOB AND THE POSTING: A STRAIGHTFORWARD EXAMPLE

Bob was worried. He had been very successful so far in his career in an international company. He had enjoyed his postings in Asia and Africa, but since the birth of his first child his priorities had changed. Now his boss was talking about a posting in a remote part of Russia, which would be difficult for his family. 'I could look for a job here in a different organization, but I enjoy working for my current company. The trouble is, I don't get on well with my line manager, and I don't think he's very sympathetic to my dilemma. What should I do?'

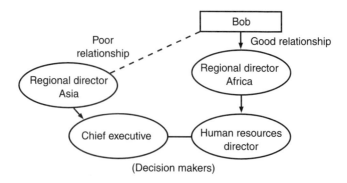

Fig. 6.5   The informal network of influence in Bob's organization

Sketching the informal network to find out who to lobby
When he sketched the informal influencing network, Bob made an interesting discovery. The decision makers were the chief executive and the human resources director. Bob's current boss, the regional director for Asia, and his previous boss, the regional director for Africa, were among the other senior managers who, together with the HR director, made up the management team.

Bob had kept in touch with the regional director for Africa, and he had always got on well with him. The regional director for Africa wanted to keep Bob in the organization—and he had a lot of influence with the HR director. Suddenly the way forward became clear—and the regional director for Africa was in town. 'When you're worried you go round and round in circles,' Bob said. 'Once you see your network mapped out it's easy.' He went off with a smile to make a phone call.

Sketching the informal network does not need to be a lengthy process (see Fig. 6.5). Bob did it with help from a couple of trusted colleagues in about 15 minutes—and his meeting with the regional director for Africa resulted eventually in a successful outcome for him. For complex situations you may need to allow more thought and discussion.

CASE STUDY 6.8   PETER SKETCHES THE INFORMAL NETWORK IN HIS COMPANY
Peter and Diana used a simple coding system (see Fig. 6.6):

- The nearer the position of the person to the general manager, the more influence the person has.
- The more influential the director, the bigger the oval in Fig. 6.6.
- Movers and Shakers who are not in the management team are in boxes in Fig. 6.6.
- Many of the relationships between the Movers and Shakers are symmetrical—they influence each other and co-operate on projects—but

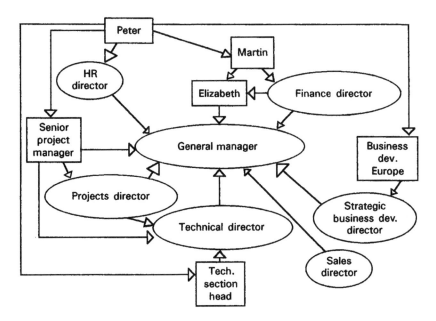

Fig. 6.6   Coalition planning: sketching the informal network for Peter's case

the arrows in the figure indicate the directions of influence which Peter can use for his coalition.

The relationship between the directors and the general manager

The general manager was primarily influenced by the finance director, the projects director, the technical director and the strategic business development director. The sales director was an aggressive man who was openly hostile to the HR division, and who had had open arguments with the HR director and Peter in public. Peter's heart sank at the prospect of trying to persuade him. However, the sales director was not much liked, so Peter was not sure quite how much influence he had—he intended to check that further with Martin.

Elizabeth—a hidden adviser

The big insight was the role and power of Elizabeth, the general manager's personal assistant. She was a quiet woman in her early thirties with an MBA from Insead. She had direct influence on the general manager, and she listened carefully to the finance director. Peter did not dare go near her unless he had a very good reason to do so. Martin played squash with her and rated her highly—he said she was not as frightening as she appeared. Could Martin talk to her informally?

The other Movers and Shakers

The senior project manager was respected by all the directors for his technical and operational skills. The general manager sometimes consulted him directly. Fortunately, Peter had worked with the senior project manager to set up a very successful project management course for the projects division. Similarly, Peter had helped to set up a skills centre for the technical section head, so perhaps she would be prepared to put in a word with the technical director.

Support from the senior project manager and from the technical section head would be essential because these two managers would be heavily involved in implementing the new scheme—they did a lot of interviewing. Peter would need to get their full and active commitment at an early stage in the coalition process. There was no way the projects director and the technical director would agree with the scheme if these two key advisers did not back it.

How about the strategic business development director? 'We've done OK with sorting out the salary package for one of the staff they wanted to transfer from the States—must have some credibility there,' Diana said. 'I get on with the business developer for Europe all right, and he owes me a couple of favours. I'll try to speed up the information he wanted on pensions.' 'Good,' said Peter, 'Now, let's see where we should start.'

Once you have mapped out the influencing network, you can try out different sequences for the lobbying. Remember that for Bob this was very obvious. For Peter, there are more options and more pitfalls.

CASE STUDY 6.9   PLANNING THE LOBBYING

Peter decides upon two lobbying rounds. In the first lobbying round (see Fig. 6.7) he contacts his allies (Martin) and those with whom he has a track record of cooperation (such as the senior project manager).

Assuming that the people in the first lobbying round will back the idea—give or take some modifications—then the second lobbying round will target Elizabeth and the other senior Movers and Shakers (see Fig. 6.8).

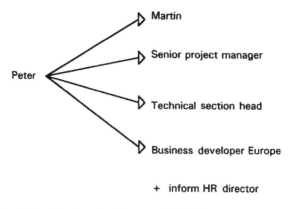

Martin

Senior project manager

Peter

Technical section head

Business developer Europe

+ inform HR director

Fig. 6.7   Coalition planning: the first round of lobbying

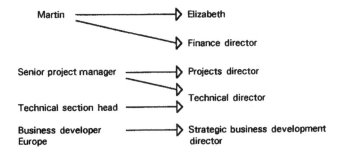

Fig. 6.8 Coalition planning: the second round of lobbying

And the third round—in so far as Peter is able realistically to anticipate that far ahead—would have Elizabeth and the directors on the list hopefully recommending Peter's proposal to the key decision maker, the general manager. By that time, however, a lot could have happened.

Key points for Stage 2: Plan your coalition

- *Lobby the informal advisers.* Elizabeth is a typical example of an informal adviser, because her support for Peter's proposal is essential. She is part of the 'shadow organization' described in Chapter 4. If she says the idea is impractical, the general manager will refuse even to consider it. Informal advisers can in effect veto an idea at a very early stage, so get to them quickly. Like the Movers and Shakers, informal advisers can be working at any level in the organization.
- *Consult the key implementers.* In the past the classic influencing route was top-down, and approval from senior managers would be the first step in coalition building. Now managers often work 'bottom-up' and go direct to the implementers to check that an idea is practical, before they invest effort in lobbying senior colleagues. This may mean going down the line, or going 'across and down' and consulting staff in other parts of your organization.

CASE STUDY 6.10 JAMES AND THE US TRANSFER—
GETTING AGREEMENT FROM THE IMPLEMENTERS
'ACROSS AND DOWN' THE LINE

The position
James is HR director for an international food products company, and one of his responsibilities is international job transfers. The director of the global

business division asked him to find a suitable manager to head up a new product centre in the USA. He mentioned Robert, who was currently working in head office in the UK, as a potential candidate for the job.

The potential candidate

James knew Robert quite well, and agreed that he had good sales and marketing experience. However, relations between the UK and the US divisions were sometimes difficult, and James suspected that he would have to do some negotiating about reporting lines in order for the US management to agree to a candidate from the UK head office. And Robert was quite a strong personality—he had matured a lot over the last few years, but James wondered whether he would have the right interpersonal skills to be accepted and respected by his American colleagues. What would the salesmen in the product centre think of being managed by a young Brit? If Robert was going to be unable to establish credibility then there was no point in wasting time on sorting out the reporting lines.

Consulting the people who count

Fortunately James was due to fly to the States the following week, so by extending his visit slightly he was able to visit the product centre concerned. He had always tried to meet the sales and marketing staff wherever possible, so he set up a meeting and raised the subject of Robert. The salesmen thought for a moment or two and said they'd give him a try—they could not foresee any big problems, provided the newcomer was prepared to be open-minded about the way of doing business in the USA.

'Support from the salesmen meant that we could go ahead,' says James. 'Once back in the UK I started the work at senior level of sorting out reporting lines and structures, so that the Dallas-based US marketing director felt reassured. I also did some coaching with Robert to ensure that he fully understood how others regarded him from the past, and how he should handle himself in the new role. By that time we'd built support for the ideas across levels and across countries, and the transfer was agreed.'

To round off Stage 2 here are some reminders:

- *Sequence is critical.* Think carefully about who to contact first. In James's case, he needed to get the salesmen's support before they heard any rumours emanating from head office. In Peter's coalition, Martin must get Elizabeth on board quickly. If this does not happen, she might hear about his proposal from other sources such as the hostile technical director, and she may form a prematurely negative judgement.
- *Timing is critical.* By lobbying too early in the decision-making process, you create space for your opponents subsequently to marshal the arguments against your idea, and to lobby and destroy your case. If you lobby too late, the decision maker might be

committed to following a particular course of action, and be unwilling to reverse the decision. Find out what the decision-making schedule could be—this is where your line manager can often help.

- *Co-ordination is critical.* Aim to be present as much as possible during the coalition-building process, to co-ordinate and consolidate the escalation of agreement. Remember that no matter how carefully you plan, you will never have total control over the situation.
- *Networking is critical.* You need a web of resources and strategic contacts at different levels who can spread the word about your proposal, and who can feed back information on developments that will be of interest to you.
- *Be guided by your plan, but not blinded by it*! Analysis is extremely valuable, but remember also to be opportunistic in your influencing. If the political wind changes suddenly in your favour, be ready to move more quickly.

Summary of Stage 2: Plan your coalition

This is the most complex of the six stages, because you have to unravel the power politics of your organization in order to plan your lobbying.

- Work out which individuals are influencing your key decision maker.
- Identify the 'Movers and Shakers' in your organization, and do not assume they are all senior managers.
- Plan a co-ordinated approach—get your allies to help.
- Talk to key implementers early to get their support.
- Select a careful sequence—aim for steady escalation of agreement.
- Check your timing—lobby at the optimal moment in the decision-making process.
- Be present throughout the coalition-building process, so you can correct any problems or exploit any sudden opportunities.
- Remember, your plan is only a guide—stay alert and flexible.

The output from Stage 2 is a plan for building your coalition, with your contacts, the sequence in which you will approach them, the people who might be prepared to help you lobby, and your timetable for influencing the decision-making process.

SPLASH—Stage 3: *Lobby and consult*

Stages 1 and 2 were your *homework*. Stage 3 is the preparation and the implementation of what Rinus van Schendelen calls your *fieldwork*. Once you have decided who to approach, you should spend some thought on *how* you will approach them.

The *consultation* in Stage 3 consists of sounding people out and hearing their views. The *lobbying* consists of talking to your strategic contacts in a planned sequence, presenting your proposal, adjusting it as necessary, asking for commitment and building 'critical mass' in your coalition. Your one-to-one meetings will comprise both consultation and lobbying. In this stage you should:

- *Describe how your idea will benefit the organization and the person* whom you are lobbying. Emphasize what he or she stands to gain from supporting your idea—at the same time, be honest about the costs and the return on investment.
- *Identify resistance, and try to uncover the causes*—some people will be open about their concerns, others may be more cautious. Listen, ask and collect as much information as you can.
- *Reframe your proposal* in a way which will make it acceptable to as many of your key decision makers as possible. This is a similar process to the refinement with your allies in Stage 1. The difference is that some of the objections and the resistance may be hard to identify openly, so you will need the help of your team and of your new allies in the coalition. (If you cannot reframe it in a way which gets early approval, your idea may be flawed and you may have to abandon it gracefully).

Tailoring your approach for your key contacts

One way of thinking about your approach is to use Table 6.1 as a guideline.

Table 6.1

1 Name of contact	2 Benefit for unit	3 Benefit for organization	4 Person's own agenda	5 Costs, investment needed	6 Risks, objections	7 Your approach

Column 1 is the list of the key contacts you have identified from Stage 2 (Plan your coalition). Column 2, Benefit for unit, describes what the person stands to gain as representative of his or her unit, or department or division.

IDENTIFYING THE BENEFITS FOR SOME OF PETER'S KEY CONTACTS

Peter knew that the senior project manager wanted to recruit a number of more experienced staff to join his division. He had had some bad experiences with recent joiners who had turned out to be disappointing. Similarly, the technical section head had had problems with recruiting senior consultants. Both would need evidence that the procedures which Peter was recommending really would help improve the quality of the selection process in their divisions.

Column 3, Benefit for organization, looks at the scheme from the company angle. Here Peter can stress how his proposal will contribute to steady growth in staff numbers, how it will help to reduce the risks associated with unsuitable recruits and how it can also help in the transfer of staff between divisions.

Column 4, Person's own agenda, addresses how the proposal will support the person's own goals. If you can find a match between your idea and the person's own agenda you will have a strong chance of getting the person on your side.

CASE STUDY 6.12   PETER REFLECTS ON THE PERSONAL AGENDAS OF HIS KEY CONTACTS

Peter read through his notes on the first round of his coalition. These are his guesses for the personal agendas of his key contacts.

Martin feels personally responsible for the company's finances. Any waste of money deeply offends him. He derives personal satisfaction from all projects which enable the organization to manage its resources effectively.

The senior project manager has been getting increasingly anxious about the overruns on some of the company's major projects. Peter knows that so far, the senior project manager has been able to pick up the warning signs in time to prevent major problems, but he is worried that the situation could get worse in the future. He has told Peter that he desperately needs at least three really good project managers to join his division.

The technical section head needs to recruit a number of technical specialists, and does not feel particularly confident about her own interviewing skills nor about those of her director. 'He still believes he can judge candidates in the first five minutes,' she told Peter. 'That's how we got lumbered with the ones I'm dismissing. Trouble is, when I discuss the candidates with him after the interviews I find it difficult to persuade him to change his mind.'

Peter needs to prove to each of these contacts how his proposal will address their individual needs and concerns. Do not use a generic approach—a sort of 'standard package' with which you present your proposal to all your key contacts. A tailored approach is far more effective, particularly if you only have limited time in your meetings. My colleague Patrick Lybaert introduced me to the WIIFY (pronounced 'wiffy') which stands for What's In It For You? and provides a helpful reminder of the importance of identifying a benefit for each person you want to influence. (I think you also have to have a good WIIFM— What's In It For Me—in order to invest all the effort required for building an effective coalition.)

Column 5, Costs and investment needed: it is tempting to stress the benefits and play down the costs, but most managers expect you to give a balanced account of both. For the senior project manager and the technical section head, the biggest problem will be the time needed to retrain themselves and their staff to use the new system. Both are currently extremely busy.

Column 6, Risks and objections, addresses the problems you could encounter during your lobbying and consultation meetings.

- What questions will the contacts ask?
- Have you all the data needed to give a satisfactory answer?
- Can you demonstrate that you have anticipated objections and that you have thought of ways of overcoming the obstacles?

In Peter's case, he needs to think about the time issue—how can he make his new scheme as easy as possible to implement? How can he reduce the time investment from the other managers to an acceptable minimum? How can he convince them that time invested in his scheme 'up front' in the recruitment process will save time in firefighting and crisis management later?

Remember also to *address the hidden worries*, which can make managers resistant to new ideas. An example in Peter's story is the vulnerability that senior staff may feel when their interviewing skills are assessed. Peter might suggest that the initial training sessions are run in small groups of managers who are at the same level in the organization, or that the senior staff receive coaching on a one-to-one basis.

Column 7, General approach, is a summary of the way you plan to run the meeting: your actions, outcomes and goals.

We can sum up these different aspects of preparation in Stage 3 as a

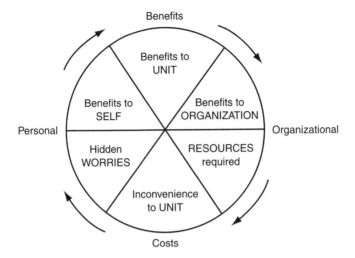

Fig. 6.9   The wheel of influence: work your way round to tailor your approach

wheel of influence, which you must work your way round (see Fig. 6.9).

Key points for Stage 3: Lobby and consult

- *Expect your proposal to go through another evolution.* Do not be too disappointed if it gets diluted or truncated in the process of acceptance. For Peter, some improvement in the recruitment system could be far better than no improvement at all. If you are lucky, your proposal may be improved and expanded.
- *Stay responsive to other people's agendas.* The more you match their personal needs, the more they will support you. Remember that some of your allies, such as Martin in Peter's case, may have to invest a lot of effort for little immediate return. Much of the 'pay-off' for contacts like Martin lies in the influence they have on the organization when they help you. Feed information through to them during the coalition process, and confirm to them how their advice and assistance has helped you with your proposal.
- *Be prepared to trade.* You may have to offer help with problems or projects outside the scope of your proposal, in order to create goodwill.
- *Aim to get explicit statements of commitment.* This will help you

to influence other strategic contacts ('Did George agree? Well in that case I'm prepared to support you, too'). Look for offers of further help in the influencing process and later in the implementation of your proposal.

- *Stay alert to signs of resistance.* It is easy to get complacent, and to think that because your contact nods and smiles the person will actively support you in the next board meeting. You must check explicitly for agreement. If your contact starts to argue, do not argue back—keep quiet and listen for clues.

- *Do not assume that because you are 'right', your contacts will automatically agree.* It takes a lot more than logical arguments to convince people to change. Remember, this is a classic pitfall of the directive, 'push' approach.

- *Resist the temptation to 'oversell' your idea.* Be honest about the costs, the effort, the risks and the inconvenience involved. Your contacts may have ideas about how to get round some of the problems, and in any case you will need their full co-operation when you get as far as the implementation stage. If you are reticent about the disadvantages, colleagues will be all the more suspicious of your proposal.

- *Do not skimp the preparation.* Some managers assume that enthusiasm on its own will win the day, but poor preparation could lose you support. Respect other people's time. Show you have thought carefully about how your proposal will affect them.

- *Keep monitoring the movements of the opposition.* You may need to organize another round of consultation and lobbying if your opponents have found some good arguments against your proposal which you need to refute, or if they have managed to get access to a key person whom you have not yet contacted. Stay in the game, and do not take your eyes off the board!

- *Be prepared to change your approach if necessary.* Occasionally you may be faced with a setback, and have to look for other sources of support. Remember the importance of grasping opportunities. The following story is an illustration.

CASE STUDY 6.13   CHANGING TACK UNDER PRESSURE—ELSA'S ORCHESTRATED APPROACH

Elsa works as a campaigner for the rights of asylum seekers in the European Union. Some years ago she was working with an action group which was lobbying her national parliament. A major project for asylum seekers had been attacked as being inefficient and ineffective. 'That's true to an extent,' said Jan, the leader of the action group. 'We are proposing some tighter budgetary controls and monitoring measures to cope with the problems. Nonetheless this project is the best that exists currently to help our target group. If parliament cuts it, a lot of suffering will result.' Elsa was asked to head up a temporary advisory committee, which would feed information through to interested members of parliament. The committee was an experiment—no-one was yet sure if it would prove its value.

The campaign for the asylum seekers had been progressing well, when suddenly there was a severe setback. One of the action group's most important allies had switched sides in the debate. A well-known woman MP who had been heading up an investigation into the rights of asylum seekers and who had previously been sympathetic was now openly attacking the project. The action group and the advisory committee were on the point of giving up.

Elsa was used to dealing with disappointments. She rang up a couple of trusted parliamentary contacts, and heard that the MP was very much under the influence of a hard-liner colleague in her political party. If the MP was putting her career first, she would not be turned round again by information, arguments or any of the normal channels. Elsa rethought the coalition process and organized an orchestrated approach.

Elsa starts lobbying

First, she contacted other MPs in other parties whom she knew were sympathetic to the cause. She explained the problem, and gave them the arguments for continuing the project and the action group's proposals for improving the administration. She asked them to raise questions in parliament at the next debate to put the woman MP and the party she represented under pressure. They agreed to help.

Next, she remembered meeting the energetic chairman of a large and influential national charity at a conference, so she rang him up and asked his advice. He was having similar problems with the woman MP on another project. 'She's out to axe a number of budgets and to make a name for herself,' he said. 'It's time she was stopped. The man who is influencing her is not popular in the party he represents—he's seen as too openly ambitious. I might be able to do something there.' He agreed to talk to some of his high-level contacts to point out how unpopular the party would become if it were associated with these sorts of budget cuts. He also contacted a number of respected journalists.

Meanwhile Elsa carried on with her own work of gathering information, supplying reports and providing arguments for the advisory committee to pass on to sympathetic parties.

A successful outcome

The project had a stay of execution, and was extended for two years—'Long enough to sort out the budget administration and tighten up the monitoring procedures,' Jan said. The woman MP lost her seat in the next election. The new advisory committee, with Elsa in it, had proved its value and was made permanent. Elsa's energy and commitment had saved the project.

How about Peter? How did he get on with his coalition? Here is the next stage in his story.

CASE STUDY 6.14　PETER'S FIRST ROUND OF COALITION BUILDING

Martin had showed Peter's revised proposal to the finance director. 'The finance director is reasonably positive,' he told Peter, 'but he doubts you will get the full scheme past the technical director, and reckons the pilot plan is more likely to be accepted. You'll have to see if one of the other directors would be prepared to run it in his division—we cannot do that because we're not planning to take on a lot of new staff this year.'

'I also talked to Elizabeth and have some good news there. First about the sales director—she says that, strictly confidentially, he's on his way out—I think he's negotiating with another company for a new job. More important, Elizabeth has worked out that she's going to have to learn about job competencies and broaden her understanding of HR matters as the next step in her meteoric rise to fame, so she's actually quite keen to get involved. That means basically she'll back your proposal. Better get your squash racket out.' Peter grinned and thanked him.

The first setback
The meeting with the technical section head did not go so well. Peter discovered that she was anxious about the conflict which she might have with her director if she supported Peter's proposal. If she had to weigh up the risks to her relationship with her boss against some intangible benefits as proposed by Peter and his scheme, would it really be worth the effort to her personally to support Peter's idea? In spite of Peter's carefully marshalled arguments about recruiting better consultants, she was doubtful. Peter could see her point. 'I'll have to find out whether the senior project manager might give the scheme a go,' he told her. 'I'll get back to you when I have talked to him. Let me know if there's anything else I can help you with—I'm sorry things are difficult for you at the moment.'

Changing the approach
Peter had to admit it—Diana was right. The pilot scheme would probably be more attractive to the management team. His chances of getting the technical director's support without the help of the technical section head were poor. He replanned his approach.

Fortunately, the senior project manager was very enthusiastic about the pilot scheme. 'We need all the help in recruitment we can get,' he said, 'and I appreciate that you guys can't do all the interviewing for us. But I'd need you to get going on this really quickly. I want to see the pilot scheme worked out in detail and costed. I'm pretty sure the projects director will go for it, but he likes to see a tidy plan so he can weigh up the risks. Can you get that to us next week?' 'I'll work over the weekend,' said Peter.

The HR director sent the fax as promised with his scribbled comments. Peter managed to catch him in his hotel. There was a management team meeting scheduled at the end of the following week and the HR director would be playing golf with the general manager on Sunday afternoon. He was prepared to sound him out gently, but he would need to be more fully briefed. 'I'll do my best to get it on the agenda,' he ended.

The next round of the coalition
Peter got the pilot proposal together on the weekend. Diana worked all day Saturday on the new costs. 'Now all we can do is wait and see how our second round of lobbying works out,' he said. 'I'll get in touch with the senior project manager on Tuesday to hear what the projects director said. Let's hope he doesn't consult the technical section head, though I think she's so busy at the moment he won't be able to talk to her. The next person on the list is the business developer for Europe—I'm seeing him when he gets back from Paris.'

An opportunity to grasp
On Tuesday afternoon Diana rushed into the office in great excitement, followed by Jacqueline, one of her many friends. Jacqueline worked in the business development division as head of public relations. She had some excellent and unexpected news. A national newspaper was running a supplement on the engineering industry, and a leading journalist had asked to interview the general manager. The journalist was looking at employment opportunities for men and women in the industry, and he had mentioned to Jacqueline that he wanted to hear about the company's recruitment policy. Light dawned in Peter's tired brain. 'When is the interview with the journalist scheduled?' he asked. 'On Thursday,' Diana explained, 'it's perfect timing—as long as we can get the general manager to understand the advantages of our scheme before he goes into the interview.' 'Now that's where we need Elizabeth,' said Peter. 'She's keen on equal opportunity issues, and she'll be interested in meeting the journalist. The general manager may want her in the interview anyway. Could we get her to prime the journalist with some relevant questions?'

Trading favours
Peter left an action with Jacqueline to talk to Elizabeth first thing in the morning, put a note on Martin's desk to keep him informed, and went off to talk to the business developer for Europe. The business developer was only moderately interested in Peter's scheme. 'We won't be affected directly by it in the short term, because we have enough staff for the moment, but I can see it could help the organization in the long run.'

The business developer paused for a moment. 'Are you planning to identify a list of competencies for business development? We've got a student in the division who's bright enough but we haven't got enough for him to do, and he's getting under our feet. Can you give him something to work on?' Peter agreed, although he knew that he and Diana would have to spend quite a bit of time training the student up. 'If I do that, will you put in a word for my scheme with your boss?' he asked. 'Will do,' said the business developer.

Monitoring progress

On Wednesday evening Peter was just about to go home when the HR director walked into his office and sat down. The news was good—the general manager was prepared to think about a change in the recruitment scheme, particularly if one of the divisional directors would champion it. The senior project manager had said his director had agreed to back the pilot scheme, which would be launched in the projects division.

Now with the journalist's interview scheduled for tomorrow there would be all the more reason for the GM to agree—with a bit of luck, the discussion in the management team on Friday would be little more than a confirmation exercise. The HR director was already happily planning some new graduate brochures 'and perhaps you could write a short article about our work to go into next month's company newsletter, Pete?' 'Our work, indeed,' thought Peter. 'I didn't see him in here over the weekend. Never mind, I suppose he did his bit with the GM, and we've almost got agreement for the pilot.'

Summary of Stage 3: Lobby and consult

- Tailor your approach to individual agendas.
- Be honest about the costs and investment involved—do not oversell your idea.
- Be prepared to trade favours and concessions.
- Expect your proposal to keep changing shape.
- Be realistic in the face of setbacks, and stay on the lookout for lucky opportunities.
- Keep monitoring progress right up to the point where you get firm approval from your decision makers.

The output from Stage 3 is *a draft proposal which is actively supported by enough of your key decision makers to make implementation feasible and probable.*

SPLASH—Stage 4: Anchor the change

Stage 4 is the *test and confirmation* of your coalition. When you *anchor the change*, you make the agreement of all your key sponsors visible to the rest of the organization. Stage 4 is also the transition between getting your idea agreed and getting it implemented. To anchor agreement, you should:

- *Check that a statement is issued in writing*—you could draft a note, a memo or e-mail, for instance, and circulate it for further comment from key decision makers. Issue a definitive version when everyone on the mailing list has agreed all the details. Depending on where you work, and on the scale of your proposal, the note may go out under your name or in the name of a more senior manager.

- *Check that the message is clearly understood*—you may need to show your draft personally to some of your contacts to ensure this really is the case.
- *Get a 'champion' to commit to your proposal in public*—the champion should be a respected manager with the power and the resources to ensure your proposal is implemented. Typically your champion could be an influential line manager who would present the agreed message at a staff meeting, for instance, or at a board meeting. If your proposal is more modest, it may be sufficient for your boss to announce that it has been approved in a weekly departmental meeting

Public sponsorship of your idea is essential if your idea, like Peter's, will have a major effect on your organization. Do not be put off by busy managers telling you that 'of course we support your idea, everybody knows that, just go ahead and don't worry'. You must have your Movers and Shakers, and especially the senior ones, visibly behind you. It's not enough for them to *say* they support you—they have to be *seen* to support you too.

CASE STUDY 6.15   THE PROJECTS DIVISION STAFF MEETING

The HR director greeted Peter warmly on the Monday following the management team meeting. 'The pilot scheme has been agreed, and the projects director has said it can start as soon as possible in his division. Good work. I'm off now to Milan, so I'll leave you to it.' Peter had heard already from Elizabeth that he had the go ahead. 'Watch your step, though,' she'd warned, 'the technical director was dead against it as you'd predicted. Get the projects director to announce it in his next all staff meeting on Thursday—then he won't be able to back out.'

Peter did not think the projects director was the type to change his mind, but in the circumstances caution was probably the best policy. He left a note for the senior project manager suggesting that the pilot scheme should be mentioned in the projects director's presentation, and offering to produce some overhead slides if that were helpful. Gerry, the student from the business development division, had turned up bright and early that morning looking hopeful. He had good slide-production skills so this was a way to get him into the project. Peter got an e-mail from the projects director direct ('a good sign,' thought Peter) thanking him for the offer, so he set Gerry to work.

The staff meeting began on Thursday promptly at 17.30. Peter tucked himself in a corner of the large conference room and listened expectantly. It was deeply rewarding to hear the projects director announce the new recruitment training programme, to be attended first by senior staff ('because we need it most,' said the director with a wry smile). The schedule was also published, reminding Peter that he must get his implementation team up and running quickly. The staff asked a few questions and expressed some interest. Peter relaxed for the first time in the last couple of weeks—it looked as though the scheme was really getting under way.

Some managers with good ideas lose interest by the time they get to the implementation phase, but follow-through is essential to the success of your proposal. If you can delegate these phases successfully that is fine—you run the risk, however, that others will not cosset your 'baby' the way you might hope!

Key points for Stage 4: Anchor the change

Because this stage marks the transition between the coalition and the implementation phases, it is a good moment to acknowledge the help people have given you.

- *Thank all those who have contributed ideas*, from all levels in the organization. Often people give you time and suggestions, then hear nothing more. If they have contributed to the acceptance of a proposal they should be told explicitly how you and the organization have benefited from their contribution. Recognition is a crucial motivator, and they will be more prepared to help you again next time.
- *Thank those who helped by suggesting other contacts or by doing some lobbying themselves.* These people will be extensions to your working network, and their efforts should be acknowledged. Your allies will also fall into this category and will share in your success.

CASE STUDY 6.16   PETER HOLDS A SMALL CELEBRATION

They had finally reached Friday afternoon. Diana was looking tired after working through the previous weekend. Gerry was reading articles on recruitment systems and coming up with intelligent questions that no-one in the HR office felt in a mood to answer. The HR director had come back from Milan full of stories about Italian taxi drivers and with an obvious need to share them. Peter closed down his computer. 'I suggest we retire to the local bar,' he announced. 'Drinks on me. Martin and Elizabeth are joining us. For once we can all finish a little early.'

- *Check that everyone understands what has been agreed.* The proposal may be much less relevant to them than it is to you, and so they may genuinely forget, or switch off in a presentation, or fail to read a memo. If in doubt, remind them in person what has been agreed.
- *Do not assume that agreement means action.* Other priorities may arise, funds could be diverted, enthusiasm can fade, and slow sabotage of good ideas is common in the best of organizations. Celebrate by all means, but then move briskly on to Stage 5.

Summary of Stage 4: Anchor the change

- Check a statement is issued in writing—an informal note or a more formal memo, depending on the scale of your proposal.
- Check everyone understands what has been agreed.
- Get a 'champion' to commit to your proposal in public, especially if your idea will impact a number of people.
- Thank everyone who has helped you.
- Keep the idea fresh in everyone's minds, and move on to Stage 5 as quickly as possible.

The output from Stage 4 is a *formal statement of the way forward, agreed and understood by all those who will play a role in the implementation of your proposal.*

SPLASH—Stage 5: Specify tasks and responsibilities

Your aim in Stage 5 is to *establish brisk progress* and keep momentum going. The keys to success in this phase are the classic management skills of planning and delegation. If you are managing a team you will find the BUILD approach helpful for gaining consensus on key decisions in your team. With larger projects, you should agree with your manager and your team the following:

- The objectives of your project
- The roles and responsibilities
- The resources and authority levels required by each individual
- Schedules, milestones and deadlines for deliverables
- Quality standards and expectations
- Help and support available from other people in the organization.

Round the table sat Peter, Diana and Gerry. They had been joined in the team by Jenny and Oscar, the two training consultants who were to design and run the training programmes, and who had also been asked to contribute ideas on recruitment procedures based on their experience with their organizations. The consultants had produced a good proposal, but Peter wanted to make some minor changes.

Peter outlined the objectives of the pilot scheme and checked that they were fully understood. 'The purpose of this meeting is to plan exactly how we proceed from here,' he said. 'We've got tight deadlines, and I know that we all have heavy workloads. The first programme will run in just under two months' time and we've got a lot of documentation to produce to back it up. I suggest we start by listing the activities—is that all right with everyone? By the end of the morning I'd like us to have drawn up a plan that we all feel happy with and that we all feel is feasible.'

Key points for Stage 5

■ *Involve your team members actively in the planning process,* and use the BUILD style of influencing for all the key decisions early in the project. This is often forgotten by managers under time pressure. The beginning phase of any implementation benefits enormously from a BUILD leadership style because of the increase in commitment you will gain from your staff. If the team is dispersed, and communication is more difficult, it is tempting for a manager to write the plan and then distribute it. The result can be disastrous.

CASE STUDY 6.18 NICK AND THE TEAM THAT FELL APART
Three consultants in three different European countries were working for a multinational. Their task was to design a two-week management training programme. The team leader, Nick, was a task-oriented 'pusher' and keen to get going. At their second meeting in London he presented his colleagues with a detailed design which he had written himself. The other consultants read it without enthusiasm. 'I thought the idea was that we'd work on this together?' one said. 'But this is much more efficient,' Nick replied. He meant well, but the team never 'gelled'. Three months later it fell apart, and Nick was replaced.

■ *Mixed teams are useful if your proposal is controversial.* You may need to set up an implementation team with people representing the different interests. You might also choose representatives from different departments, countries, levels in the hierarchy, or disciplines, for instance. The advantage of this approach is that by involving representatives from different interest groups right at the start you can avoid misunderstandings and conflicts later in the implementation phase. You will need, however, to invest extra effort in the early stages of your team.

- *Watch out for problems in communication.* Words and phrases may have different meanings for different people, even if both parties are speaking English. Set up ground rules for checking for understanding
- *Do not rush teams with a high level of diversity*—they generally take longer to settle down to the task. Invest in some form of socializing and team-building activities, even if this is simply a sandwich lunch together. Involve your team members in all the key tasks. In teams with a high level of diversity, your written plan could be the first demonstration of the team's ability to work together, as well as an opportunity to get used to each other's working styles before the team starts on the actual project.

Summary of Stage 5: Specify tasks and responsibilities

- Agree objectives, roles, deadlines and resources—apply the principles of effective delegation.
- Involve all your team members right from the start in the planning process.
- Use mixed teams with members from different interest groups if your proposal is controversial.
- Watch out for problems with communication.
- Allow diverse teams enough time to get used to working together at the start of the project.

The output from Stage 5 is *an implementation plan agreed and supported by implementation team members and any other managers affected by it.*

SPLASH—Stage 6: *Hold regular reviews*

To implement a proposal you need influencing stamina. Commitment can so easily fade, and you need to be constantly working at *reinforcing the change, removing obstacles and renewing interest.* This is why you need reviews, to:

- Check progress against plan
- Demonstrate to the rest of the organization what you have achieved
- Publish your successes and the benefits you have achieved for the organization
- Pick up early warnings of fading enthusiasm
- Take corrective action
- Look for new opportunities for improvements
- Revise and update your plan.

The other problem for serious influencers is that generally you only get one stab at success. If your initial plan fails for any reason, senior managers, champions and decision makers have usually moved their focus to other projects, and they will be reluctant to reopen the discussion. You cannot afford to lose speed or to make mistakes. *Keep moving forwards* (see Fig. 6.10) by:

- *Checking that the 'new' behaviours are consistently used and rewarded*—observe how middle-level staff follow the new initiative and comment on their progress to their managers, for instance; keep an eye on more senior colleagues to ensure that they are also following new procedures
- *Finding ways of reinforcing the change*, such as reminding colleagues in management meetings how the new procedure is helping the organization
- *Smoothing out problems* that have arisen in the wake of change, such as resistance from some of the managers who did not fully support the initial proposal and who are now trying some sabotage
- *Setting up an 'after-sales service'*, to monitor progress after the implementation of your proposal
- *Setting up new initiatives* to reinforce the changes you have implemented: refresher courses, for instance, or new projects to introduce other, related improvements to another part of the organization.

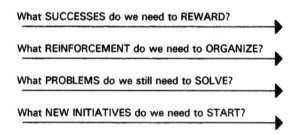

Fig. 6.10 Questions for your review

CASE STUDY 6.19 THE TEAM REVIEW

Peter consulted his file—it was six months since he had scribbled his first ideas in the kitchen. He was now writing up the minutes from the review meeting. The pilot scheme had certainly been a success, but the big challenge now was follow-up.

A lot had happened in the organization. The technical section head had left to set up her own business as an independent consultant. Peter had seen her around, working now as a contractor on a highly specialized project—she looked a lot more relaxed. She had been replaced by a Canadian who was very keen on HR matters and had already had a chat with Peter about the recruitment scheme. 'We'll have to see how he settles in,' Diana said. 'If he does well, he'll be a very useful ally.'

Progress

In the management team there had been some important progress. The projects director had extended the pilot scheme so that all staff involved in interviewing could attend. Once the finance director heard this, he said he was ready to put his staff on a training course, to everyone's delight. The sales director had gone, and the one remaining opponent was the technical director, but Elizabeth told Martin that she thought he would give in under pressure eventually. She had now moved the focus of her attention to business development, but she remained a friendly and useful adviser to the HR team. How about the general manager—would he ever attend a course? Peter doubted it, but now that so many of the other directors were supporting the new scheme it did not really matter.

The problem of the follow-up actions

There were a number of loose ends to be tied up. The projects division had made some suggestions for refining and clarifying the admin side of recruitment: improving the forms and the screening procedures, for instance. Peter had also promised to tighten up the competency lists that had been used during training. Unfortunately, Gerry had been such a success in the HR team that the business developer for Europe had reclaimed him for his division, leaving a gap in the team. The result was that many of these follow-up actions had not been completed. Both Peter and Diana were very busy on other projects—he would either have to find a new team member or simply finish off these details himself.

Reinforcing and maintaining progress

Maintaining standards was another problem. Staff had started out very enthusiastic after the courses, but for some there had been a gap of a couple of months before they could actually apply their interviewing skills in practice. Some of the senior managers had found that it was more difficult than they had thought to change their old ways—Peter could see from their scanty interview reports that they had slipped back under pressure to some bad habits.

Broadcasting success

They needed to broadcast more widely the progress they had achieved. Before he left the team, Gerry had drafted a short report on the outcome from the new scheme. Senior members of the projects division had used the new procedures and techniques to recruit two new project managers. The new joiners seemed to be performing well, and the interviewers had said they felt much more confident about their questioning techniques as a result of the course they had attended. 'We must remember to complete Gerry's report and distribute it to the management team,' Peter said.

Next steps

Peter disliked practical details—somehow it was never as much fun to follow through progress as to engineer it in the first place. It was clearly necessary, though, and the team had been helpful. The list of follow-up actions was as follows:

- Peter to sort out updating of all documentation
- Jenny to arrange coaching sessions with senior staff
- Oscar to design a follow-up day for all staff who had already attended training courses
- Peter to sit in 'sample' interviews for staff who had attended the courses, and to give feedback as required
- Diana to organize new training schemes in other divisions and to co-ordinate extension to pilot scheme in projects division
- Peter to complete Gerry's report and talk to HR manager about presenting it in the next management team meeting.

'There's still the problem of the technical director,' Peter reflected. 'If the new sales director turns out to be another hard-liner, we may have problems in the long run. I'd better stay in touch with the new technical section head—take our Canadian friend out to lunch perhaps. We may need to think about the next round of coalition building, just in case.'

Key points from Stage 6

- *Maintain the momentum.* Some managers are natural perfectionists who derive satisfaction from following through on details. Others, like Peter, have to fight against boredom and lethargy at this stage, in themselves as well as in others.
- *Look for new initiatives to provide fresh interest.* Diana, in Peter's case, will hopefully enjoy the challenge of extending the new recruitment scheme to the other divisions.
- *Look for new people to help.* Gerry, in Peter's story, had enjoyed the challenge of doing routine work in a new environment. If you have not the time or energy to do the necessary follow-up, see if you can find a new helper who will take the work on and enjoy it.

- *Broadcast your success*—do not assume people are aware of what you have achieved. Reminding people of your progress will boost morale in your own team too, particularly if you share the credit.

Summary of Stage 6: Hold regular reviews

- Check new behaviours are used and rewarded
- Smooth out any remaining or emerging problems
- Set up your 'after-sales service'
- Publicize your successes, sharing the credit
- Get some new initiatives going

Reviews help you to maintain motivation, to make your project visible, and to keep interest, effort and resources coming your way.

Summary of coalition building

SPLASH gives an overview of the key stages in coalition (see Fig. 6.11):

S Start with your allies
P Plan your coalition
L Lobby and consult
A Anchor the change
S Specify tasks and responsibilities
H Hold regular reviews

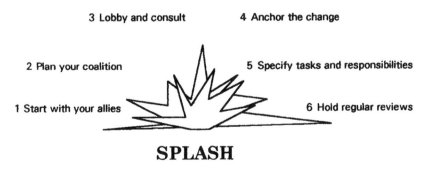

3 Lobby and consult   4 Anchor the change

2 Plan your coalition   5 Specify tasks and responsibilities

1 Start with your allies   6 Hold regular reviews

SPLASH

Fig. 6.11 Reminder of the SPLASH stages

- *Plan, but at the same time be an 'opportunistic influencer'*, ready to deal with problems or grasp any lucky chances that come along.
- *Stay flexible.* If you are dependent on support from a number of people in order to get acceptance of your idea, then you must expect your idea to change and evolve.
- *Identify the Movers and Shakers and the informal advisers* in your organization, so you can use those contacts when you need them.
- *Remember that coalitions are highly dynamic.* You will never be able to control the situation fully, so keep your eye on the ball and stay in the game.
- *Tailor your approach to the person.* Pay particular attention to individual agendas and address costs as well as benefits.
- *Share the credit*—coalition building is a team activity.
- *Follow through to the final stages*, so you keep up the momentum. You need to have influencing stamina if you really want results.

Notes

See Moss Kanter (1983), Kotter (1985), and Pfeffer (1994). See also John P. Kotter 'Leading change: why transformation efforts fail', *Harvard Business Review*, March-April 1995. Peter Block has a good section on lobbying in *The Empowered Manager—positive political skills at work*, Jossey-Bass, 1990. Kathryn Vagneur contributed the idea of the press conference. If you want more material on cross-cultural teams, see Sue Canney-Davison's article 'Leading and facilitating international teams' in *Cross-Cultural Team Building*, Mel Berger (Ed.), McGraw-Hill, 1996.

Dutch readers with an interest in the workings of the European Union could also consult M. P. C. M. van Schendelen's *Gelijkhebben of winnen?* Amsterdam University Press, 1995, and *Lobbyen, hoe werkt 't?* by Bennis, Pauw and van Schendelen, SDU, The Hague 1990.

7 Strategic networking: how to build a web of co-operative relationships for your work

The need for a network

'It all sounds so political—so manipulative,' said the young engineer on a management course. 'And it would take me away from my real work.' Increasingly, however, networking *is* the real work, because without a network of established relationships you cannot get results. As one experienced manager put it, 'Your ability to get things done depends largely on the quality of your network. It's what makes the Movers and Shakers so effective.'

A network in the context of influencing is a web of co-operative relationships between colleagues at work—both inside and outside your formal organization. People in the network help each other with information, resources and advice, and that help is acknowledged and returned. An interpersonal network is based on trust, and to build trust you need face-to-face contact. Electronic networking can support interpersonal networking, particularly in information exchange, but it cannot replace it.

A good network is essential if you want to build coalitions with the SPLASH approach described in the previous chapter. Even if you are not particularly ambitious with your influencing projects, you will need a network just to solve everyday problems. In the new, flatter organizations, where senior managers are too busy to intervene in interdepartmental disputes, a co-operative relationship with colleagues is an essential part of our work. And networking is not manipulative, because a networking relationship will only be effective if it is based on a track record of genuine, mutual help.

Here is a typical cautionary tale to demonstrate what happens if you do not have an established network.

CASE STUDY 7.1 NO NETWORK: HARRY CANNOT GET SUPPORT FOR THE NEW SYSTEM

Harry was an IT consultant, a quiet clever man respected for his technical expertise. He was working in a high-level project team for a large government organization, and he reported to a client project manager. Harry's task was to help in the upgrading of a major system, but the more Harry looked at the system, the more convinced he became that the client would do better to scrap the current system and invest in a new one. He talked this over with his client project manager, who basically agreed.

The problem was how to proceed from there. The client project manager guessed that budget would not be a problem, but he was reluctant to do anything other than talk to his own boss. The budget was managed by a large and powerful department where Harry knew no-one. Indeed, he knew few people in his own organization who could help—he had joined a year ago and gone out straightaway to work on-site. Being a shy man, he had scarcely any contact with his own account manager, let alone the sales staff or the strategic business unit manager. He really had no idea where to start. Did he have the energy to contact them all from scratch? Or was it really easier to drop the whole idea of a new system? Harry sighed and went back to the upgrade.

Networks are particularly important if, like Harry, you want to do something new or different.

From lone ranger to team player

Another reason to develop your networking skills is the change in attitudes towards performance. Whereas previously individual performance was valued above all else, senior managers are now expecting their staff to be good 'corporate citizens' as well. Joseph de Feo is Director of Group Operations and Technology at Barclays Bank, where he has led a drive to help Barclays become a world leader in financial services. He believes that the old individualistic mentality is past history. Using a favourite baseball analogy he says that 'Of course everyone wants to hit a home run—and organizations reward home run hitters. What we want now in this organization is team players with high batting averages.' Many organizations, like Barclays, are investigating ways of directly rewarding team as well as individual performance.

Failure to co-operate and network constructively with colleagues can cost some managers their career.

CASE STUDY 7.2   NO TEAMWORK—STEPHEN WILL NOT CO-OPERATE WITH HIS COLLEAGUES

Stephen was sales director of a small products company that formed part of a larger European organization. His numbers were good, and his staff were loyal, but Stephen had a poor reputation for co-operating with colleagues in sister companies. Each time an opportunity for collaboration arose, Stephen would either drive a very hard bargain or would back out of the deal, complaining of the incompetence of his fellow managers. Paula, his boss, put up patiently with both his complaints and those of the other managers, and did her best to help Stephen see that co-operation on the larger projects was essential if the organization overall was to increase market share. But Stephen remained adamant. Eventually Paula had no choice but to move him from his position. Stephen was sent to head up a start-up operation in China, and Paula replaced him with a manager who worked more collaboratively.

Uses for networks

How can you use your network to improve your performance at work? Here are some examples.

CASE STUDY 7.3 NETWORKING FOR INFORMATION: PAUL AND THE BUSINESS OPPORTUNITY

Paul is managing director of a contract furniture company in London. He has a network which includes architects, suppliers, designers, salesmen, but also head-hunters, journalists and key industry figures who have retired. 'The network is a crucial source of information about trends and opportunities in my business,' Paul says. 'I do the figures in the evening, so I can meet people during the day.'

NETWORKING FOR MANAGING RISKS: ALEX SPOTS A PROBLEM

Alex is the manager of a Polish company which distributes a range of products. He was on a management course, in a session on objective setting. A plant manager, working in Italy, offered one of his own objectives as a basis for review. He described a production target for one particular product planned for distribution in Poland. The objective was framed according to all the guidelines recommended by the trainers, but Alex interrupted the discussion. 'Is that target realistic?' he asked the Italian colleague. The Italian hesitated. Alex continued 'If you think you're going to get into difficulties, let me know now. A target which is lower by 10 per cent would also be OK for me, as long as I know well enough in advance and as long as you can really make it. Let's talk about this over lunch.' By spotting the problem early, he was able to agree a more realistic action plan and avoid what could have been a major risk.

NETWORKING TO UNDERSTAND THE CULTURE: BEN AND THE TECHNICAL ASSISTANTS

Ben is working as an expatriate engineer in the Middle East. The organization where he is working employs not only Europeans, but also a number of workers from India to carry out administrative tasks and to work as technical assistants. The Indian staff have a very efficient network of their own—'They know most of what is going on in the office.' Ben likes and respects his technical assistant and has built up a good relationship with him. In return, he has gleaned a great deal of useful insights into the organizational and local culture 'and as I was a complete newcomer to the Middle East that has been very useful'.

NETWORKING FOR CLIENTS: RIA RECRUITS HER STUDENTS

Ria is program manager of the Executive MBI at the Erasmus University in Holland. Since the programme started in 1989 she has built up a large network of past alumni. She tries to get her routine work out of the way before 08.00 so that she is available during the rest of the day to answer the phone and meet people. Her contacts help her by acting as references for the quality of the course and hence attracting a steadily growing stream of new students. They also recommend speakers and sometimes contribute as speakers themselves.

Ria enjoys keeping in touch with alumni, and sends them a note or gives a call to congratulate them when they are promoted. She organizes special lectures to which she invites key contacts, and if there is an event such as a graduation ceremony she makes a mental note to 'get round' all her contacts and ensures that she has talked to them all. 'Without the network, we wouldn't get the students,' she says. 'The network is the job.'

Your network can help you to:

- *Collect information:* about developments in your own organization and in other organizations, for instance, about the way in which your local and organizational culture works, about trends and techniques in your specialist area, for benchmarking and 'best in class' purposes, or to find out more about the movements of people who may be important to you—anything which may help you in your job
- *Get advice and ideas* on how to tackle difficult areas, how to make the most of new opportunities, how to get hold of additional resources
- *Get feedback* from internal and external customers on the progress of your project, for instance, or on the service which your unit is providing
- *Avoid conflicts and misunderstandings,* by giving you forewarning, for instance of conflicting expectations from your clients, which you will have to reconcile
- *Solve problems and manage risks,* by enlisting the help of colleagues whom you have helped previously, or (like Alex) by spotting problems at an early stage
- *Set up new contacts* which are important for yourself and for your organization.

Networking also enables you to get out of the office, find some inspiration, work on projects which may be more interesting than your routine work, get some recognition from people who will actually be grateful for your help and generally to put your own job into a wider perspective.

The downside of all this activity is, of course, the time that networking can consume, and the effort involved in meeting new people, particularly if you are not by nature a gregarious person. The solution is to plan carefully who you want to meet and why, and this brings us to the subject of strategic networking.

Setting up and auditing your own strategic network

'People often mistakenly think of networking as random socializing,' said Win Nyström of PCM (Positive Career Management) in Brussels. 'That's why I prefer to talk about *SCOR—the Strategic Cultivation Of Relationships.'* Win's phrase is a bit of a mouthful but it does indeed describe much more accurately what networking is all about. Before we start looking in detail about how to set up or review your network, however, here are a few important reminders.

- Networking is about *mutual help*. If you exploit a strategic relationship solely for your own ends, that relationship will not last.
- Networking requires a considerable *investment of time,* so you should be selective about who to include in your network, you should be willing to make time available to help your contacts, and you should be prepared to drop or to delegate contacts if necessary.
- Strategic networking is *work-related*. Network contacts can, of course, become friends, but you should not confuse the professional process of strategic networking with the spontaneous development of friendships.

Three steps to an effective network

A simple but useful way of thinking about networking is to break it down into three steps (see also Fig. 7.1).

1. *Choose your focus:* where do you need help?
2. *Identify the person:* who could help you?
3. *Develop the relationship:* how can you contact the person? What help can you offer him or her in return? What should be your first action to get the relationship going, or to develop it so that you are both actively helping each other?

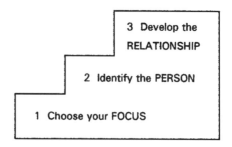

Fig. 7.1 Three steps to effective networking

Choosing the focus for your networking contacts

One way of reviewing your focus in your existing network is to sort out your current and potential contacts according to *short-term* versus *long-term goals*, and according to *organizational* versus *personal focus* (see Fig. 7.2).

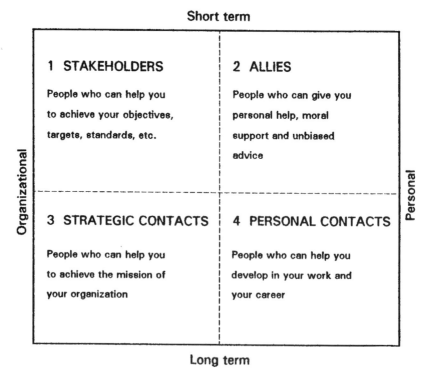

Fig. 7.2 Choose the FOCUS for your network activity

Your short-term contacts are the stakeholders and allies who can help you over (roughly) the next twelve months. If they are people whom you trust, and with whom you share longer-term objectives, you may also develop a long-term relationship with them. As far as your current job is concerned, however, short- to medium-term contacts are the people who are in a position to help you *now*.

When you develop contacts for long-term goals, you could be planning for anything up to five years ahead, or indeed longer if you feel that is realistic. With strategic and personal contacts you may have only a limited direct benefit now, but you cultivate the relationship primarily because of its medium- to long-term potential.

Sorting your contacts according to an organizational versus a personal focus might sound strange given that strategic networking is always intended to be work-related. However, all staff are now being encouraged to take personal responsibility for their own career and professional development, and it is in this context that you should think of a personal focus for work contacts.

Allies and personal contacts will help you at work primarily because they value their relationship with you—these contacts have a personal focus. Stakeholders and strategic contacts will help you at work because they want to achieve the goals and mission of their organization—these contacts have therefore an organizational focus. If you changed job, you might hand your organizational contacts on to your successor, whereas you would maintain and retain your personal contacts yourself. The trend towards shorter stays in particular functions means that managers have to develop their ability to build and rebuild their networks fast and effectively.

The lines between the quadrants in Fig 7.2 are dashed because some of your contacts will fall into several categories, and because relationships change and evolve over time. For instance, Jim, a Mover and Shaker, could be a valuable stakeholder in quadrant 1, helping you to achieve your current goals. Jim could also become an ally over time as the two of you get to know and trust each other. If Jim were then promoted and moved to another, influential part of the organization, he could become a strategic contact for you. This might look very efficient for your network, but if anything happens to disrupt this relationship—if Jim moves to another country, for instance—the loss to you will be all the more significant. The purpose of mapping your relationships is to check that you have a reasonable spread of contacts for your different purposes. We will now explore the different quadrants in more detail so you have a chance to check the effectiveness of your own network.

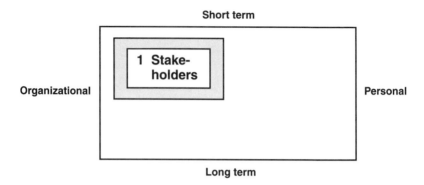

Fig. 7.3   Focus on stakeholders

Quadrant 1: Stakeholders

Stakeholders can offer short- to medium-term help for your current job (Fig. 7.3). They can help you in any or all of the following ways:

- Giving you access to extra budget, staff, expertise, equipment, senior staff, etc.
- Supplying you with relevant information
- Guiding you through the procedures used by your organization
- Offering you advice in new or difficult situations
- Coaching you so you can develop new skills.

If you fail to build constructive relationships with your stakeholders, they also have the power to hinder your progress considerably.

To identify your stakeholders, start by reminding yourself of the scope of your current job. What targets and objectives have you been set for roughly the next twelve months? What are your organizational goals? What will you have to do, and how and when will you do it? What are your key quality standards and service goals?

Now think about your answers to the next three questions:

1. *What are your indicators of success?* How will your success in your job be measured? What sort of feedback will you need in order to judge your progress and your success? And who exactly will assess your progress and judge your success?
2. *What are your critical success factors (CSFs)?* What are your priority areas in your current job—the key activities which will

have a major impact on your achieving your objectives? CSFs are about the way in which you achieve your objectives, and they are often not obvious. If you manage all your CSFs effectively, you should have an excellent chance of success. If you neglect any one of them, this could seriously threaten your objectives. Aim to identify four or five CSFs for each of your main objectives—you can read an example later in this section.

3. *What are the main risks which could sabotage your success?* The answers to this question should overlap with your answers to question 2, but often the 'risks' question will provide a different perspective and an additional insight.

Now start listing the individuals who can:

- Measure your success and judge your progress
- Help you with your five CSFs
- Enable to you avoid the main risks which could threaten your work.

These are the key contacts to cultivate for your stakeholders quadrant.

Stakeholders can come from any level and any part of the organization—it is not just the senior staff who can help you. Often staff further down the formal hierarchy can offer you valuable information. Networking 'across and down' can be very helpful. One senior line manager said that 'it's only by having good contacts lower down the organization that I really find out what's going on. Without them I'd be entirely in the dark.' Information about progress in projects was a component of one of his CSFs.

To show how you can apply this type of analysis, here is the case of Roland, a project leader responsible for designing and building a modification to a large factory.

CASE STUDY 7.4 ROLAND IDENTIFIES HIS CRITICAL SUCCESS FACTORS FOR HIS PROJECT

Roland identified the following critical success factors for his current job:

1. 'The client must be fully satisfied with the installation (and this client is quite difficult to please).
2. My team must establish open, friendly and professional contact with the operations staff (so that we can agree and discuss any changes to the design and ensure a smooth handover with minimum disruption).
3. The composition of the team must be maintained throughout the lifetime

of my project (I don't want any of my most senior engineers to be whisked off onto other projects—that's a major risk).

4. I must stay up to date with the details of the imminent reorganization in my organization (to keep my team informed, and to maintain contact with my key internal stakeholders).'

Identifying the people
For each critical success factor, Roland identified the following stakeholders:

1. *(Client satisfaction):* the client himself—in this case, the operations manager, his team and all those who gave him informal advice. Roland added his own manager to the list, and also key suppliers and the quality assurance manager and her team to help with any technical problems.
2. *(Good relations with operations):* the operations manager and his team, a junior member of Roland's team who socialized with staff in operations, and Roland's neighbour, who was supervisor of one of the operations teams.
3. *(Team composition stays stable):* Roland's boss, colleague project leaders who were well informed about other projects, the human resources manager and his team, a couple of other managers at the same level as Roland's boss who might have had their eye on Roland's senior engineers.
4. *(Stay up to date with company reorganization):* the boss again, Roland's friends in the public relations department, an ex-colleague who was a member of the works council, and the departmental secretary.

If this analytical approach appeals to you, you might like to fill in some of the critical success factors for your job at the top of the columns on the following table. You can then fill in the names of your most important stakeholders in the spaces below each CSF.

Stakeholders who can help you to achieve your short-term goals

CSF 1	CSF 2	CSF 3	CSF 4	CSF 5

Quadrant 1: questions for reviewing your contacts

Filling in the names is fine, but now you need to assess whether you have identified your stakeholders correctly. Here are some questions to help you check.

1. *Is there a CSF column which is scarcely populated with names?* Check how important this critical success factor really is: if it is high priority, you had better start planning to cultivate some more contacts right now. Occasionally you might identify an entire department where you know no-one, or you might discover that many of your former contacts have left that department and moved on. Start thinking about who you should meet and how you can meet them.

2. *Are there any people whom you feel should be stakeholders, but who do not fit easily in your matrix of CSFs?* Check that you have not forgotten another critical success factor for your job, which might even be more important than those you have listed so far. One senior project manager gave the following example. 'I'd noted down the name of my previous client, because I realized he could also have an influence on the success of my current project. Then I thought of adding the name of the man who will be client on my next project—they both work in the same organization. This led me to identify another critical success factor—to manage the reputation of my organization in the eyes of the client.'

3. *Is the distribution of names across your matrix reasonably even?* If you have one column which is black with names, or which includes contacts whom you see a lot, you may need to review your use of time. Have you been spending a great deal of time with people whom you know well, at the expense of extending your network with the contacts who could be more strategically important to you? Do you need to set up contacts with some new stakeholders—in different departments perhaps?

Check the quality of your relationships with the stakeholders you have named

Tick the names of people with whom you already have a good relationship, and where:

- You have regular, friendly contact
- You have established some common goals and interests
- You have a track record of mutual help.

Put an asterisk next to the names of key contacts which you need to develop. These could be people whom you have:

- Not yet met
- Met, but with whom you have not yet established a co-operative relationship
- Met, but where the relationship is slightly strained or tense.

These are the people in whom you will have to invest effort soon.

Have you just started in a new job? Meet your stakeholders now
The stakeholders in Quadrant 1 can offer help now and in the medium term, so if you have just started a new post you need to get out networking as soon as possible. Many of us when we are moved to a new position spend our time reading up on the new subject area and getting familiar with the content of the job. This may not be the best way to settle ourselves in.

CASE STUDY 7.5 NETWORKING EARLY IN THE JOB
Andrew is a civil servant whose task is to formulate advice on policy matters, and to do this he relies on his network of contacts both inside his own organization and outside with other influential advisers in different organizations. His previous job had been very different and more office-based. 'When I moved to this position,' he says, 'I realized I'd have to get going quickly. I spent the first two weeks out of my office meeting people. I had a messaging system so that people could always find me while I was moving around, but I made a conscious decision to spend my time setting up information sources and meeting the key people who could influence my work. In my job the contacts are as important as the content.'

Building relationships is often easier when you are new to a job. You have a good excuse for asking naive questions—once you have been in the post for longer you risk looking foolish if you try to fill the gaps in your knowledge. Your new contacts will also be curious about your views and happy to make time for you. If you are a client, for example, then your contractors will be anxious to get to know you. Another advantage of networking as a newcomer is that you can often sort out the small as yet unresolved problems which your predecessor had never got round to handling. The result is that you will already have created a small pool of goodwill.

Maintaining your relationship with your stakeholders: what can you offer in return?
Do not contact your stakeholders only when you need them. Find out how they might need you. One technical specialist who worked mainly on her own commented 'I hadn't realized that I had to invest in my

network—I thought it was just there for me to use when I had a problem.'

Often there are minor tasks which you can help colleagues with, as another manager described. 'I do the cost estimates for some of my colleagues. They find it a hassle, whereas I don't mind. You have to be careful not to take on too many of these chores because some people will take you for granted. Most people are sensible, though, and they'll help me out when I need a hand. It's a form of teamwork.'

Many senior managers derive satisfaction simply from sorting out difficulties for their organization. They may not expect you to be able to help them in return. Check you give them follow-up information, so they can see how their help has contributed to the success of your project. Other contacts may appreciate information from your part of the business, introductions to other people who could be useful to them, or pieces of technical information which enable them to stay technically up to date. If your stakeholders are your peers in the organization you can set up your network in such a way that the mutual benefits are obvious, as in the following case.

CASE STUDY 7.6 A NETWORK OF STAKEHOLDERS FOR MUTUAL HELP—HANS GETS GOING

Hans is a technical specialist who enjoys working primarily on his own, and who was reluctant about networking. When he thought about his critical success factors, however, he realized that he needed more contact with colleagues in the offices next to his in the corridor where he worked. 'We all assume that our tasks are quite separate,' he said, 'which is why we haven't talked much. But I wonder if we've been reinventing the wheel or doubling up on effort. If we meet now we could check. But won't it look odd if I suddenly walk into their offices for a chat?' 'Suppose you order some sandwiches and send them an e-mail inviting them to lunch?' another colleague suggested. 'What have you got to lose?' After some jokes about his budget, Hans went ahead. The lunch meeting did indeed reveal some misunderstandings that the group could sort out, together with some discoveries of new technical ideas, and a tentative network of the self-contained specialists along the corridor was born.

How big should your network be?

The size and scope of your network will depend on your job, and most people have more network contacts than they realize. Roland's task as project leader in the earlier example is reasonably narrowly defined, so a network of about 40 regular contacts in his stakeholder quadrant could be adequate. A minimum number of contacts would be about 25—that is what a specialist like Hans in the case above would need. If your network is smaller than that, you could be getting quite isolated.

Leaders of larger projects might need 60 to 80 regular contacts, rising to 200 contacts if they include longer-term strategic contacts. The total number of organizational contacts for managers with liaison jobs could easily be 1000. The larger networks require a great deal of time to maintain and organize, which is why sales and marketing directors, for example, will need assistants to help them to keep track.

Quadrant 2: Allies

Allies are the people whom you trust and with whom you have a more personal relationship (Fig. 7.4). They can help you by:

- Sharing sensitive information with you
- Offering unbiased opinions and advice
- Giving you moral support
- Keeping an eye open for opportunities for you
- Warning you when you are about to do something stupid.

Allies are essential to you if you want to exert influence in any organization, because they form the 'home base' from which you can launch coalitions and other initiatives. A high level of mutual trust is what distinguishes a relationship with an ally from a relationship with a friendly stakeholder. Over time, of course, a stakeholder can become a trusted ally. With both stakeholders and allies, however, the emphasis is on short- to medium-term support. If your ally changes jobs, you may or may not stay in touch—some allies become friends, others eventually disappear out of your life except perhaps for a Christmas card.

With an ally you can be yourself, and this helps managers cope in times of rapid change and negative stress. You can share good news and

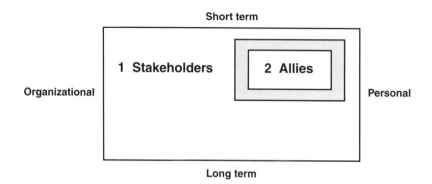

Fig. 7.4 Focus on allies

bad—your allies will rejoice with you in times of success and commiserate in times of hardship. Here are some other examples of ways in which allies help.

CASE STUDY 7.7 JESSIE AND THE JOURNALISTS— MUTUAL MORAL SUPPORT

Jessie works in public relations. She has developed a network of contacts with the media, and some of those contacts have become allies. 'A couple of freelance journalists have moved up the ladder at the same rate as my own career has progressed. We help each other with leads and information. And since we've all been through good times and bad, we provide each other with a fair amount of moral support as well. In stressful environments, that's really important.'

Another way in which allies will support rather than compete is by warning you of impending trouble. Rivals will keep quiet and watch you get into problems. Allies will intervene in time for you to avoid the worst. Here is a story from a senior manager.

CASE STUDY 7.8 MY ALLY WARNED ME JUST IN TIME

'I'd thought of a really good way of reorganizing my part of the business. Of course, it meant changing roles, and territories, for several of my peers. One manager, Ian, would have been particularly affected—his patch would have been considerably reduced, but since he'd been pretty ineffective I thought no-one would object. My boss had been openly critical of Ian, so I assumed he would support me. Luckily I talked it through briefly with one of my colleagues who is also a mate. He told me that Ian was now in the boss's good books— he'd just pulled off a major sale. I backed off just in time. I'd have looked a real fool in the board meeting, and I'd have made some very powerful enemies.'

Allies will protect your interests, and they will protect your back if you are working in a hostile environment. If allies become too close, they form cliques which may be detrimental to your organization, so judgement and a sense of integrity are also important in the relationship.

Allies can also confront and challenge you in difficult times, to make you see sense.

CASE STUDY 7.9 HELPING MARY TO RECOGNIZE HER FAULTS

Mary was looking pale and tired. She was in the midst of an ongoing battle with Mike, her boss, and that was bad news, because the legal department where she worked was just about to be reorganized and staff would be cut. Mary was a skilled lawyer, but she had a reputation for being uncompromising.

Her colleague, Graham, liked and respected Mary, but he was not blind to her faults. 'She was heading straight for trouble,' he said. Over a number of discussions he helped her to change her perspective.

'I was really quite tough with her,' he said later. 'She didn't like what I said, but she knew I was only doing it for her sake. In the end she agreed to talk things over with Mike and they came to a compromise. Mike was promoted, she kept her job—it all worked out all right.'

Identifying your allies

Here are a number of questions to help you identify your actual and potential allies. You can probably think of some other functions that your allies fulfil, but this is just to get you going.

Your allies—who do you know who

- Shares sensitive information with you?
- Chooses to support you, rather than compete with you?
- Tells you about attractive opportunities?
- Warns you when you are about to make a mistake?
- Confronts you with constructive feedback?
- Is genuinely delighted for you when you are successful?
- Will genuinely commiserate with you when times are bad?
- Gives you support and time by listening and acting as a sounding board?

Everyone needs allies. It does not matter what your job is, or where you are in your organizational hierarchy, or how large or small your organization may be. I think you need a minimum of three to five allies for the sake of your mental and emotional health. If you have lost some allies because they have moved or retired, for instance, then you will need to develop some new ones. If you have to change organizations, it will take you time to replenish your stock of allies because personal relationships depend so much on shared experience and trust. As always with new contacts, you may have to make the first move.

Quadrant 3—Strategic contacts

Strategic contacts (see Fig. 7.5) can help you to achieve the long-term mission of your organization by:

- Giving you access to new markets, projects and clients for your organization
- Keeping you up to date with trends in your technical, political, social and economic environment

- Providing you with feedback for your strategic planning
- Giving you information to help you develop and refine your products and services
- Providing tacit or active support for you and your corporation in times of crisis.

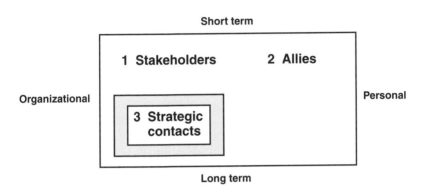

Fig. 7.5   Focus on strategic contacts

Strategic contacts might include former stakeholders who helped you with your short-term goals. Most will be more speculative contacts from inside and outside your organization, which you develop for their longer-term potential.

Are strategic contacts relevant to you and your job?
Just one comment before we tackle strategic contacts in more depth. Many staff imagine that developing strategic contacts is the responsibility of senior managers alone—'I can see it's important, but it's not really part of my job,' as one middle manager put it. 'And I really haven't got much to offer the senior people who would be strategically useful to me.' If you are a middle manager or a technical consultant, just before you skip this section you might like to read the following advice from a chief executive.

CASE STUDY 7.10   'WHAT IS IMPORTANT IS PRACTICE.'
'It's really important for all staff to practise strategic networking, just to develop the skills and to get used to the idea. Otherwise you can feel really lost if you get promoted to a job where it's part of your role.
   I'd suggest you find any area where you feel you can make a contribution. You may feel that you're not in a position to offer much to very senior contacts,

but you can still join a technology user group, for instance, or a trade and industry association, or any professional organization or institute. Give it a go—see who you meet. Women managers could try the women's networks. Associations outside work could be useful practice grounds—school associations, golf clubs, charities and religious organizations all offer the opportunity to meet people who could be potentially interesting to you. Some may turn out to be a waste of time, but at least you will have got used to the idea of networking. Others can turn out to be lucky hits.'

You should be trying out your skills at this broader kind of networking in at least one context. Where are you currently practising your strategic networking skills?

Identifying activities for networking effectively
Often you can identify activities which will help you to glean strategic information and hence develop new business for the future. Again, you cannot always predict which events will prove to be most useful for your organizational mission, so you have to be prepared to invest time and effort and then hope for the best. Here is an example.

CASE STUDY 7.11   SPEAKING AT CONFERENCES TO GLEAN INFORMATION FOR THE LONG TERM
Judy Larkin is a corporate relations consultant with a business of her own. She cultivates opportunities to be a speaker at academic and industry events. She has just accepted an invitation to talk at a leading university on a two-day programme on marketing and corporate communication. 'It's a lot of work, but these events are valuable opportunities for me to gather information on the internal and external communications problems faced by corporations today. By improving my understanding of those problems, I can "sell in" a high-quality service and develop new business over the longer term more effectively.'

Which events could be most useful for you? Conferences are opportunities for making new contacts—which ones do you attend? You may also find opportunities to take on positions in professional associations, for instance, where you can attain a higher profile and where some of your target contacts actually approach you first.

Identifying your strategic contacts
Long-term planning can help you to select the contacts you should be developing. We have talked already about using your stakeholders from your network to help you manage risks in the short to medium term. You may also want to identify longer-term risks and opportunities, and

to foster relationships in anticipation. The following is an example from the public sector.

CASE STUDY 7.12 NETWORKING TO PRE-EMPT PROBLEMS AND EXPLOIT OPPORTUNITIES IN THE FUTURE

Peter van Zunderd, a district chief of police in Holland at the time I interviewed him, was responsible for maintaining friendly and peaceful relations with the 20 000-strong Turkish community in the large city where he worked. He had set up contacts in advance with influential and respected elders in the Turkish community. He took time to build a solid and unhurried relationship with them so that if problems arose, mutual respect and understanding had already been established. 'The network gives a sense of security to Dutch and Turkish communities alike,' he said. 'We know that problems can be tackled directly and discreetly at an early stage, to preclude more serious crises. By setting up a strategic network in advance, we can all promote peace in the community.'

'Peace in the community' is the mission which Peter was working towards, and his contacts with the Turkish elders contributed towards the realization of that mission.

Identifying strategic contacts from your long-term stakeholders

You can identify other long-term strategic contacts from your wider pool of stakeholders. Your primary stakeholders will probably be your staff, your customers and, if you are in the private sector, your shareholders. Other stakeholders who can be significant for you in the medium and long term are your suppliers, distributors, partners, competitors, and also the key representatives of :

- Local communities (as in the previous example in the Turkish community)
- Government and public bodies
- Unions and works councils
- Industry/regulatory bodies
- Investors
- Special interest groups
- Representatives of the media etc.

CASE STUDY 7.13 IDENTIFYING A STRATEGIC CONTACT IN THE COMPETITOR ORGANIZATION

George is on the committee of an industry association related to the industry sector in which he works. He has cultivated a networking relationship with his opposite number in a major competitor. 'At the moment we're both fairly careful, because this is a highly competitive market,' he says. 'In the longer term, however, the contact could be very useful—if we have to deal with environmental issues which affect the industry, for example, and our two organizations decide to work together. You never know—and he's a nice chap to have a beer with.'

Another manager pointed out that you need strategic contacts outside your own organization and outside your own industry sector, if you are interested in longer-term benchmarking activities and becoming 'best in class'.

Many managers will be particularly interested in developing strategic relationships with their customers, so we will now address that category of stakeholder in more depth.

Developing strategic contacts with your clients and customers

Who are your long-term clients and customers, inside and outside your organization? Which of your customers and clients are likely to have most influence over the next few years? If you can identify some potential 'high flyers', you may be able to rise with them, as in the following example.

CASE STUDY 7.14   DEVELOPING A LONG-TERM RELATIONSHIP WITH A KEY CLIENT

'A few years ago I met a manager in one of my large client organizations. I established contact with her although my staff were not working directly for her at the time. When I heard that she'd been promoted to another position in a new organization, I went in to congratulate her. I told her that I wouldn't disturb her in the first few months of her new job—I'd wait for her to settle down first. In fact she called me two weeks after she'd moved. She'd been given responsibility for managing a project with a very tight deadline and a mixed team of staff both from her organization and from mine. I helped her by organizing additional training for her staff, by assigning some of my best resources and by committing to a tight delivery. The result was a great success for her. She's now a lifelong friend of my organization.'

For the manager, the woman client became a valuable strategic contact—she is now in a position where she is powerful enough to help him and his organization with his long-term strategic goals. The story continues as follows.

DEVELOPING A RELATIONSHIP WITH HER BOSS

'In time I handed over the contact with her to my successor, and they're getting on fine. Her boss has now also been promoted to another organization, and he's been in touch with me. My task now is to develop a strategic relationship with him.'

AND WITH A NEW COMPANY

'Meanwhile there's been another interesting development. The same client encouraged us to join forces with a different company which has unique technical expertise. By doing this we could address her needs more effectively. Our relationship with this new company has progressed very well—we are now working together and delivering our services to some important new clients. Internally we call this sort of networking the "spider web technique".

Many managers are working hard at developing relationships with their clients or suppliers which are much closer than the relationships of the past. Sa'ad Al-Hilli, an experienced sales manager, described how he has helped clients in the past to develop their careers inside their organizations, offering them both personal and organizational advice. He has just set up a 'Ski Workshop', where clients and suppliers can combine business issues with sport and relaxation Another senior manager invites selected clients to attend some of his key strategic meetings with his own staff, so that they gain a better understanding of his organizational mission. Suppliers are increasingly prepared to take part in solving the problems, sharing the risks and 'sharing the pain' of their clients in order to develop a stronger strategic relationship in the interests of all the organizations concerned.

Exploiting chance opportunities
Not all relationships with strategic contacts are so carefully planned. Some are formed quite fortuitously, and managers must be prepared at times to take a risk.

CASE STUDY 7.15   SPECULATIVE NETWORKING—A LUCKY ENCOUNTER
'I met a senior German banker on a programme at Insead. We got on well together, and I proposed to visit him next time I was in Munich. I wasn't sure whether he really wanted to make the time for me or whether we could really establish any mutual benefit in the relationship, but he was an interesting man and it seemed worth following up. The outcome was much better than I'd expected—when we met he described to me a problem he was having in his organization and suggested that my people might be able to help. It was only a small project, but I thought we could really be of some service to him. From there we went on to identify a number of mutual interests—we were quickly able to spot some opportunities. That's how it goes with this sort of networking—sometimes you're lucky.'

Another type of strategic contact—opinion formers and influencers
Opinion formers and influencers are the people who help to create the political, business and social climate in which your organization operates. They may be leading journalists, for instance, or scientists, academics, industry spokesmen or politicians with an interest in your field. The more senior your role, the more interested you may be both in contacting opinion formers and influencers and (potentially at least) in becoming an opinion former and influencer yourself.

CASE STUDY 7.16   BECOMING AN 'OPINION INFLUENCER'

Peter van Zunderd, the district chief of police described earlier, was both pleased and amused to find himself unexpectedly in this role. He had given a well-received talk on crowd control at sports events at a conference in the States. Six months later, he received a phone call from a Canadian radio station, and was asked to give his opinion on police intervention at the final of the Stanley Cup, which had been played in New York and had been followed by riots in Vancouver. Subsequently he was contacted again for his views, this time by his colleagues in the Canadian police who wanted his advice. Some time later, Peter received the evaluation report from the police chief of Vancouver. His views had been incorporated into the new policy section.

This kind of recognition is always gratifying because it builds your credibility, particularly if you are tactful and professional in the way you express your views.

Another reason for developing good relationships with opinion formers and influencers is that their responses can be critical for your organization in times of pressure and crisis. Judy Larkin points out that 'If something goes wrong, many of your stakeholder groups might be sceptical about the behaviour of your organization. If you don't have good relationships with your key opinion formers, you may find yourself and your corporation confronted with escalating criticism. If you have good relationships with, say, some leading journalists, they will already know something about your operations, and they'll feel they have access to reliable information through you. They may be prepared to be openly positive about your organization, or at least to restrict themselves to a few neutral comments. Most importantly, they will be prepared to give you the benefit of the doubt.'

Meeting strategic contacts—organizing events
Many managers are starting to work more closely with colleagues in corporate relations, for instance, to organize internal events which will bring the people whom you want to meet into your organization. Cultural and sports events can be successful, though you need to

research the interests of the individuals you want to meet in order to design an event which will be attractive to the right people. Evening or lunch-time seminars on a 'hot topic' with carefully chosen expert speakers work particularly well because the guests stand to gain as much from the event as their hosts. Attention to detail pays off—if you show that your organization has put careful thought into seating plans, selection of guests and topics, then your strategic contacts will soon learn that your events are worth attending.

Developing your strategic contacts

- In which organizations are you currently practising your networking skills?
- Which events are particularly useful for you to meet strategic contacts?
- Which long-term contacts could help you avoid problems and manage potential risks?
- Who are your key long-term stakeholders?
- Which relationships could be particularly useful for you to invest in personally?
- Who are the key opinion formers and influencers in your field?
- What sorts of events could you organize internally in order to attract strategic contacts?

Quadrant 4: Personal contacts

Organizational life has become so volatile that it makes sense for all of us to develop contacts who can help us personally and professionally.

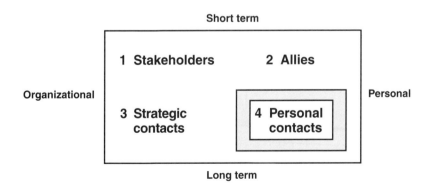

Fig. 7.6 Focus on personal contacts

Personal contacts (Fig. 7.6), support your long-term development in any or all of the following ways:

- They enable you to place your problems in a broader organizational context
- They place their experience, expertise and wisdom at your disposal
- They build your confidence and self-esteem by showing an interest in you
- They give you access to other contacts who can help you achieve your goals
- They stimulate you to develop new insights and new areas of knowledge.

A personal contact is someone who at some stage in some way or other has committed to help you over the longer term to achieve your personal goals.

Mentors—important personal contacts

One important example of a personal contact is a *mentor,* who takes a long-term professional and personal interest in a colleague who is less experienced. Some organizations are setting up mentoring systems in order to promote these contacts, with varying degrees of success.

You can contrast mentoring, with its broader scope and longer time horizon, with coaching, which is more tightly scoped and intended for short- to medium-term results. Coaching focuses on the development of work-related skills. Once the person has demonstrated that he or she has acquired that skill, the coaching is complete.

Mentoring is much more open-ended, and is usually a much more extensive commitment. It is often described with family metaphors. As one manager put it, 'A mentor is more like a parent, or an older sibling—it's a more personal, long-term commitment.' Japanese organizations talk about the 'elder brother' relationship. Some organizations will have 'godfathers'—senior managers who can offer guidance and a broader organizational perspective to their selected 'godchildren'. The following is one senior manager's description of his relationship with a mentor who has helped him significantly over the years.

CASE STUDY 7.17   A CHIEF EXECUTIVE TALKS ABOUT HIS MENTOR

'I go to him when I feel I'm out of my depth—when it's not obvious to me what I should do, and I have no experience to fall back on. He's managed a large number of businesses very successfully, so a problem that's new to me will nearly always be familiar to him. He helps me to put the problem into context. I don't always follow his advice to the letter, but he always manages to give me a

trigger that jolts me out of my indecision. He's very challenging and probing—
he doesn't say a lot, but he seems to have a sense about where the confusion
lies. And he's very good at being available—if I leave a message with his
secretary that I'd like to talk to him, he always gets back to me promptly.'

Another manager said 'I have a couple of ex-clients who seemed for
some reason to take a liking for me. Over the years they have made
time for me—to listen, to offer advice, to help me become more
confident. I have been very lucky to have those relationships—they have
made an enormous contribution to my personal development.' By
giving you their time, mentors demonstrate faith in you, and that can
make you feel more confident and more able to see a way forward out
of a difficult situation.

What do mentors get out of the relationship with less experienced
staff? Personal contacts are unusual in that the relationships are not
fully symmetrical—the personal contact appears at least to be giving
more than he or she is receiving. Managers who mentor have quoted
the following benefits.

CASE STUDY 7.18   BENEFITS OF MENTORING
'I do a lot of voluntary work with organizations. It's a reaffirmation of my
worth—after a bad day where my boss has kicked me around, I feel at least I
can do some good elsewhere. It stops me feeling disempowered.'

'I can re-use my experience. When I help line managers in my role as non-
executive director, I can apply the things I learned when I was managing similar
companies—without going through all the hassle of running the company myself.
With very little input and no direct responsibility, you can have a lot of influence.'

'It keeps me in touch. It's easy to forget the problems that young engineers
face. It keeps my feet on the ground.'

Who are you mentoring? And who are your mentors? Ideally you
would have two, one inside and the other outside your organization.
Often it takes time to find a mentor, because of the 'personal chemistry'
involved. You could start by asking a potential candidate for some help
on a current problem, then follow up and inform the person about how
you applied the advice. In the follow-up contact you could express not
only your appreciation but also your interest in developing the
relationship, and you could then see how the person reacted.

The door-openers
Another type of personal contact is the 'door-opener'—the natural
networker who can put you in touch with other useful contacts over the
longer term, and who enjoys doing so. The following is an example
from an engineer.

CASE STUDY 7.19   THE CONTRACTS ENGINEER—A NATURAL 'DOOR-OPENER'

'I have got a drawer full of CVs from people who have contacted me at work and asked me for help. I'm regularly in touch with a wide range of contractors and outside organizations. It's particularly important now that so many companies are making staff redundant. I'm happy to help people if I can.'

Door-openers are particularly useful for people looking for work. Some managers have friendly long-term relationships with head-hunters, who are natural door-openers because of their formal role. Other contacts with door-openers are more informal and speculative. Jennie Hawks, who has worked with disabled students, advises them to make contacts at university with anyone whom they think could help them to get jobs later: lecturers, visiting speakers, friends, friends' parents and their contacts and so on. One of the ways in which you can return favours to your personal contacts is to act as a door-opener yourself and to offer help to their children with work placements, projects or travel plans, etc. In cases such as these a strategic plan is still helpful, but the main aim is to spread your net wide.

Innovators and stimulators

A third category of people in this quadrant are the innovators and stimulators—people who supply you over the longer term with new ideas and information. In a world where knowledge is power, these contacts are valuable supplements to the standard sources of information such as the Internet, membership of professional associations, subscriptions to specialist journals and so on. The following is an example.

CASE STUDY 7.20   MY PROFESSOR HELPS ME STAY UP TO DATE

'My old college professor has been a particularly useful contact over the years. He has stayed very active in the fields of scientific research that are useful to my work. He has the time to read the literature and to talk to the researchers. He's been very good to me personally, sending me extracts from journals, flyers about technical conferences, providing me with contacts and so on. Once or twice I have been asked to help with some technical problems that have been particularly challenging—my professor put me in touch with some researchers who gave me very valuable information. Staying up to date with current technology is essential for my career—without his help, I simply wouldn't have the time.'

Identifying your personal contacts

Who do you know who

- Makes time available for you to talk through personal and professional problems?
- Helps you to gain a broader perspective on your work?
- Expresses a professional faith and interest in you?
- Puts you in touch with other people who will help you in your development?
- Invests time in helping you to stay up to date with developments in your field?

Reviewing your strategic network

At this stage you might like to review your network, with your personal and organizational goals in mind. Check the size and the spread of your network across the different quadrants. Fill in the names of key individuals in each of the quadrants (see Fig. 7.7).

Short term

Organizational		**Personal**
1 STAKEHOLDERS People who can help you to achieve your objectives, targets and standards over the next twelve months, e.g. 'Movers and Shakers', stakeholders and contacts in your own line, elsewhere in your organization and in external organizations	**2 ALLIES** People who can give you personal help, moral support and unbiased advice e.g. your own team, other work contacts whom you trust	
3 STRATEGIC CONTACTS People who can help you to achieve the mission of your organization, e.g. longer-term stakeholders, opinion formers, key customers and clients inside and outside your organization	**4 PERSONAL CONTACTS** People who can help you to develop personally and professionally, e.g. mentors, 'door-openers', innovators	

Long term

Fig. 7.7   Review the focus, identify the individuals

Developing the relationships

Once you have identified a potential network contact, how should you approach the person? Start by checking what the other person stands to gain from networking with you. What is the personal and organizational benefit for him or her? The mutual business benefit provides you with your opening line when you approach any new contact. This is reassuring for those people who are naturally shy, and who equate the hurdle of talking with a new network contact with that of approaching people at social events. An example of an opening line for a marketing manager talking to a logistics manager, for instance, is 'I have got another big promotion campaign planned in three months' time. I know that these campaigns have caused problems for you recently. Could we talk together to see what we can do to make things easier for both our departments?'

How should you contact the person if you have never met him or her? You have three basic options for getting in touch with the person you have identified. The first option is to contact him or her direct, introducing yourself and stating the mutual benefit. You could call the person up, walk into his or her office, or send a note or letter, depending on the organizational culture in which the person is working. The second option is to ask one of your existing network contacts to introduce you, explaining the mutual benefit. If you do this you must keep your original contact fully informed of your progress—you will find more about this in the Code of Conduct section below. The third option is to find an indirect opportunity for developing the contact. You could join a task force or committee, for instance, where you have a contribution to make but where you will also have a chance to work alongside your target contact.

What if the person then does not want to spend time with you? Sometimes the person will not see a direct benefit in spending time with you. That's fine—it is not a personal rejection of you, it is simply a comment on the other person's priorities at work. You could ask the person if he or she can suggest someone else whom you could contact, where the mutual interest is more clearly defined. Junior sales staff sometimes make the mistake of contacting people who are too senior in the client or buyer organization, and have to start again lower down the organization. You may also have problems with perceived 'equivalences' if you are in an organization with fewer levels than the organization in which your target contact is working. You may need to explain your role and responsibilities to your contact in detail, so that he or she can gain a better understanding of your power base. The steps to effective networking are reviewed in Fig. 7.8.

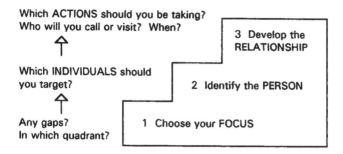

Fig. 7.8   Reviewing the three steps to effective networking

Developing networking relationships is usually much easier than people think. It is largely a question of convincing yourself that it is worth the effort, and then taking the plunge. Can you identify two people whom you should contact? And can you specify one networking action which you will take this week?

A 'jump-start' to networking: the alternative to the analytical approach

If all this strategic analysis looks too much like hard work, and you prefer a faster, intuitive approach, you might like to try the 'jump-start' suggested by Roger Hayes. Roger is Director General of the British Nuclear Industry Forum and he estimates that his own network includes around 2500 contacts, but he offered the following approach for someone starting from scratch:

- Identify ten *key contacts* who will be essential to you over the next year (see Fig. 7.9).
- Discuss your list with colleagues, to get a consensus on your target contacts and to check that you will all be working in the same direction.
- Focus on those contacts in the first three months, then review progress with your colleagues and agree a further list.
- By the end of twelve months your network should have grown to roughly 100, and you should plan again for the following year.

This approach gives you a small and easily manageable core of contacts. It would be ideal for a small start-up operation: if you had been sent to head up a sales office in Prague, for instance, you could quickly organize a programme of meetings and public relations events. Roger warns, however, that after about six months you should use the more detailed strategic approach, because otherwise your 'jump-start

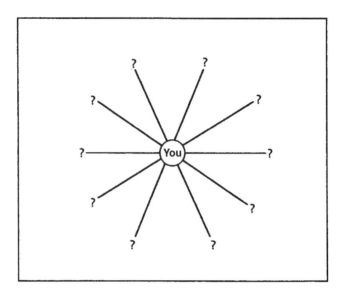

Fig. 7.9   Jumpstart to networking: ten key contacts

network' could become narrowly focused and oriented too much to your short-term goals.

A code of conduct for ethical networking
To maintain and extend your network, you have to work ethically and follow certain conventions.

Rule 1: Invest up front
Once you have selected a networking contact, be generous. You should aim to be in a position where people owe you favours, rather than the other way around. Some managers underestimate the services they can provide to others, so here are some reminders of types of help you could offer:

- Listening to someone's successes
- Showing personal interest in them
- Suggesting other people with relevant experience whom they could contact
- Offering advice and information about study courses for their children

- Helping them stay up to date with relevant extracts from newspapers, journals, Internet references (this is where electronic networking is useful)
- Acting as a sounding board when they have problems
- Offering them a break to cheer them up (lunch, or a drink)
- Helping them to solve minor, irritating problems (such as paperwork if you are in a foreign country)
- Acknowledging their help and contribution by informing senior staff
- Acknowledging their help simply by thanking them and telling them how their advice helped you
- Inviting them to meetings, presentations, conferences which could be of interest.

You can expect your networking contact to follow the same rules, and to be generous with helping you. If that is not the case you can consider dropping the contact, though this is always a risky thing to do—your rejected contact might yet reappear in a position with enough power to make you regret your decision.

Rule 2: Be honest about your objectives

Be clear to yourself and to the other person about what you want out of the relationship. If you hide your motives you will lose the other person's trust and respect at a later stage. Be explicit about your intentions in an early letter, perhaps when you are confirming arrangements for a first appointment. This gives you a basis for exploring the areas where you can help each other. It is also a helpful protocol for removing any potential misunderstandings between men and women.

Rule 3: Keep your network contacts informed

'It's about not letting people down,' said one manager. 'You must always let the person know what you've done with the information or advice you've been offered.' Win Nyström recommends following a strict protocol to ensure that your contacts are kept fully informed. Suppose you ask Joe, an existing contact, to introduce you to Sally, whom you have identified as a strategic contact but whom you have not yet met. Joe agrees to help you, and you should now keep both Joe and Sally informed:

- Send Joe an e-mail/fax/note/postcard to thank him for the introduction

- Ring Sally to arrange the meeting
- Confirm the arrangement with Sally in a short note, giving your purpose for meeting her, what you think she could gain from the meeting, and your thanks for her time
- Call or send a note to Joe to tell him you have set up the meeting, and to check whether he now wants to give you more information about Sally to help you prepare for the meeting.

Next, we will assume that you have had the meeting with Sally, and that she has given you at least some of the information or advice or contacts which you wanted. You have also tried to identify areas where you can help her. After the meeting you:

- Send her a note within 48 hours to thank her for her help
- Inform and thank Joe
- Contact Sally within six weeks of the initial meeting, to let her know what you did with her information or advice, and with something to help her—an article or cartoon, a piece of information or a contact which could be useful to her. This demonstrates that you have invested in the relationship with her
- And, of course, you let Joe know what you have written to Sally.

Yes, it is a lot of work, but when Joe does you that initial favour by introducing you to Sally he is making himself vulnerable. If you offend Sally or fail to impress her, Joe could lose some credibility on his own network. He needs to feel reassured that you are taking the process—and his needs—seriously. If you follow the rules, then Sally will introduce you to some of her contacts, and your network will increase in range and influence.

Rule 4: Respect people's time

'There's an awful lot of writing and paperwork in your Rule 3,' said one manager. 'Isn't that rather bureaucratic?' A phone call may seem easier, but it is also an interruption. Written notes and e-mail can be read at the person's convenience, and that is what respecting a person's time is all about. Similarly, your phone calls and meetings should be thought through and planned, so that no contact time is wasted.

Rule 5: Maintain the relationship

Networking relationships decay very quickly if they are not managed and maintained. Herma Volwater, an account manager, points out that 'People will reproach you if you don't get in touch—but they'll only do that once. If it happens again, they'll drop you.' Failure to get in touch causes loss of face. Roger Hayes suggests that you should plan at least three face-to-face meetings with your key contacts per year. In the case of external contacts, the meetings can be backed up by invitations to work functions, a copy of your annual review, Christmas cards, etc.

Rule 6: Delegate your contacts with care

Typically, the contacts which you delegate are the short-term stakeholders, who have helped you with your short- to medium-term goals. Check whether you want to upgrade them to strategic or personal contacts before you hand them over to your successor. You can, of course, continue your own relationship with the person as a strategic or personal contact while your successor is building a relationship with the same person as a stakeholder.

If you decide to delegate a networking contact, do so tactfully. Many stakeholders dislike losing the initial contact and having to build a relationship with a new person. Explain why you have handed over the contact (because of a change in your job, etc.) and check in the first few months that the contact is being properly managed.

Be particularly careful if you are working in an organizational or national culture which 'manages by relationships'. One manager working in Egypt said that he was quite taken aback by the evident distress his Egyptian contacts experienced when he said he was going to be posted back to Europe. He had to work very hard to help his replacement get some measure of acceptance before he moved on.

Occasionally you have to drop a contact altogether, because there is no longer any benefit in the relationship for you. Ideally you would suggest other people for the contact to get in touch with, and then 'bow out gracefully' with reasons of work pressure or a change in your working role. An alternative is to let the contact decay by failing to follow up phone messages, and in some circumstances this can be the best solution. If you do not delegate and drop some of your contacts your network may become unmanageable and inefficient.

Rule 7: Be cautious when you share information

Sharing information is an essential element in maintaining your network, and this is another area where tact is required. Trial and error build trust—you offer a contact a small nugget of information, and wait to see how she uses it. Does she respect her source, and use the information discreetly? Does she offer you something worth while in return? 'Often you throw out a small fish to catch a bigger fish,' said one manager, 'and a small fish to you could be a big fish to the other person.' Timing is crucial in information exchange: news of a reorganization is top secret and highly valuable one month, confidential but still interesting the next month, and open news and hence of no value to your contact the third month. Knowing at which point to divulge or dig out the information is crucial—and a matter of judgement.

Rule 8: Remember the importance of face saving

Watch what you say about other individuals, whether they are your colleagues or your contact's colleagues. If in doubt, play safe. 'Always save face on both sides,' said Herma Volwater, working with a large organization. 'Never criticize people directly—your contact may wonder what you say about him behind his back. When someone criticizes a contact, and looks at me expectantly, I'd always be careful and say something like "of course he's under a lot of pressure." The message is clear enough.'

Using your network to get things done

Here is a last case to illustrate how you can solve organizational problems by drawing on your allies and stakeholders from a well-established network and by applying some of the suggestions on influencing and coalition building from the previous chapter. This is how Sarah, an internal consultant in a multinational organization, went about gaining support from her colleagues for an interesting but time-consuming project.

CASE STUDY 7.21   USING YOUR NETWORK ETHICALLY AND EFFECTIVELY—SARAH AND THE COURSE DIRECTOR DILEMMA

Sarah had just been given an interesting opportunity. In addition to her usual role as human resources consultant, she had been asked to take overall responsibility for a two-week residential management course. The course was scheduled to run six times a year in the company training centre, which was located in a different country from the one in which Sarah worked. The design of the course was no problem since she had already been involved in the course development, but her workload was heavy and she knew she would be unable to be present in the training centre for the full twelve weeks which had been scheduled. The challenge for Sarah was therefore to find some colleagues who would be willing to share the load as course directors in the training centre and who would put in the effort required to make the residential courses really successful.

'I thought about a number of colleagues who might be interested in helping to run the course as a developmental opportunity for themselves, and who would have the skills to do the job,' she said. Sarah had regularly helped her colleagues when they had been stuck, so she was able to draw on the goodwill she had established. However, these courses represented a serious commitment of time and effort, so she could hardly present her request as a minor favour. Sarah planned to run three of the six courses herself, and to ask three of her colleagues to act as course director for each of the remaining programmes.

No manipulation! Sarah plays it straight

Sarah thought hard about her approach. 'I always play it straight when I'm asking for support,' she said. 'I've been subjected to pressure myself by other people asking for help, and I think it's manipulative if people downplay the amount of work involved. You might take on a task and only later discover that it's much more work than you'd thought. Other manipulative tactics include the "Could you just?" type of request, or the use of flattery along the lines of "Oh, you're so good at this, it will be easy for you to sort it out." And I don't like it if people are artificially humble, or if they imply that you will be letting them down personally if you don't give them a hand. All these so-called "clever" tactics make people feel resentful later, and they won't help you again. Of course, if you "undersell" the opportunity you won't get any help either, so you have to choose an approach which will be both ethical and effective. I prefer to:

- Describe what the personal benefits and opportunities are for each of the colleagues I approach
- Explain the work involved, giving them a realistic idea of the minimum and maximum effort they would have to contribute
- Give them all time to think over the opportunity and to make up their minds without feeling pressured.

In this case, I also thought carefully about how we could organize the project to maximize the development opportunities for each person and to share out the interesting work as well as the routine chores.'

Identifying the benefits for each individual

Sarah selected three colleagues who could help. One was James, an experienced project engineer who was running a number of technical courses very successfully. James was an energetic man who was getting a little bored in training, and Sarah reckoned that he would welcome the challenge of running a management course for a change. He had already expressed an interest in some of the content of the new course, and if he were to be course director for one of the six courses he would have an ideal opportunity to further his own learning. He would also be able to check the interface between the management course and some of the advanced technical programmes which he was running, and he could meet some of the 'leading-edge' speakers from the business schools who would be contributing to the course.

Another potential course director was Brian, an old ally of Sarah's who had recently retired from his job in marketing. Brian had settled down very happily in his large house in the south of England where he was a keen gardener, but Sarah knew that he would welcome the opportunity to spend two weeks in the training centre, to catch up with his former colleagues and to interact with the course participants. Brian had helped with some of the initial development of the course, so Sarah thought he would be interested to catch up on some of the developments. As long as the course dates did not clash with his commitments (primarily sporting fixtures and visits to France) Sarah reckoned that Brian would be keen to help.

The third of Sarah's targets was Carole, an economist from another part of the business. Carole's experience to date had been limited to two locations and one area of the business. Sarah thought that a prime benefit to Carole of the course director role would be the chance to meet managers from different parts of the business, and to work with participants from a variety of cultures and backgrounds. Carole was a competent but shy woman who would probably benefit from a bit of networking herself, and managing one of the management courses was a perfect opportunity to do that.

Following through to success

The outcome was positive—to Sarah's delight, James, Carole and Brian eventually agreed each to take on one course. Sarah then checked with the course directors' own managers that they were happy with the plan, and got their agreement in writing. She thanked each of the new course directors personally. She made sure that there was plenty of space for discussion, and that her colleagues' ideas about the course were implemented and acknowledged. She then switched her attention to setting up the team, defining roles and responsibilities and integrating the ideas of each of the new course directors. She also worked behind the scenes at removing administrative obstacles. Once the courses started running, she made sure that all the course directors were working well together and that there was a smooth handover after each event. 'It's been a most successful programme,' Sarah said, 'we've all enjoyed the experience of working together and we've learned a lot from one another.'

What made Sarah successful—some conclusions

Before she started:

- Her network was already in place
- She was 'in credit' with her colleagues—she had helped them out in the past
- She thought about the benefits personally and organizationally to each of her colleagues

When she presented her request:

- She framed the request in terms which appealed to each individual
- She was open about her objectives

- She was honest about the effort involved
- She did not put her colleagues under pressure—she gave them time to think
- She did not act manipulatively

Once they had agreed:

- She allowed space for discussion and integrated her colleagues' ideas
- She thanked them each individually for their contribution
- She anchored the decision by checking that the stakeholders' managers approved the plan for them to help as course directors
- She followed through with careful project management.

Summary of strategic networking

You need a network in order to solve problems, collect information, obtain access to resources, get feedback, avoid misunderstandings, get advice, ideas, and new contacts.

Networking is the *strategic cultivation of relationships,* and is based on mutual help. The three key steps to networking are (1) choose your *focus*, identify the *person*, develop the *relationship*.

Audit your network across the quadrants (see Fig. 7.10). Use the 'jump-start' system of 10 key contacts if you prefer—but update it. Observe the networking code of conduct:

- Invest up front
- Be honest about objectives
- Keep contacts informed
- Respect people's time
- Maintain the relationship

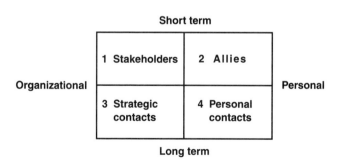

Fig. 7.10   Recap on the quadrants

- Delegate your contacts with care
- Be cautious when you share information
- Remember the importance of face saving.

Use your network together with SPLASH coalition building to get results.

Notes

The questions for identifying your allies are based on material from *Build your own rainbow* by Barrie Hopson and Mike Scalley, published by Lifeskills Associates, 1984.

Wayne Baker's *Networking Smart*, McGraw-Hill, 1994 offers a great deal of sound advice on networking in an American environment. Dutch readers may enjoy the descriptions of influential business executives and politicians in the Netherlands in *Je kent wie je bent* by Jos van Hezewijk and Marcel Metze, Balans, 1996. *The Secrets of Savvy Networking* by Susan Roanne, Warner Books, 1993 is chatty and readable but will not appeal to everyone's taste in Europe.

For a comprehensive list of some of the networking help you can offer, see *Influence without Authority*, by Allan R. Cohen and David L. Bradford, John Wiley, 1990.

8 Working with resistance: finding ways of moving forward

What is resistance?

Managers and consultants who want to implement change will inevitably encounter resistance—the direct and indirect expressions of anxiety and opposition. Here are some examples which will probably look familiar to you.

CASE STUDY 8.1 'WHY CAN'T HE TAKE CRITICISM?' ANDRÉ ARGUES

Katherine was trying to give some feedback to André, one of her team members. He had behaved aggressively to a younger colleague in a recent progress meeting, and had upset the other members of her team. Katherine had set up a private meeting with André to raise the issue with him. As she started to talk about his behaviour, however, he leaned forward, interrupted her and began energetically to defend himself. Each time she tried to explain what went wrong in the meeting he cut off her sentences with 'Yes, but...'—and started defending himself again. Katherine felt increasingly irritated. 'Why can't he take criticism?' she wondered.

'WHY WON'T SHE HELP?' HELEN GOES QUIET

Tom was manager of a project which was crucial to the business objectives of his organization. He was working to very tight deadlines, and needed extra resources from other projects to help him cope with a setback. He was presenting his case in a departmental meeting, with his two colleague project managers and the line manager present. One of his colleagues agreed straightaway to give Tom some computer time. The other colleague, Helen, was much less enthusiastic. 'It's all very well,' she said, 'but if you take two of my senior staff my project is going to suffer.' The line manager reassured Helen that he would fully understand if she could no longer make her targets. She said nothing, but did not look happy. 'That's agreed, then,' the line manager said. 'Make a note of it in the minutes.' Helen remained silent for the rest of the meeting. When Tom tried to catch her later in the corridor she walked off. 'I didn't mean to upset her,' Tom said later to the other project manager. 'You were prepared to help—why couldn't Helen do the same?'

'WHY CAN'T HE ACCEPT THE NEED FOR CHANGE?'
BILL BROODS

Bill had been operations director of his division for over 10 years. A new chief executive, Margaret, had been appointed, and a major reorganization was under way. Bill had been carefully consulted, along with all his senior colleagues. He felt torn in two—his head recognized the need for change, but his heart was heavy at the thought of removing old friends and colleagues from posts where they had worked loyally for years. He honestly did not know how he would get through the next few months.

Right now Margaret was presenting the reorganization to a group of 70 senior staff. Bill was gazing sadly out of the window, not looking at the overhead screen where she was pointing to the company results. Bill's shoulders were slumped, and he was sitting at an angle away from his chief executive. His face was pale and drawn. Bill's behaviour did not escape Margaret's keen eyes. 'There's trouble,' she thought. 'Bill said that he agreed with the changes, but he's still not backing me fully.'

In each of these cases:

- The person expressing the resistance feels anxious and threatened
- The manager who is faced with the resistance feels puzzled and frustrated
- Both parties can end up feeling angry and misunderstood.

Resistance is about logic, but it is also about emotions, and to deal with it effectively you have to recognize and respect those emotions. Some types of resistance are relatively easy to understand. If staff have not been adequately informed about the reasons for an organizational change, or if they feel they have not been suitably consulted, for instance, then they could well react with anger or scepticism. The solution is to explain the change more fully and more effectively, and to use a sensible consultation process wherever possible. You can read more about this in Chapter 10.

Resistance is also a matter of perception. The staff who felt they were not informed about the organizational change may accuse management of deliberately keeping them in the dark. The real reason could be a lack of co-ordination between the senior managers. The staff may be reacting defensively to a perceived threat, not a real one.

Perception also plays a part in how we interpret the behaviour of people who are showing resistance. In the cases of André, Helen and Bill, their managers and colleagues might blame them for being obstinate and obstructive, even childish. For the person concerned, however, the resistance is entirely normal and rational.

André knows he is impatient, and does not like that trait in his own personality, but he has no confidence in his own ability to change. He has heard this sort of feedback for years—it just makes him uncomfortable. He does not know what he can do about it. He also feels that the incident in the meeting is not all his fault. The team member had produced some poor-quality work, and André thinks that Katherine should be stricter about the technical standards of junior staff.

Helen believes she will be penalized for poor performance if she agrees to Tom's request. She thinks Tom is a nice guy, but resents him for putting her in a very difficult position personally. She cannot say anything about this openly in the meeting, and does not feel there is much point in explaining her worries to Tom—after all, there is nothing he can do about it.

Bill's strength as a manager is his concern for his staff. That concern is causing him a lot of distress, which he feels unable to explain to Margaret for fear of appearing weak. He is also worried about his own future. If some of his experienced staff are losing their jobs, there could be a real risk that Bill might lose his job too.

The concerns of André, Helen and Bill are all understandable. Unfortunately, the underlying reasons for the resistance are such that they feel unable to explain them—hence the confusion and the frustration. The resistance is expressed indirectly—Helen, for instance, feels under pressure from her line manager, but she reacts mainly against Tom. Tom is puzzled and hurt, and assumes she is just being difficult. A vicious circle can easily result, with relations between the two people deteriorating steadily.

The bad news about resistance is that if you do not spot it and work with it sensitively, your own behaviour can easily make the resistance worse. If you get impatient with André, Helen or Bill they will be less, not more, likely to co-operate with you. You have to recognize and understand resistance in order to respond appropriately.

Resistance is an opportunity, not an obstacle

Managers who are good at 'engineering' change recognize that resistance is a necessary part of the transition process. Gary Steel is currently working in a management team to implement a major change. He has had a lot of experience with dealing with resistance. Gary's view is that 'You won't get real change in people unless they get uncomfortable, and unless, with support, they can deal with that discomfort in a constructive way.'

Chris Parker is a consultant who advises senior teams working with change. He points out that resistance should not be dismissed as an inconvenient block in the path of progress. 'It's a positive statement about people's commitment to their own needs and values—an honest defence that we should respect.' So you have to surface resistance, and not suppress it. In this chapter you will find many suggestions for how to do this, but before we go any further here is an example of a manager who with some considerable discomfort learned to work with resistance rather than against it—and achieved fine performance in his team as a result.

CASE STUDY 8.2   JOHN LEARNS TO WORK WITH RESISTANCE

John had been made responsible for marketing and R&D in a large pharmaceutical company. A pleasant, mild-mannered man, he regarded his strength as teamwork, and he felt that a harmonious atmosphere was essential for the creativity needed in his unit. His personal style was reflected in the quiet, respectful tone with which he addressed his staff. They liked John, and soon realized that he expected them to treat each other with the same careful consideration. After a few months, however, John realized there were problems in the performance of his unit. Comparisons between the output from his team and from teams in other locations showed that his staff were not as flexible nor as fast as some of their colleagues. John asked a consultant for help.

The consultant observed that there was a pattern of exaggerated politeness in the communication between team members. This meant that open discussion and debate were almost non-existent. As soon as any signs of resistance emerged in the group, John would intervene with comments like 'Look, stop fighting, we're a team.' John's fear of conflict was repressing the creativity of the team.

The consultant showed John that he had to change part of his own style. 'Resistance is the life blood of creativity,' the consultant explained. 'It doesn't kill a good idea—it speeds the creative process up. You've got to surface it and let people explore their disagreements.' Hesitant at first, John showed a lot of courage in altering his approach. 'When people get angry now, I can see it as a sign of their commitment,' he told the consultant later, 'and it has been rewarding to watch the energy and productivity increase in the team'.

If you can treat resistance as an expression of integrity rather than intransigence, you will be able to work with it rather than against it. That will give you a much greater chance of achieving genuine, lasting change. And you do not need to be a psychologist to be effective—you simply need to understand:

- The causes of resistance
- The signs of resistance
- How you should respond when you spot resistance
- What you must avoid doing and saying in order not to make the resistance worse
- How you should behave with your staff and with other colleagues, in order to avoid unnecessary resistance in the first place.

Common causes of resistance

So resistance is a normal part of any change process—but what causes it in the first place? You can think of resistance basically as a response to a threat. Examples of typical threats are the fear of loss of security, loss of control, loss of territory or loss of status—all of which make people feel vulnerable. Another kind of threat could be some impending and unpleasant action that the person will be required to undertake, such as having to implement an unpopular procedure, confront a difficult boss, or move long-serving staff, as in Bill's example.

Feelings of confusion and uncertainty are an important part of resistance. A sales supervisor told to open up a new area of business may feel very unsure where to start. At the same time he might feel unable to share his uncertainty with his manager, for fear of appearing incompetent.

Understanding resistance requires you to have a bit of imagination, but once you are aware of the main causes, some patterns quickly emerge, as in the following examples.

CASE STUDY 8.3 FEAR OF LOOKING FOOLISH

A client was talking unusually frankly to the manager of a consultancy firm. The client was explaining why some of his colleagues were unwilling to employ the manager's senior consultants. 'They know your people are good—that's just the problem. If they bring your consultants in, their colleagues will wonder what's wrong with them—are they too stupid to cope with their problems themselves? However, if they bring in more junior staff from other consultancies, they can say that the junior staff are just 'extra pairs of hands'.

FEAR OF LOSING TERRITORY

A divisional director had been looking for some time for a new section head. When one high flyer was proposed, the divisional director got decidedly nervous. 'I know he's good,' he told the human resources director, 'but I'm not sure he's got the experience for the job.' The two men trusted each other, so the HR director took a risk and 'read between the lines'. 'Robert tends to overreach himself—is that what's really worrying you? You're thinking that before we know it he'll be running the whole division.' The divisional director nodded reluctantly. 'In that case we need to define Robert's role very carefully,' the HR director said.

It is easy to dismiss other people's fears as irrational and childish. The truth remains that if we were confronted with such problems, we might well react irrationally also.

Signs of resistance

Once you understand roughly what causes resistance, you will find it easier to recognize it in your interactions with others. In our cases so far there have been direct signs of resistance—such as when André argues openly with Katherine—and indirect signs, such as when Bill turns away from Margaret and looks out of the window. The direct expressions of resistance are easy to spot, but the indirect signs are much more subtle and easy to overlook. How many signs of indirect resistance you can identify in the following case?

CASE STUDY 8.4   WHAT'S THE MATTER WITH CHARLES?

Two consultants, Simon and Anne, had been talking to Charles, the general manager of a company in northern France. They were reviewing the situation on their journey back to the office. It was their third meeting, and Charles was paying their expenses, but to be honest they were getting nowhere.

Charles had asked them to design a training programme on performance management. The module looked straightforward enough—the consultants had completed similar work successfully before. Initially Charles had been friendly and helpful, but when they asked about his training needs he became evasive. Each time they presented a design, Charles found something wrong with it. When they tried to explore his objections, he would move away from talking about the workshop and change the subject to a much broader discussion on the performance of his staff in general. Then his usual, cheerful manner would change—he would sit back from the table, look down at his hands and appear worried and withdrawn. He would talk repeatedly about 'the problems with the staff', but when the consultants gently probed, he would back off and change the subject yet again.

Finally they all agreed on a compromise design, and the consultants breathed a sigh of relief. At the last minute, however, when they had tried to reserve some dates for the workshop, Charles had been reluctant to commit himself. 'And that really didn't make sense,' said Simon on the way back to the office. 'He may well be busy over the next two months, but to put it off for six months seems very odd.' 'And yet he said it was an urgent training need, and he wants us to come back again to talk next month,' remarked Anne. 'I just can't get my arms round the problem.'

Indirect signs of resistance

Some of the indirect signs of resistance from Charles are when he:

- Reacts evasively when asked about training needs
- Changes the subject away from the workshop design
- Repeats the key phrase 'the problems with the staff'

- Changes his non-verbal behaviour, sitting back, looking down
- Refuses to set a firm date for the workshop.

Other examples of indirect resistance are when people fail to come on time or to prepare for meetings, when they fail to follow up on actions, or when they put blocks in the path of progress by saying things like 'we must first study this in more detail'.

Each time Anne and Simon think they have made some headway, Charles changes his mind. Many are the consultants who would give up and blame the client at this point. However, these shifts in Charles's behaviour are themselves indications of resistance and hidden worries. Later, when Anne got to know Charles better, she discovered that he had been worried about his own career. He had been afraid that his own senior management would interpret the performance problems with his staff as a failure on his part to manage the plant successfully. The training modules were genuinely intended to help his managers, but he feared that, as his subordinates became more skilled, they would notice his shortcomings too. And although he liked the consultants, he did not trust them enough initially to share his concerns openly with them.

People showing resistance often feel buffeted by ambivalent feelings. One moment Charles was positive and open—then, as his personal doubts came flooding back, he became vague and withdrawn. No wonder the consultants felt confused. Peter Block in his book *Flawless Consulting* suggests that another way of spotting resistance is to monitor your own reactions during a meeting. If, like the consultants working with Charles, you feel impatient, bored or frustrated, this may be a sign that you are dealing with the inconsistent behaviour so typical (and so understandable) of resistance.

The iceberg model: direct and indirect signs of resistance

Figure 8.1 shows some examples of signs of resistance, represented as an iceberg to show that the indirect signs, hidden under the surface of the water, often reveal anxieties which are deeper and more personal. Note that resistance is not just conveyed verbally, in words. Many of the indications are non-verbal, conveyed by the person's tone of voice, eye contact, gestures, stance and so on.

Resistance is a stress response, so typically it is a behaviour which is different from the person's norm. A quiet person suddenly becomes very angry. A friendly person becomes withdrawn. The range of ways in which people signal their resistance and their discomfort is very wide

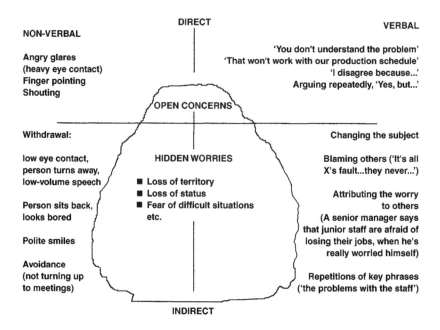

Fig. 8.1   Signs of resistance—the iceberg model

indeed. The better you know the person, the easier it is to spot resistance. The more the person trusts you, the more likely he is to respond to your careful questioning and to tell you what he is really worried about. Unfortunately, if you do not know the person well, the resistance is harder to identify and to explore. If you are not both persistent and sensitive, the other person will succeed in deflecting and distracting you, and your good idea will die here.

Working with resistance in one-to-one cases

So once you have spotted the signs of resistance, what should you do about it? Let us go back to the case of Katherine, trying to give feedback to her team member, André, who had behaved aggressively in the team meeting. On a bad day, she might be tempted to tell him to shut up and listen—she could over-rule him and instruct him to change his behaviour in future. Because human beings are such complex creatures, once in a while this PUSH approach might work. Katherine might be able to shock André into compliance and use her hierarchical position to force him to obey. The chances are far higher, however, that the meeting would end in André's sullen defiance, and André would have suffered loss of face. His resentment of her approach could make the next team meeting an uncomfortable and unproductive event for everyone.

Other managers might adopt the 'Let's talk about this calmly like civilized human beings' type of approach. Here you are repressing André's anxieties, rather than exploring them. He is being treated like a child, or like a robot. Unless you find out what his problems are, it is very unlikely that you will help him to change.

You have to deal with resistance fast if you are to find a satisfactory solution. The longer you leave the problem, the more difficult it will be to solve it. Ultimately, if Katherine does not get André to change his behaviour, she may need to remove him from the team. To work with resistance effectively, you must use a BUILD approach, and the key priorities to bear in mind can be summed up in the 3S model (Fig. 8.2).

1 SUPPORT the person

Support is an essential part of getting the person to open up and explain his or her concerns—that is why it is priority number one. If you can show that you understand the person's reactions, you will get a lot further both in understanding the problem and in finding a way forward. One way of demonstrating support is to show that you can understand the other person's concerns—that you do not think he or she is being stupid. In this way you legitimize the anxiety. Another simple way to offer support is to tell the person about times when you have experienced similar problems yourself.

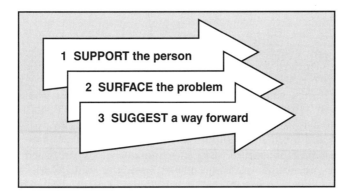

Fig. 8.2 Working with resistance—the 3S model

CASE STUDY 8.5   SUPPORTING ANDRÉ

Katherine listened attentively to André, and eventually he admitted that he had had similar feedback before. He knew he ought to control his temper with colleagues, but occasionally ('If they're being really stupid') he found that very difficult. And he felt that his impatience was normal—'They should think harder before they come up with such dumb ideas.'

Katherine also had a quick temper, but she had learnt on the whole to control it. She told André that occasionally she found it hard to be patient in meetings too. She described to him times when she had had to breathe deeply and count to ten. She observed that André's behaviour towards her had now changed—he was sitting back, looking more relaxed.

Resistance is always a sensitive matter. If you ignore it, it usually becomes worse. If you overstate it or misinterpret it, you risk offending the other person. The essential element when you support others is to enable the person to retain his or her dignity at all times. The best approach is to move cautiously, summarize regularly and keep checking with the person that you really have understood what is worrying him or her.

Saving face is an essential part of supporting the person. People need to preserve their self-respect if they are to let go of their resistance and work with you to find a way forward. As an illustration, here is how Anne, one of the consultants working in France, got on with Charles, the general manager who seemed so reluctant to organize the training workshops. You may remember that Anne and Simon had spent a great deal of time talking to Charles and designing the training modules, but that Charles had been reluctant to commit to any dates.

CASE STUDY 8.6   SUPPORTING THE PERSON— HELPING CHARLES TO MOVE FORWARD

Back in the office, Anne was writing a note to Charles. Her colleague had been whisked off to another, more promising project, so she had to tackle Charles now on her own. Tactfully but clearly, she described the consultants' observations—that the problem Charles was facing seemed to be broader than just designing the training modules, that there seemed to be some reluctance on his part to organize the dates, and that she would like to address these issues in her next meeting with him. Putting this in writing was risky, but doing nothing seemed riskier still. And she knew she could count on the fact that Charles seemed to like her.

Anne finds the face saver

There was a worrying pause of a couple of weeks before Charles' assistant rang, but the response then was positive. In the meantime Anne did some homework. Her own Paris-based organization was small, but it was networked with a much larger company which specialized in high-level seminars for top executives. One such seminar was on performance management. Her contact in the training organization owed Anne a favour, so he agreed that she could have one free place on the next seminar coming up. 'Perfect,' Anne thought, as she thanked him.

Success
In the meeting with Charles she invited him to talk, and she listened attentively. Sure enough, he kept coming back to 'the problems with the staff'. Anne was conscious that he probably would not want to raise his worries with her directly, but over lunch she casually mentioned the possibility of the free place at the seminar. His face showed little expression as he consulted his assistant— could she spare him for the three days? She thought that was just about possible. Anne rang her contact to confirm the place. And to her surprise, as she finished her phone call Charles's assistant handed her a list of possible dates for her training modules. Anne was in business.

Anne helped Charles in two ways: she ensured that he did not look weak in front of his assistant, and she found a way for him discreetly to enlarge his skills and expertise. She also offered him options, rather than 'boxing him in'.

2   SURFACE the problem
Once you have established some support for the person showing the resistance, you will find it much easier to work on identifying the worries and defining the problem. If like many managers you are tempted to jump to solutions, you may find the BUILD acronym helpful for remembering the behaviours you should use in order to keep on track and focus on the problem:

B   ack off
U   nderstand
I   nvite the person to explain
L   isten
D   emonstrate that you have understood.

The hardest part for most managers is to follow the first step—Back off! It is so tempting to flood the person with all your best arguments and to try to beat him intellectually and emotionally into the ground. Instead, you should change your approach and let him talk—so that you can Understand what it is that is worrying him. Hence the importance of Inviting the person to explain.

A classic example of a useful question at this stage is simply 'What's the problem?' Veterans of communication courses will recognize the need here to ask open questions and to explore the underlying concerns. The best questions are often the simplest ones. To get André to talk about the meeting where he had behaved aggressively, Katherine could ask him:

- What do you think went wrong?
- How did you feel at the time?
- How do you think the others felt?
- What do you think you could do differently?
- What would you find difficult about changing your behaviour? and so on.

Listening is vital, and this means that you have to be patient and make time available, even if you have to stay late or come in early. Listening is a sign of respect for the other person. Pause after you have asked an open question, to give the person time to think. Your interviewee needs that elapsed time to consider what his concerns really are, and whether he is prepared to tell you about them. If Katherine rushes André, he may clam up and she will be none the wiser, so she must give him space. If you suddenly spot signs of resistance, and do not have the time to listen, stop the process and say that you would like to set up a new appointment to hear the other person's concerns in more detail.

Finally, summarize the other person's worries—to Demonstrate that you have understood.

CASE STUDY 8.7   WORKING WITH ANDRÉ— *SURFACING* THE PROBLEM

André was talking more quietly and reflectively. 'The trouble is that when I feel deeply about something my emotions just get in the way,' he explained. 'I want the team to produce really high-quality work, and I don't always feel that the others take the project as seriously as I do. When they make silly suggestions, that really annoys me and the words fly out of my mouth before I can stop them.'

'So your intention is to maintain high standards,' Katherine summarized, 'and you don't mean to upset the others—but you don't know how to control your reactions. Have I got that right?' André nodded. 'I agree that we should address the problem of the technical standards, and I will think about that. But can you see from your side that if you snap at some of the younger members of the team, that makes them nervous. They then don't dare to ask questions if there's something they don't understand—and that can cause them to make mistakes.' André nodded again. 'So what do you think we can do to improve the situation?' 'I'll try to stop biting their heads off,' said André, 'but I'm not sure that it will always work.'

3   SUGGEST a way forward

Understanding the problems which underlie the resistance is an excellent start, but your emphasis in the next step is on finding a practical way forward. If you start to impose your ideas, the resistance will reappear, so you should aim to integrate your ideas with those of the other person in order to find a next step which is acceptable to both of you.

CASE STUDY 8.8 SUGGESTING A WAY FORWARD WITH ANDRÉ

'How about this?' said Katherine. 'You do your best to be patient with the junior team members. I'll talk to them again about the importance of quality control. If you do lose your patience at any point I'll give you a discreet signal to back off.' 'Right,' nodded André. 'And you don't have to be too discreet—I'll understand.'

'Looking at the longer term, I wonder if it would help if you coached two of the team members,' Katherine suggested. 'You are the most experienced member of the team. We could give a part of your routine work to one of the other team members to free up some of your time. If you did some coaching you'd have a direct impact on the quality of work, and you could prevent some of the quality problems. What do you think?' André thought for a moment. 'That would really force me to practise being patient,' he agreed. 'I could give it a try.'

A lot depends here on the goodwill of the team members and on André's priorities—how important it is to him that the team functions well, and how prepared he is to examine honestly the effects of his own behaviour. But by using the 3S approach, Katherine has worked with André's resistance rather than against it, and this has given them both the best chances of success.

Each manager will use his or her own way to work with resistance. Here is a case from a senior consultant who builds both 'face saving' and practical assistance into his consulting approach.

CASE STUDY 8.9 SUPPORTING THE PEOPLE: RESISTANCE FROM SENIOR STAFF

'Senior managers can feel very vulnerable bringing in consultants like myself from outside. They know they need the help, but they don't like having to ask for it from an outsider, and they need reassurance. I tell my client that it is normal for managers of large and complex organizations to find themselves suddenly confronted with large and complex problems, and that it is always easier for outsiders to take an objective view. My underlying message is that the problem is not due to any incompetence on their part—it's just an inevitable part of their job. Together we have all the skills and expertise to handle it.'

Surfacing the problem
Then I tackle the main, underlying concern—how can my client present his case to his boss? Often my proposed solution to the consultancy problem involves

some major change, and this is what worries my client. He wants to appear reliable, responsible and in control, but if he suddenly changes direction he risks looking the opposite. Because he's senior, all his staff will be feeling vulnerable too. I raise these issues directly, saying again that they're a normal part of management and that we will find a way to tackle them.

Agreeing a way forward

Typically what I do is to go through the presentations that the client and his senior managers have made over the last couple of years, and to check all the policy statements they've made in public. We put together a series of new presentations, explaining the benefits of the change and presenting it as a logical continuation from their previous work. I do all of this quite openly with them in a series of meetings, so that by the time they present to their board they are fully prepared. They have a clear vision, they feel personally secure, they know where they want to end up and they know which steps they have to take first. Both the managers and the organization benefit.'

In the examples so far, the managers have found a 'win/win' solution to working with resistance. This is not always possible. Sometimes staff in organizations have to give up territory and status, knowing they will get little or nothing in return. One senior manager who had worked with union representatives during major reorganizations said that 'Most union reps are people with a genuine mission. You have to remember that, when they take up traditional postures. Talk to them off-site, where you can build trust and speak freely without committing yourselves. People will often be prepared to make sacrifices as long as you treat them with respect and help them to retain their personal dignity.'

Avoiding unnecessary resistance—good managerial practice

So far we have seen how to work with resistance on a one-to-one basis. Before we progress to looking at resistance in groups, here are a few reminders about what you can do as a manager to avoid unnecessary resistance in your staff and colleagues:

- *Check your communication.* Resistance is often an expression of confusion. Be clear and consistent about objectives, expectations, performance measures, priorities and assumptions.
- *Be constructive with criticism.* People will often perceive criticism as a threat. Point out what the person does well, put the criticism in context and check the person agrees and understands. Make sure the person gets any help that he or she needs in order to improve, follow up your meeting and acknowledge the progress

that the person makes. These steps will help you to make criticism less threatening, and more effective.

■ *Avoid blame—it triggers resistance.* Use the same constructive approach if you want to give feedback to a colleague who is at the same level or more senior in your organization. Sometimes managers go through months of frustration with their boss, for instance. Finally they explode, and they express all their resentment in vivid detail. Emotive attacks, although often understandable, are rarely effective. Cross out your more aggressive statements in your memo—force yourself to be constructive. You can pre-empt resistance and increase the chances that your readers will be receptive.

■ *Choose an approach designed to reduce resistance.* People who are used to influencing from a limited power base are often very skilled at avoiding any small comments or actions that can trigger unnecessary resistance. The following account comes from the wife of a manager working for a multinational. She is active in a number of voluntary organizations but has no formal role in her husband's organization. On several occasions she has helped to set up initiatives to support other spouses, and this has brought her into contact with managers in various departments.

CASE STUDY 8.10 CHOOSING AN APPROACH WHICH IS UNTHREATENING—AND EFFECTIVE

'It's not easy working from a position of no formal power. On several occasions I have been quite taken aback by the amount of opposition I have encountered—to what seemed to be quite straightforward requests. But managers in all organizations are understandably sensitive to setting precedents, and to the costs which can be entailed. I have gained insights into the way in which organizations work which I have found very interesting—and I have learned to be careful.

As soon as I spot something that needs doing, I find someone sympathetic and senior, and I paint a clear picture of where I'm coming from. I have to show I'm independent and open—I'm simply a representative, not a deputation or a pressure group. I keep watching the faces of the people I'm talking to—if their face muscles start to tighten, I back off. If you're aggressive you get nowhere, so if I take anyone along with me I choose people who are sensible and quiet.

My starting point is to explain the problem and to say: 'This is what I'd thought of doing—how should I go about it?' If you ask for advice, rather than aggressively selling an idea, you get a better response. You have to be prepared to translate any proposal into "company speak"—to explain what is needed, why, and how much it will cost. They are always short of time, so if you tell them clearly what you expect from them they are more likely to agree.

The other important point about influencing in these circumstances is to see the problem from the other person's perspective—to remember that they've got a point. As long as they feel comfortable with your proposal, they're usually prepared to be reasonable.'

■ *Use your network, to set up co-operative relationships in advance.* Remember that networking helps you to manage risks, including potential resistance. Managers in head offices, for instance, are particularly vulnerable to opposition from other parts of their organization, because staff in operating companies will typically feel that 'We do the real work—head office sends the memos'. By building co-operative relationships early you can pre-empt unnecessary resistance.

How to handle resistance in groups

Working with resistance from an individual is tricky, but resistance from a group is much more complex. One of the most common forms of group resistance is the organizational myth. Most managers have to confront a myth at some stage in their careers, so in this section we will explore the concept of the myth and you can read a number of ways of dealing with them.

A myth is a statement issued by a group which feels under attack. A common format is 'We tried that in 1991 and it didn't work' or 'Senior management will never accept that'. The purpose of the myth is to act as a defence—to help the group feel stronger, to divert attention away from any proposal which the group finds threatening, and ideally to stave off the attack altogether. One senior manager described the following example of a myth which had initially caused him great frustration.

CASE STUDY 8.11   AN ORGANIZATIONAL MYTH:
'OUR CUSTOMERS AREN'T INTERESTED IN AN
INTEGRATED PRODUCT SERVICE'
'Our management team was working on a reorganization of our product division, to offer a more flexible service to our customers. Many of our product managers had worked for the organization for years, and they weren't happy with the proposed changes to their jobs and territories. The spokesman for the product managers came up with the most extraordinary tale—he told the team with great conviction that our customers weren't interested in an integrated product service. I knew this wasn't true, because I'd just commissioned a survey into customer needs and I had some of the preliminary findings in front of me. But even after I showed them the findings, the product managers were just as confident that our reorganization would be a complete waste of time.'

The myth as a protective wall

The myth is like a wall that the group builds round itself. It is a shared version of events that gets elaborated and reinforced as time passes or as the threat draws nearer. It is also an effective way of saving face and concealing the real worries—in some cases the individuals may be unaware themselves of what is really making them anxious.

Myths create camaraderie—as one manager put it, 'We had a "Dunkirk spirit" where the group bonded together in the face of a common enemy'. A myth supplies an emotional need, and the bigger the group of people that believe it, the more effective it becomes as a defence.

The problem with myths is that they can be very persistent. A carefully crafted myth can slow down change and sometimes sabotage it altogether. And some people will never accept a change, so they have to move or leave before the change can really get under way. Often, however, the people who are showing this form of resistance are staff who are very useful to the organization, so you have to find other ways of helping them let go of the myth and confront the real and legitimate problems underlying it.

How myths evolve

When you work with resistance, it is helpful to understand how the myth has evolved. Here is a typical example.

CASE STUDY 8.12   FRANK AND THE ORGANIZATIONAL MYTH

Frank had just joined a large organization which contracted in a lot of technical experts from other bureaus. Part of his new role involved managing the contracts for these experts. Frank soon noted that one of these experts had a contract with the organization which seemed unduly generous. When he raised this issue with his colleagues they agreed with him, but they also said that 'the expert will never accept a change'. They repeated this statement several times, with much shaking of heads. When Frank said that he was quite prepared to raise the issue himself with the contractor, they told him that 'unless you've got powerful contacts with senior managers, you will get burned'. The implication was that they did not have these contacts, and neither did Frank. Frank was puzzled—he could not see why this was all such a problem. What was going on?

The two myths created by Frank's colleagues were 'He (the expert) will never accept a change' and 'Unless you've got powerful contacts, you will get burned'.

Frank's colleagues created the myths because they had tried persuading the expert and had failed. They did not know what they could do differently in order to succeed, and they did not want to look stupid in front of Frank, so they invented a new version of events in order to save face. As with all resistance, the more you argue logically against it, the more entrenched it becomes. When Frank insisted that he was prepared to tackle the contractor himself, the colleagues backed up the first myth ('the expert will never accept a change') with a second myth dressed up as a friendly warning ('unless you've got powerful contacts, you will get burned').

Dispelling organizational myths—the options

So once you have spotted a myth, what should you do about it? If you think back to the two basic influencing strategies, you will recognize that you have two main choices.

You can use a PUSH strategy, where you identify the myth, but then go ahead with your original course of action anyway. This option is viable if you have good personal credibility, if you can get the backing of senior management and if you are reasonably confident that you can solve the problem. Frank had come from outside the organization, and he had good credibility, so he opted successfully for this approach.

CASE STUDY 8.13   FRANK TAKES DIRECT ACTION

Frank went straight to his boss. 'Have you any objection to my talking to the expert?' he asked. 'Go ahead—I think you will find it difficult to change the contract, but in principle I'm right behind you,' was the response. Frank planned the meeting with the expert carefully in advance. Together they agreed objectives for the coming period, defined the scope of the expert's work and discussed what the expert's contribution was worth on the open market. The result was that the two men quickly reached a new deal that was satisfactory to them both. And Frank wasn't 'burned'—on the contrary, he scored high in his appraisal.

'Everyone was frustrated by the problem, but no-one was prepared to take action,' Frank said later. 'They had ended up frightening each other with their tales of punishment. Once they saw that it was quite possible to change the contract, they started taking action with other experts too. And of course they had a "face saver"—they could say that it was easier for me because I had come from outside. I didn't argue with that because there was some truth in it.'

So Frank led by example, and his colleagues were able to live comfortably with his success. If, like Frank, you have reasonably high credibility with the people you are trying to influence, you can afford to take a risk, ignore the myth and go ahead with your proposal anyway. If you do not have good credibility and the backing of your management, myths are harder to manage.

A BUILD approach to dispelling myths

Many staff who have to work with a myth will not have the power base to enable them to confront the problem head-on. Internal consultants, for instance, often have a hard time convincing their colleagues in different departments to follow their suggestions. If you are in this position, you will need to use the BUILD approach to help managers to explore the myth and to discover the truth and the anxieties behind it. Once the managers have confronted their real worries, they can start to take positive action themselves to tackle the problems. As is often the case with the BUILD approach, you will need to invest more time and effort to get results. Hank Williams from Learning Curve offers training and mentoring to internal and external consultants. Many of the suggestions which follow in this section are based on Hank's experience.

Here is an example where a consultant enabled a group to explore a myth.

CASE STUDY 8.14   RICHARD AND THE NEW SECTION HEADS: WORKING WITH AN ORGANIZATIONAL MYTH

Richard had been working as an internal consultant to support some senior managers on a project to set up a major change. The project had run very smoothly so far, and his task now was to explain to the middle management layer—in this case to six section heads—some changes in key procedures which were part of the new scheme.

The meeting did not run quite as Richard had expected. Several of the section heads were relatively new to their posts and uncertain about their roles. He had started off with a short presentation, but from the questions which followed he soon sensed that the section heads were feeling unsettled and hostile. A heated discussion broke out. Richard realized he had to change his tack, and putting his papers aside he asked them what was bothering them. He instantly got an energetic and indignant response: 'How can we be expected to manage our sections when we don't know what's going on? Our managers never inform us.'

First spot the myth

Suppose you were in Richard's place—what would you do? The first step is to spot the myth. Words like 'never' are signs of potential resistance. Rationally, the statement does not make sense—is it possible that the senior managers really *never* inform the section heads? Emotionally, the statement reveals a deep well of frustration and insecurity, which is legitimate from the group's point of view.

Change the agenda

Your first reaction should be to slow down, take a deep breath, remember the BUILD acronym and Back off. Don't argue. You could suggest that the group change the initial agenda, and explore the problem of the lack of information instead. You will not be able to use a PUSH approach and continue with his initial script—if you try, you run the risk of losing control of the meeting.

Use the 3S model—but take each step more slowly

Use the 3S approach, but take each of the steps more slowly, and explore the problem in more detail, because the myth is a cover for a number of different individual needs and problems.

1   SUPPORT the people

Do not let your questions sound like an interrogation, or the group will retreat in unison behind the myth, emerging only to attack you. Explain that you want to help, and that you can understand their concerns. If they say that they do not want to talk about the problem, do not impose your help—close the meeting and retreat to think the problem over. If the group trusts you they will usually be prepared to talk about the problem.

2   SURFACE the problem

Get some specific examples to illustrate the problem
You could open up the discussion with questions such as:

- Can you give me an example of when your managers failed to inform you? What happened exactly?
- How did this affect your work?
- Why do you think they did not inform you?

You can then start gradually and tactfully to expose the myth by exploring times when the senior managers were more helpful:

- Can you think of any times when you have been properly informed? What happened then? How did that affect you?
- Are there any managers who do inform you? Can you give me an example?

This will enable you to scope the problem. You may also want to get a historical perspective, to give you and the managers a sense of the scale of the problem:

- How long have you been aware of this problem? When do you think it started? Has the problem always been there? Do you think it has stayed the same, or do you think the situation is getting worse?
- What have you done so far to improve your relationships with your managers? What happened? What are you planning to do now?

Keep summarizing to check that you have understood, and to prevent your exploration from sounding like an examination.

Identify the individual needs

You should now have enough information to help the managers to emerge from behind the wall of the myth and to start specifying their individual needs. This is a sensitive point in the process, because if the managers start to feel threatened then the myth will reappear in a form which will be more compelling for them than ever. In some cases you may decide to continue with this process in one-to-one meetings, where the individual managers will not be distracted by the reactions of their colleagues. Check the timing of your one-to-one meetings, however. Once you are out of the way, the managers may revert to the myth and the comfort of group solidarity. Richard decided to tackle this stage in the process with the whole group. He continued as follows.

CASE STUDY 8.15

'We've collected some examples of when you've felt you were left in the dark. Let's look now at what it is you really need from your managers. Who'd like to start?' Richard asked. The section heads came forward one by one with their needs. Anneke had started in her post a month ago, and felt she was not getting enough guidance and coaching. Mohammed said he was unsure about his objectives. John said he agreed with Mohammed, and that he was having trouble prioritizing his workload.

Mario and Hans said that their managers had made their objectives clear enough, but that they could do with some more feedback on their performance. They had both been in their positions for over a year, and neither had had an appraisal. The remaining section head was reasonably positive when pressed about his manager, but said he would stay in the meeting and help his colleagues in the discussion. 'Good,' said Richard. 'We're making progress.'

3 SUGGEST a way forward

Next you should specify the individual outcomes for each manager. Your aim here is to construct a really attractive alternative to the myth.

The section heads need to feel confident that by working towards their own outcomes, they can solve the problems which caused them to hide behind the myth in the first place. Useful questions are:

- What could your manager do that would make a real difference for you? Can you give me an example?
- How would that help you in your work? How would that affect your performance?
- If your manager could only make one change or take one action to help you, what should that be?
- What can you do yourself to improve the relationship?

CASE STUDY 8.16   RICHARD HELPS THE SECTION HEADS TO SORT OUT THEIR OUTCOMES

Anneke said that if her manager could explain to her the budget cycle she would already feel more confident. 'I don't really understand the current system, so I can't put your proposed changes into any context.' Richard said he could understand why she had sounded so confused when he had tried to answer her questions.

Mohammed said he could at least draft a note giving his understanding of his objectives, and then check whether his manager agreed—'That might open up the discussion'. John needed an hour with his manager to check out his priorities—'I really feel completely confused at the moment, and the proposed organizational change will increase my workload.' Mario and Hans said they both needed an appraisal within the next month or so. Their managers kept deferring the date, and they really were not sure how they could persuade them to take the appraisals more seriously. 'Let's come back to that one in a minute,' said Richard. 'I may be able to put in a word with them myself.'

Action planning

The section heads now have an accurate understanding of their problems, and an idea of their desired outcomes. The next step is to do some solid action planning, so the section heads know how to get from the present, uncomfortable situation to their desired solution. Questions for this step are:

- What actions can you take?
- Which action will you take first?
- What could get in the way of progress?
- What can you do to prevent/overcome that problem?
- Who else/what else could help you?
- Do you feel confident that this will work? If not, what else do you need?
- When will you start?

Agree follow-up

Agree some follow-up, either with yourself or with some other member of staff, to monitor progress and offer any further support. You can of course offer some direct help yourself, perhaps (like Richard with the timing of the appraisals) through your own networking contacts.

A complex case: handling an inter-team conflict

This chapter closes with a case where the manager has to work with different kinds of resistance under considerable time pressure. The context is a handover from one team to the other. Handovers often cause conflicts, because of the high standard of communication and co-operation required. If there are tensions between the different groups, then resistance and organizational myths quickly emerge. Again, prevention pays. John Stubbs, a senior engineer working in a major multinational, points out that with proper risk management and an effective network of stakeholders you can pre-empt many of these problems. Occasionally, however, a manager inherits a dilemma which he has to solve, as in this story.

CASE STUDY 8.17   RESISTANCE FROM ALL SIDES—
THE PROJECT LEADER AND THE HANDOVER

The situation

Michael had just been appointed to take over as project leader from Philip, who had unexpectedly fallen ill. Michael had been working in head office, so he was familiarizing himself with the project and the team. The purpose of the project was to design a minor addition to an existing facility which had been in operation for several years. The chief executive of the local organization was a dynamic and demanding leader, and the plant had been highly successful in meeting its production targets. Much of this success was due to the efforts of the operations group, led by Tony.

The problem

Michael had originally been excited at the prospect of his project leader role, which represented a big promotion for him. Once at the site, however, he quickly spotted that all was not well. Communication between the project team and the operations group was poor. Relationships were strained, and Michael was taken aback to hear the open hostility of the project team towards the operations group. When he asked some members of the team about meetings with the operations group, the team member said flatly that they were a waste of time. 'There's no point in trying to talk to them,' the team member said. 'They never attend the meetings anyway. They're a conservative bunch, and they've been critical of our work from the start.' Michael found this very worrying, especially as the handover was due to commence in two weeks' time. He called Tony to set up a meeting for the following day.

The team's version of events

Meanwhile Michael talked to one of the more experienced team members to find out what had been going on. Michael's predecessor had apparently had a 'personality clash' with Tony. The two men simply did not get on. And there had been some problems with design suggestions put forward by Tony's team at the start of the project. All this had happened before the team member had joined the team, but for some reason only half the suggestions had been integrated by the project team into their design. 'Of course, Phil could be a bit arrogant at times,' the team member said with a grin and a shrug, 'but he was a great guy to work for.' Michael said nothing. He'd never met Philip, but he'd heard that he could be difficult.

The story from operations

Michael's neighbour was a friendly older woman called Jean, who was responsible for the administration for the operations group. He spotted her in the canteen and went over after lunch to join her. She confirmed that Tony had been furious when half his group's suggestions had been rejected. 'As I remember, Philip gave him no real explanation—he was really very off-hand with our staff. Of course, Tony isn't always easy either—he believes in proven technology, and isn't keen on anything too fancy or innovative. The operations group think your lot are a bunch of inexperienced hobbyists—I'm sorry to say this, but I think you should know. And it's a pity that the operations staff have been so preoccupied with the maintenance problems that have arisen recently. That's made the situation worse between the two groups, because Tony's had to cancel several meetings with your team. He's very worried that your design will be full of holes. I suspect that both groups are preparing their defences for the chief exec, in case the whole thing turns out to be a disaster.'

Michael analyses the problems

Back in his office Michael had a quiet think. The personal relationship between Philip and Tony had been poor, but at least as a newcomer he had a chance to set up his relationship with Tony in a more constructive way. Both groups in the conflict were 'stereotyping' and blaming the other, so he had to cope with some deeply embedded organizational myths. And it looked as though he'd have some serious technical problems to confront, because of the lack of co-operation between the two groups since the start of the project. He had gone through the files but found no satisfactory explanation for the rejection of the operations group's suggestions. On the other hand, Michael knew that deadlines could have a motivating effect, if only he could persuade both groups to stop fighting and start co-operating.

Jean's comment about the groups marshalling their defences was another worry: if they had already invested so much effort in 'covering their backs' there was a risk that they would not be prepared to change. Some of the team members were due for a transfer, so they could well feel that the handover was Michael's problem—and not theirs.

Michael was uncomfortably aware that there was something else he had to consider. Everyone in the team knew that this was his first post as project leader. Michael had the full support of his own line manager, but head office was a long way away. And Philip had been very popular with at least some members of the team. If Michael criticized his predecessor, even indirectly, the whole team could turn against him—at the very time when he urgently needed their support. He contacted a couple of the more experienced members of his team, to ask for their opinions about how he should run the meeting, and to get their support. They agreed they would back him in the meeting.

The team meeting
He called a team meeting for four o'clock, in order to prepare for the meeting with Tony the following day. He knew he would have to be careful about saving face for the team if he was to lead them in a different direction. 'The situation is radically different now, with the handover coming up,' he said. 'I can understand that you've had a lot of problems with the operations group in the past, but we need to put that behind us and plan for the immediate future. You're the ones with the technical experience of the project, so I need your help to prepare properly for tomorrow's meeting.' The team members said again that Michael would never get Tony to co-operate. 'That's my responsibility,' he replied, 'but I'll need information from you first. If this handover turns out be a disaster, it won't do any of us any good. Tony will feel under pressure too—the chief exec will be watching him as well as us.'

Michael guessed that he had half the team with him by now. The other half carried on criticizing the operations group. 'You're new,' they said. 'You have no idea about what's gone on.' Michael listened to the catalogue of complaints, so they could air their resentments and hopefully get them out of the way. 'I can understand how you feel,' he said again when they paused for breath, 'but now we have to concentrate on the future.'

Gradually the mood of the meeting changed, and with varying degrees of enthusiasm the whole team settled down to planning the meeting and the handover. The more constructive team members led the way in making a list of the essential items, and the negotiable items. After the meeting, an exhausted Michael reviewed the situation. He had the team more or less behind him. Now he needed to come out of the meeting with Tony with a satisfactory outcome so that they would continue to support him.

Lobbying Tony—some informal preparation
Michael packed up his papers and walked into the lift. On his way out he made a detour to Tony's office. He knocked and put his head round the door. The other man was working at his computer. 'Have you got a minute?' Michael asked. Tony nodded and beckoned him in without a smile. 'About tomorrow's meeting,' Michael said. 'I realize there have been problems, but with the handover coming up I'd like us to make a fresh start. I wondered if there was anything in particular you want to have on the agenda, so I can do some extra preparation if necessary.' Tony thought for a moment, then mentioned a number of technical points he was worried about. Michael said he would look into these first thing. Tony finished the conversation with a reference to Philip. 'Your predecessor was not much help,' he said. 'Let's hope you can do better.' With that he went back to his computer, and Michael left the office.

The meeting with Tony

Michael had spent the previous evening reading the files and checking that he was thoroughly prepared for Tony's questions. He'd arrived early at the conference room which he had reserved. Tony was a few minutes late, but gave a brief apology. Michael started by outlining the purpose of the meeting and agreeing an agenda. He then listened to Tony's account of the problems in the past. Michael guessed that Tony had felt humiliated by Philip's treatment of his group's suggestions, and wanted to demonstrate that he himself would treat the colleagues in the operations group with more courtesy and respect. Listening carefully to Tony's story was one way of showing that respect. Both Tony's story and his own team's version of events seemed somewhat exaggerated, but that hardly mattered now—if he could get the relationships to improve, he would be a long way on the road to progress. Finally Tony had finished, and Michael gave him the same response as he had used with his own team. He agreed that it all sounded very frustrating, but repeated that now they had a good opportunity to work together more constructively. He continued in a more practical vein, giving Tony the answers to the technical questions he had raised. They went on to tackle the items on the agenda.

The results

They were both pleased with the outcome from the meeting. They had agreed a plan for organizing the handover. Both had stressed their priorities, and both had made some concessions. The technical problems were considerable, but they were not quite as serious as Michael had privately feared. 'Grounds for cautious optimism,' he thought.

Michael was able to demonstrate to his team that he had defended their legitimate interests. He agreed with Tony that two project team engineers should work in Tony's part of the office with his technical experts on the most pressing technical issues. Michael chose the two team members who were most constructive as well as technically expert, and he stressed to them the need for proven solutions. The weeks ahead could still be tough, but they had come a long way to solving the conflict.

Learning points

Michael was working with low to medium credibility with both his own team and the operations group, so he applied primarily a *BUILD approach*.

He used *lobbying and consultation* effectively—with his own team members, with Jean from the operations group, and most importantly with Tony.

He concentrated initially on his own team, in order to operate from a strong base. He used the *3S model* with both the team and later with Tony. He *supported the two parties* by listening attentively to their complaints, and by saying he could understand how they felt. He was aware that the versions he was hearing were highly coloured, and probably factually incorrect, but he listened anyway in order to improve the relationships and to show both sides that he was treating them with respect. You may have noted that he was careful not to get drawn into taking sides—he retained his neutrality as a newcomer, which was his greatest asset in the conflict.

Michael was also careful not to make any of the resistance worse. He avoided criticizing Philip, and kept his opinions of his predecessor to himself.

He tried to *surface the problem*, for instance by attempting to find out why the design suggestions had not been adopted, but when that was unsuccessful he emphasized the need to look to the future—this gave all sides a *face-saving* excuse for working more co-operatively together. In both the meeting with his team and his meeting with Tony, he prepared carefully and *suggested a way forward* for organizing the handover.

Finally, he arranged for engineers from the two teams to sit together and to work on the most pressing technical problems together. This was a way of anchoring the change to a more constructive way of working together.

Watch out for stereotypes and organizational myths where you work

Negative stereotypes of other groups are a common type of organizational myth. They are particularly prevalent when the interfaces between the groups are fragile and tensions are rife. Each group then blames the other for performance problems, as in Michael's case, and the groups may end up investing more effort in 'covering their backs' than in improving communication.

You can prevent a conflict by stepping in as soon as you spot a myth emerging. Do not let your staff blame the other group—make them realize that they are also responsible for any drop in performance. Talk early to the manager of the other group and discuss the problem with him or with her. You could then schedule a meeting for both groups together, to discuss problems with working procedures and ways of improving them. Stress the organizational goals which are common to both parties. By intervening early you can pre-empt personal attacks and get the situation back on track. You can read more about sorting out interfunctional conflicts in Chapter 10, but the safest way to avoid conflicts altogether is to use mixed teams with members from both groups working together from the start of the project.

Summary of working with resistance

- *Resistance is a response to a perceived threat*. Resistance is a normal part of any change process. It is often an expression of the individual's integrity. You have to respect the emotions of the person expressing resistance in order to solve the underlying problems.
- *Signs of resistance* are verbal and non-verbal, direct and indirect. Be particularly alert for the indirect signs—they are easier to miss. Deal with resistance promptly, using the 3S model:
  1 SUPPORT the person
  2 SURFACE the problem
  3 SUGGEST a way forward
  together with the BUILD behaviours: Back off, Understand, Invite the person to explain, Listen and Demonstrate that you have understood.
- *Avoid unnecessary resistance* by clear communication and adequate consultation during the change process. Make your expectations and objectives explicit to staff. Be constructive when giving feedback, and avoid blame. Use your network.
- *Organizational myths* are defences invented by groups in the face of a common perceived threat. If your credibility is high, you may be able to use a 'push' approach, otherwise use the expanded version of the 3S model.
- *Intergroup conflicts* require application of the BUILD approach, and the 3S priorities, including the principle of face saving. Prevent inter-group conflicts from developing by challenging any myths and stereotypes which emerge. Setting up mixed teams at the start of a project is one way of avoiding inter-group conflicts.

Note

For the most practical guidelines on working with resistance, see Peter Block (1981), and William Bridges' excellent *Managing Transitions—making the most of change*, Addison-Wesley, 1991.

Part III
APPLICATION OF *BUILD* SKILLS: INFLUENCING KEY INDIVIDUALS AND GROUPS

Influencing key stakeholders: building good relationships with the people who matter to you at work

At work you will have a number of people who have a critical impact on your success—your key stakeholders. Your own manager will usually be a key stakeholder, and so will some internal or external clients. If you are in a matrix organization you will have two or more managers, each of whom could be a key stakeholder. You may also have a senior team member whom you regard as a key stakeholder, or a colleague in another unit who has an exceptional influence on your work. When the relationship with a key stakeholder goes well, you can get excellent results and have a lot of satisfaction. When the relationship goes badly, you can feel frustrated and anxious.

In this chapter we will look at how to audit the effectiveness of your relationships with your key stakeholders, how to lay a strong foundation for a successful relationship, how to intervene in the relationship when problems arise, and how to survive if the relationship becomes really difficult. The final section offers suggestions for working effectively with stakeholders from other cultures.

Auditing your relationships

You could start by identifying for yourself one of your key relationships. Which of the following statements would describe the relationship most accurately? Give your relationship a Grade from A (excellent) to G (very bad).

A We have an excellent, open relationship. We achieve good results and enjoy working together.
B We get on well. We achieve good results on the whole, with no serious problems.
C We are having some problems working together. I am wondering

whether I should wait and see if things improve, or whether I should take action.

D The problems are getting worse—I must do something to improve the relationship.

E I have tried improving the relationship, but I have not made much progress.

F I am getting really fed up. I will be very glad when one or other of us moves on.

G The situation is hopeless. I have either got to stick it out, or get out.

David Cormack is an international consultant specializing in multicultural team development for a number of major organizations, and he is also a Director of the Scottish Ambulance Service. He points out that your perceived need to intervene—your willingness to do something about the relationship—changes according to how you evaluate the relationship (see Fig 9.1). At points A and B, where the relationship is basically fine, you do not feel much need to intervene actively. At points C and D you are getting increasingly dissatisfied, but you are hopeful that you can make an improvement, so your motivation to take action in the relationship is high. This can be a very constructive turning point in a relationship, where you can make substantial changes for the better and you can upgrade your relationship to a B or perhaps even an A. If you intervene inappropriately, if the other person is not

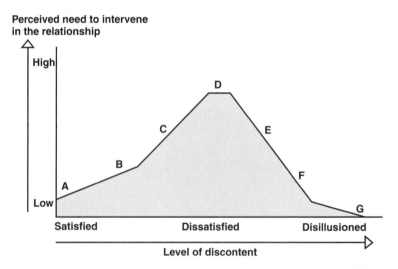

Fig. 9.1 Discontent in a relationship and the perceived need to intervene

open for change, if you do not persevere long enough or if you are simply unlucky, the relationship can deteriorate further. Points E, F and G reveal increasing disillusionment. The worse the situation gets, the less you feel motivated to make an effort with the other person. By point G you have given up, and this can have a negative effect on your performance, your self-esteem and your health. If you are a line manager, it will also inevitably affect the morale and the work of your staff.

We can classify grades A to G as follows (see Fig. 9.2). A and B are both Class 1 relationships, productive and enjoyable. Grade A relationships are exceptional, and depend on a high level of maturity, shared goals and values, and a real affinity between the individuals concerned. Grade B relationships are based on a similar level of mutual trust, but may suffer from occasional, minor friction, and may fail to meet some of the hopes and expectations of one or both parties. A Grade B relationship is nonetheless constructive and effective on the whole. To consolidate Class 1 relationships, you must understand the other person's agenda and preferred way of working, and make minor adjustments when needed in your working relationship to accommodate both people's needs.

Grades C, D and E are Class 2 relationships, where you are experiencing problems. The need in Class 2 relationships is to find some way of intervening to resolve these problems and to improve the

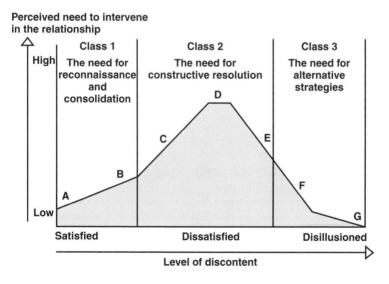

Fig. 9.2   The different needs for each class of relationship

relationship. Grades F and G are Class 3 relationships, where you need to develop some alternative strategies to help you get out of the relationship with minimal damage, or simply to enable you to survive until one or other of you leaves.

Class 1 relationships: the need for reconnaissance and consolidation

If you have graded your relationship an A or a B, it could be that you have 'clicked' from the start and that the chemistry between you was right. Or perhaps you are just embarking on a relationship, and the initial phases have gone smoothly. It is very easy then to get down to work and not to invest any time analysing the relationship itself, on the basis that 'if it ain't broke, don't fix it'.

There are pitfalls with this approach, however. One is that you may be being a little too complacent. The fact that you have had no problems so far does not mean that you will automatically avoid misunderstandings later. Some people have little contact with their manager because they work in different locations, or because the manager is away much of the time. Under sudden pressure, the relationship may prove to be more fragile than they had thought.

Another pitfall in Grade B relationships is collusion. When a consultant and a client are working together, for instance, the consultant may feel reluctant to disagree with the client in case this disturbs the existing harmony. The consultant colludes with the client by supporting his or her view of the world rather than challenging it. The added value offered by the consultant in the longer term is then limited, and the true level of openness in the relationship is much lower than appearances would suggest. One internal consultant working for a major corporation described a difficult moment in his relationship with his client.

CASE STUDY 9.1   TAKING RISKS FOR THE SAKE OF THE RELATIONSHIP

'You must be willing to take risks and gradually surface the more sensitive areas in a relationship. I was working recently with a senior manager and 20 of his top staff. They were going through a major reorganization of the business. It was really difficult to get him to face up to how much this would affect people personally. I asked him how much the change would affect him, and got an evasive answer. So I challenged him—"If it isn't affecting you personally, what's the point of running the workshop?" When he saw that I was ready to walk away from the project if he wasn't prepared to be honest with me, he opened up. That's when our relationship started to become more genuine.'

Grade A and B relationships which have been tested with some conflict, or which started out less auspiciously and where both parties have been obliged to do some thinking, are generally more robust.

You can ensure that your relationship has a solid foundation by doing some sensible fact finding. Reconnaissance and consolidation enable you to maintain the relationship at a Grade B and to prevent it from slipping to a Grade C. If you are lucky enough to have a Grade A relationship with your stakeholder, then by investing some additional effort you can ensure that you really are making the most of your partnership.

Your first step with any relationship is to identify your key stakeholder's agenda and objectives. You can then go on to identify his or her expectations, capabilities, preferred working style, and personal preferences. It is also wise to check any sensitivities and risk areas in the relationship.

Personal liking, or 'rapport' as it is sometimes called, plays a strong part in the relationship. If you feel an affinity with the other person, the ease between you will promote communication, and good communication promotes trust. Often the affinity is based on shared interests—you may both be sporting fanatics, or wrestling with the problems of bringing up teenagers, or you may come from the same part of the world. If a personal affinity does not exist initially, it is worth trying deliberately to find interests which you share outside work. Once you have discovered you have something in common, the chemistry between you will often improve.

In Grade A relationships, your stakeholder will also make an effort to understand your agenda, working style and preferences. In Grade B relationships, realistically you will probably be doing more of the adjusting, on the basis that if you make the effort to adjust you will have a better chance of influencing the person. If you agree with your stakeholder's agenda, and are satisfied with the results you are achieving, then the effort of adjustment will be worth while. We will now consider each type of reconnaissance in more depth.

Class 1 relationships: identifying the stakeholder's agenda

You must know what your stakeholder is striving for, both personally and organizationally. Here are some examples of managers who recognize this requirement.

CASE STUDY 9.2 A CONSULTANT WORKING WITH A SENIOR MANAGER

'I have to know his agenda. When I started in this job I went to his own advisers and asked: "What does he want? What else does he need?" At first they were quite cautious, so I insisted—I repeated the question twice, three times. I said to them that if they didn't tell me what he needed, I couldn't help him. Now we've got a good open relationship between all of us.'

'WHAT HAVE YOU DONE LATELY FOR ME?'

'I've worked for a number of managers in the private and public sectors. In my experience they all have the same question in mind: "What have you done lately for me?" They're interested in your contribution to their careers and their organization. If you have done something concrete, it gives you a halo effect which improves all subsequent interactions. If you haven't, you will be operating from a much weaker position, and you have to bear this in mind when you plan your next meeting.'

A DIRECTOR TALKING ABOUT HIS CHIEF EXECUTIVE

'Pierre wants to grow the company to a thousand people. That's his operating framework. If you cannot explain a proposal to him in terms of that framework, he won't listen to you.'

Aim to build up a detailed picture of your stakeholder's agenda. It is easy to assume that all managers are rampant careerists, and to stop exploring the person's needs any further. Your manager may indeed be planning on a couple more promotions, but what else is he or she working for? Examples of organizational agendas are:

- A more international approach
- Major profit growth
- Cost reductions and increased efficiency
- Moving into 'state-of-the-art' technology
- More autonomy and devolution for business units
- Cross-functional teamworking
- Better customer orientation
- A flatter organization.

Organizational and personal objectives often overlap in practice, but examples of more personal objectives are:

- More recognition for his or her department
- A more 'human' working environment
- Better development of young talent
- A major career step before, say, forty-five
- A last challenge and opportunity to achieve something before the manager retires

- A chance for the manager to prove himself or herself after having suffered a failure
- Job security, by avoiding major risks
- Recognition, by taking major risks.

Check the context in which the person is operating, and the constraints which he or she is under. Where does the person fit into the politics of the organization? How powerful is he or she? How well does your stakeholder get on with his or her manager? How much do their agendas and styles overlap? How much recognition is your stakeholder getting? How much is he or she being developed and supported? You may want to link your analysis of your stakeholder's agenda with some observation of the person's tolerance for stress, capacity to take risks, and general level of motivation. How much does he or she really enjoy the job and take it seriously?

By identifying the agenda and the context you can position all your proposals to highlight the benefits, as the examples earlier in this section have shown. This is assuming that you basically agree with the agenda, and, of course, this may not always be the case. Voicing major disagreements may downgrade your Class 1 relationship to Class 2 or even 3, and requires careful thought and planning. Minor disagreements should be manageable inside a good relationship. Handling disagreements in public is a classic area of risk, so we will address this in a later section. Your first step in any relationship is to find out the person's agenda so that you know where you stand.

Identifying and agreeing expectations

With any stakeholder, there are a number of expectations which you need to clarify and agree, preferably at the start of the relationship. The delegation interface, where your manager or client hands over a task to you or agrees with you a set of objectives, is often the point at which problems arise. Each party in the handover may have different interpretations of what has been agreed. The interpretations can be entirely reasonable, but if they differ widely this will cause problems later, particularly at appraisal time when both parties may have different opinions on the quality of work delivered. Realistically there are bound to be some misunderstandings, because you will both still be making assumptions, but you should aim to minimize these.

The key to negotiating a better match between expectations in a working relationship is to address not only what you are going to deliver but also how you are going to deliver it. It is often the 'how' that causes the problems.

CASE STUDY 9.3   FAILURE TO CHECK OUT
EXPECTATIONS—ESPECIALLY THE 'HOW'

One technical manager got into a heated argument in an appraisal with a
project manager reporting to him. The human resources manager was called in
to help resolve the ensuing conflict. The technical manager said that the project
manager had achieved her targets 'but she's got the wrong attitude. She's gone
about her work in the wrong way.' The HR manager was surprised to hear the
comment, because the woman concerned had seemed competent and sensible to
him.

When he explored the problem further with both parties, he found that the
technical manager had failed to explain to the project manager how he wanted
her to work. The technical manager was very keen that she should take a tough
commercial line with the client, but he had never said this explicitly to her. The
project manager had assumed on her side that she should make some sacrifices
to the client in order to demonstrate goodwill in a potentially long-term
relationship. She had failed to check explicitly with the technical manager
whether this was what he expected. The misunderstanding, low trust and
hostility between them was a result of poor communication on both sides.

With managers who are experienced and mature you could agree
expectations by asking questions such as:

- How will you measure my success?
- What are the priorities—in what I have to achieve and how I
  should achieve it?
- How much freedom can I have? What are the boundaries of my
  authority?
- What feedback can I get from you on my performance?
- If I need help, coaching or advice, where and how can I get it?

Some of your stakeholders may regard this type of conversation as
unnecessary, and get irritated or confused if you try to identify their
expectations directly. You may have to use a more indirect approach,
by asking questions such as 'I plan to tackle the problem like this—
what do you think?' Similarly, you can check out your manager's
assumptions about your level of autonomy and reporting with questions
such as 'How much do you want to know as we go along?' or 'How
close do you want to be to the project?' Space discussions out over a
period of time, so that the manager has time to prepare and to get used
to the process.

Careful observation over the longer term will also enable you build
up an accurate picture of your stakeholder's expectations. One technical
expert said of his manager: 'I have worked with him for some time
now, and there are five ways in which he measures the success of his
staff. You have to know your "dossier", work hard, fit in with the

cultural norms, come to him early if you have problems and keep him thoroughly informed.'

With long-distance stakeholders it is particularly important to identify the person's agenda and agree expectations as early as possible in the relationship.

Recognizing and managing differences in working styles

Once you have gained agreement on the expectations of both parties in the relationship, you can go one step further and start analysing any differences in your working styles which could cause potential problems. Some of these differences may emerge very early in the relationship—you may feel surprised or irritated by an unexpected reaction from the other person, for instance.

Many of our preferences in working style are fixed by the time we are adults. We see our way of working as 'right' or 'normal'. Our preferences help us to generate our personal strengths, but they can also create blind spots. If you can understand some of the major differences in working style between you and your stakeholder, you can make some adjustment in order to meet both parties' needs. The aim is not to change either the other person or yourself, but to find a way of working effectively together.

Some people are uncomfortable about the concept of fitting in with what their manager or client wants. They may fear that they are becoming corporate chameleons with no identity of their own, or they may simply resent having to 'do all the running'. There is a big difference between adjusting to work-style preferences and selling out on your values. Adjustment to preferences is part of organizational life. Your values are your business, and should be defended as part of your integrity. Tony Taylor, a senior manager in a major corporation, explained his approach to a group of young managers on a training course, one of whom was protesting that he did not see why he should alter his way of working just to suit his boss.

CASE STUDY 9.4   LOOK ON YOUR MANAGER AS YOUR INTERNAL CLIENT

'I see my boss as an internal customer. I think of him as a Category A client. In our business, we have Category A, B and C clients, and we offer each category a different level of service. Category A clients get an instant response—as near as we can manage. If my boss says, "Tony, could you do this when you've got time?" I do it now. I don't regard that as "creeping"—I respect my boss and I offer him a high level of service. See your manager as your customer, and usually you will get on fine.'

Occasionally you may find that you are having to adjust too much for comfort, and this is a sign that your relationship has slipped from a Grade B to a Grade C. One manager, for instance, described how her boss only took her suggestions seriously if she presented them very forcefully. 'I had to stand up and thump the table, then he'd listen to me.' She felt that this more aggressive behaviour fitted ill with her own personality, and she had got to the stage of wondering whether to take a risk and say something. In her case, the problem was resolved by the departure of her boss. The working relationship lasted only a year—'I could put up with him for that length of time, and in fairness, I learned a lot from him technically.' Most of the adjustments you have to make won't be so uncomfortable, and are more a question of appreciating different ways of getting the same good results.

One example of a difference in working styles is the priority you attribute to the task or to the people. It is a preference identified by C. J. Jung, Katharine Briggs and Isabel Briggs Myers. People who put the task before the relationship reason that if you set up the task properly, good relationships will follow. People who put the relationship before the task feel that if you get the relationships right, good task performance will follow. Task-oriented managers regard motivating their staff as a means to an end, whereas relationship-oriented managers see motivation largely as an end in itself. You can be very effective (or ineffective) with either preference. However, if you are working with someone whose preference is very different from your own, you will have to adjust your approach in order to work together effectively.

People who put the task before the relationship

Task-oriented staff are interested in results, feedback, objectives, targets and standards, deadlines, milestones and resources. They tend to trust ideas and facts in preference to feelings.

CASE STUDY 9.5 LEARNING TO WORK WITH TASK-ORIENTED COLLEAGUES

Rosemary was divisional head in a products company. Her organization had a culture which was warm and friendly, but it had just merged with a company where the culture were much more task-oriented. 'I soon noticed the difference. There was none of the friendly chat I was used to—the meetings were run with strict agendas, and all the discussions oriented around procedures or objectives rather than people. It seemed very cold and impersonal at first. I had to learn to be much more concrete and businesslike in my approach, and to talk in terms of targets and standards. If I talked too much about the people issues, the others just ignored me. I got used to it though, and I found a role for myself in encouraging my new colleagues to concentrate a little more on team building and on sorting out some of the underlying tensions between individuals. I think we've all gained from the interaction.'

Guidelines for working with task-oriented staff

- **Be brisk and businesslike.** Keep discussions work-focused—people with a strong task focus see social talk as a waste of time. If you are relationship-oriented this may feel very unfriendly, but remember that people's needs for social contact vary widely.
- *Present ideas in terms of targets, results, return on investment, etc.* Collect the relevant data.
- *Be clear about objectives, standards, level of authority.* Remember that any vagueness about objectives and performance measurement can frustrate task-oriented stakeholders, and cause them to lose respect for you.
- *Do not expect task-oriented people to be sensitive towards you—* usually they are not! Find support elsewhere if necessary from your network.

People who put the relationship before the task

Suppose you are task-oriented—how should you handle people whose priorities are the other way around? Relationship-oriented managers regard people as important individuals in their own right, and they will often trust their own feelings more than hard facts and logic. Here is an example of a task-oriented manager who had to adjust to a relationship-oriented environment.

CASE STUDY 9.6 LEARNING TO WORK WITH STAFF WHO VALUE RELATIONSHIPS

Henk was strongly task-oriented, and a great believer in objectives and standards. When he started work as a senior technical consultant managing a team in a government department, he got a shock. 'My client, Michel, worked in quite a different way. He ran his team like an extension of his family. There were cakes when people had birthdays, they went out for meals together, and they seemed to take an enormous interest in each other's families and lives outside work. If anyone got upset about anything, the whole team got involved. I couldn't believe it. When I criticized a team member for a piece of technical work which was of poor quality, in what I thought was quite a diplomatic way, Michel showed me that he disapproved. I had to adapt my style to match his. First, I realized that the staff in Michel's organization were very sensitive. Comments which would have seemed normal to people in my own organization could easily upset them. Second, everything revolved around people and teamwork. Getting on with the others was more important than being a technically brilliant individual. I realized that it was better for me to delegate work really carefully, and offer help and coaching, than to throw people in the deep end and then expect them to correct the mistakes. And I had to show a lot more personal interest in my team. It took a lot of adjustment, but I think I have become a better manager.'

Guidelines for dealing with staff who put relationships first

- *Show personal interest.* These are people who are concerned with building and maintaining friendly relationships—including with you. If you treat them like robots they will feel very demotivated.
- *Express appreciation of the person's contribution.* Relationship-oriented staff value warm, personal praise. Criticism can easily be interpreted as a sign of personal rejection. Henk invested effort in delegating and coaching in order to avoid having to give criticism later.
- *Offer support with problems*, using the 'How can we tackle this?' approach. Support works much better than confrontation with relationship-oriented staff.
- *Invest effort in team building.* Relationship-oriented staff work at their best in an emotionally harmonious climate. If you allow some time for socializing at the start of a meeting, they will settle down better to the task subsequently.

Identify your stakeholder's strengths—not just the weaknesses

By examining contrasts in working styles you can become more open to your own strengths and weaknesses and to those of your key contacts. On a bad day, we are only too aware of the other person's weaknesses. To maintain relationships at a healthy Grade A or B, it is important to take a balanced view of what your stakeholder has to offer, as the following story illustrates.

CASE STUDY 9.7   THE MANAGER WHO TOOK LITTLE INTEREST IN THE RESEARCH

Maria was a research scientist with a passionate interest in her specialist field. Her boss had come from another part of the organization, and although originally he too had been a physicist, Maria reckoned he was not a very good one. 'The first year he took over our team, he didn't seem at all interested in our research,' she said. 'Quite honestly we couldn't see what his added value was to our team. We're quite a close knit group, but he spent most of his time away from the office visiting other parts of the organization and meeting senior staff.'

By the end of the second year, however, Maria had changed her opinion. 'We made an exciting discovery,' she said, 'and it was then that our manager came into his own. All those contacts of his suddenly came in handy—he was able to publicize our success and get hold of some additional budget. He's now due to move, and I must say I'll be sorry to see him go. In retrospect we've been a dream team.'

Maria's manager had a motivational drive based on what David McClelland calls the need for power and influence. Maria was much more task-oriented, so her manager's strengths had been in an area which she initially underestimated. You can check for yourself if you are overlooking a colleague's strengths, and missing an aspect of potential synergy between you, by filling in a simple matrix as shown in Fig. 9.3. You may want to discuss the result with one of your allies, to ensure that you have been fair.

Admittedly, with some individuals it may be genuinely harder to find a list of useful strengths—we will tackle some more difficult cases in subsequent sections. On the whole, however, this approach enables you to take a more balanced view of the other person's contribution.

Once you have understood your stakeholder's agenda, and you have researched any of the differences in work style where you will need to make adjustments in your own way of working, then you can look also at the personal preferences of your stakeholder. These may seem trivial, but they are still important for a smooth working relationship.

Identifying your stakeholder's personal style
Identifying someone's personal style is largely a matter of observation

	Strengths	Weaknesses
Maria	Technically sound Good team player	Not interested in organizational politics (and did not recognize this as important)
Her manager	Large network of powerful contacts Good at selling ideas	Out of touch with recent technical developments Away from the office too much

Fig. 9.3   Look for complementary strengths

and experience. The aim is to make your life and the life of the other person a little easier, by respecting some of the manager's personal habits. Here are some examples:

- *Knowing when it is appropriate or not to raise problems:* 'You have to be careful about approaching him with problems. Don't go to him early in the morning, or after he's just returned from a business trip and is still sorting himself out. He needs some peace and quiet first—then he's fine.'
- *Knowing when to offer support:* 'If he comes back from the monthly operations review he is sometimes fed up—he gets frustrated by the attitude of some of the other division managers. He needs to be able to let off steam, so I listen to him and try to cheer him up.'
- *Knowing how to present decisions:* 'She has a favourite formula. She likes to have material presented to her as follows: we identified these issues, talked to these people, and suggest these ways forward. It's a question of phrasing and positioning. You should know the kinds of arguments that your manager can easily accept, so that she can follow through to the conclusion that you want. Ideally she should get a good feel for what the answer will be before she gets to your recommendations.'

These examples show how you can 'humanize' a relationship by being attentive. With reasonable bosses and clients the service will be mutual—they will cheer you up when you need it too.

Dealing with the sensitivities

Some areas of your relationship with your stakeholder will be particularly sensitive. These are the hidden quicksands where you can easily get into problems without intending to do so. Classic examples are issues of trust and loyalty, dealing with disagreements in public, and issues of face.

Sensitivities are like tripwires—you often become aware of them only after you have made a mistake. If you think back to the concept of resistance described in Chapter 8, you can see that sensitive areas include any actions which could be perceived by your stakeholder as a potential threat.

Trust and loyalty

Trust is a key ingredient in a first-class relationship. If a manager feels that his staff are loyal to him, he will allow them far more scope in their work. Managers who do not perceive their staff as trustworthy will monitor them more closely, restrict their freedom and focus more on their mistakes than on their achievements.

Sometimes, however, a manager may misinterpret the intentions of a person reporting to him, and this can cause the manager to doubt the loyalty of his subordinate. Here is the story of one sales manager's experience.

CASE STUDY 9.8   'HE WORRIED ABOUT MY LOYALTY'
Luis is sales manager for southern Europe for an international company. He is a dynamic, enthusiastic manager who has risen through the ranks of his organization very rapidly. The sales director to whom he reported was initially very friendly to him, but then the relationship started to deteriorate.

'It was after a quarterly review, run by our chief executive. The chief exec was flying to the States after the meeting, and as I had to visit one of our American suppliers in the same city, I flew to the States with him and we sat next to each other. After my return to Europe, my director seemed a lot cooler, and I couldn't understand why. I got on well with the chief exec, but naturally I was careful about what I said during our conversations on the plane. And I respect my director, so I wouldn't have said anything critical anyway. In the end I took the director out for a meal, and over a few glasses of wine I tried to find out what was wrong. Eventually he hinted that he'd felt a bit uncomfortable about my trip with the chief exec. I didn't tackle the issue directly—I didn't want him to feel at all foolish—but I told him in depth what the chief exec had said, and he relaxed a little.

'The next time I flew to the States with the chief exec, I scheduled a meeting with my director before I took the flight. We work in different locations, and that always puts a bit of strain on a relationship. Anyway, I agreed with him which issues I'd raise with the chief exec, and I rang him immediately on my return to tell him what the chief exec had said. It hadn't occurred to me that my director would be so sensitive about my talking to his boss—but I can understand it now, and our relationship has recovered.'

Most managers are sensitive about what their staff say about them to their boss, or about what their boss says about them to their staff. Trust and loyalty are also tested in meetings where other people are present. Few people like it if their manager criticises them in front of their manager's boss, or if their staff suddenly raise a problem of which they were unaware in a meeting with senior colleagues. These are all situations to be taken seriously, and to be avoided wherever possible.

Handling disagreements

Similarly sensitive is the issue of disagreement in public. One senior manager described his approach as follows:

'I don't mind if the managers reporting to me disagree in private meetings with me—that's part of a healthy, open relationship. Disagreement in public is out of the question—outside our one-to-one meetings we must present a united front.'

Another manager learned to handle disagreement with his boss in the following way:

'I warn him in advance if I think we are going to disagree in a meeting where others are present. I tell him I'm going to be arguing in favour of a particular course of action. That way he's forewarned, and he can see it's not personal. He can also prepare how to handle it, and he appears in control in front of his colleagues. I learned to do this after I realized how sensitive he was about disagreements in public, even quite minor ones. When I once asked him in a meeting what his purpose was in setting up a project, he took it quite negatively. We have a very good relationship, but this is an area where I have to be careful.'

Issues of face and visibility

Public status is especially important for people who, like Maria's boss in the earlier story, are driven by the need to exert power and influence. If you deprive a person with this drive of an opportunity for visibility, you will discover another area of sensitivity. This is a mistake sometimes made by people who are more interested in efficiency than in impact, such as the consultant who told the following tale.

CASE STUDY 9.9   'I'D DEPRIVED HER OF AN OPPORTUNITY FOR STATUS'
'For years I had worked for Thérèse, a client in a large government organization. We got along fine, until I made the following mistake. I was due to run a large meeting with staff from a number of departments, as part of a long-running fact-finding exercise. The organization had a very formal culture, so Thérèse always opened these meetings by introducing me to the attendees, and then after a while she'd return to her own office and I'd carry on alone.

   On this particular morning Thérèse was late. We waited and waited—the other people were getting restless. After 40 minutes I started the meeting myself. Five minutes later Thérèse arrived. I gave the attendees a question to consider and slipped out of the room to talk to her. She was white with anger—so furious she could hardly speak. I realized then that I'd deprived her of one of her few opportunities to exert her authority and demonstrate her status in public. I'd aimed at effectiveness—I'm task-oriented—and in doing so had taken away her moment of impact. I realized instantly that it was a bad mistake, and apologized profusely. I felt like a small child—she made me promise never to do it again.'

Thérèse, like Maria's boss in the earlier example, is motivated by the need to exert influence. Stakeholders like these are very sensitive about where they are placed at a formal dinner, how they are addressed in public, where they are standing when a photograph is taken, how much recognition they are given when other important people are present, and whether or not they are invited to attend particular meetings. If you observe this pattern in your stakeholder you should plan carefully how you will meet the person's needs. Avoiding any area of sensitivity—however minor it may appear to you—will give you a much higher chance of building a successful relationship with your stakeholder.

Bridging the gap in Grade B relationships—using your network

The emphasis throughout this section on Class 1 relationships has been on making an effort to understand and accommodate your stakeholder. This is equally important for Class 2 relationships which you want to improve. Ideally it should be a mutual process, and in Grade A relationships this will be the case. In Grade A relationships, your needs for personal support and professional development, for instance, will also be met. Grade B relationships will be based on an overlap of agendas and working styles, but will fall short of some of your personal needs. A common example of a shortfall is when a manager or client fails to give you all the credit you feel you deserve.

One way of bridging the gaps is to use your network. Voluntary projects inside or outside work could provide you with some of the recognition, stimulus or support that you could be missing, for instance. By being creative with your time and energy you can achieve a satisfactory balance. Another solution is to develop your sense of realism—many people still operate the 'no news is good news' feedback system, and it is often only the really good Grade A managers who are generous with praise.

Before we move on to the problems of Class 2 relationships, you may like to reflect on the subject of stakeholder relationships from a different angle. Who among your work contacts would select you as a key stakeholder? Would they evaluate their relationship with you as a Grade A or a Grade B? If not, why not?

Class 2 relationships: the need for constructive resolution

Class 2 relationships are hampered by problems. In Grade C relationships, you have noted the need for change but are not yet sure whether you should take any action. Grade D relationships are so unsatisfactory that you feel you should intervene in some way to improve the situation. Grade E relationships have deteriorated further. You have tried but failed so far to get an improvement, and you may be wondering whether to give up.

Class 2 relationships are nonetheless characterized by a basic commitment on your part to get the relationship right. The boundary between Class 2 and Class 3 relationships is critical—once you cross over the boundary, you basically abandon hope of improving the situation. That step is under your control. David Cormack says that 'the relationship never goes beyond the rescue point unless *you* decide to give up. Class 2 relationships require you to pay a cost in terms of effort, and in terms of making yourself vulnerable. Until your stakeholder is also prepared to put his or her payment on the table, you have to pay the cost for both of you. And there's no guarantee that the relationship will come out right. If the relationship is still important to you, however, you will carry on making the effort and paying the cost.'

In Class 3 relationships, the final payments are made, and the ultimate cost to the individual may be greater. Organizations are generally unwilling to take the side of an employee against that of the manager, or to support the case of a consultant against a client. On the whole we are expected to sort out difficult relationships, and when we give up, it is often we who are punished.

Class 2 relationships can provide valuable experience if we can live with and learn from some of the more painful bruises to our egos. One senior consultant who was himself a supportive manager said that 'it's important for people to encounter at least one bad manager early in their career. They learn about organizational realities, and acquire a sense of self-reliance'. In this section we will address some of the ways in which you can rescue relationships, and enjoy the satisfaction of getting your stakeholder back on track. First, however, here is a warning about Grade C relationships.

The perils of the 'wait and see' approach

In Grade C relationships there is always the temptation to wait and see if the relationship improves by itself. The 'wait and see' approach enables you to avoid the direct risks of confrontation, but it also has inherent risks. If you wait too long, the problem can erupt into a crisis—and that can be a very unpleasant experience, as Philippe, a technical specialist, discovered.

CASE STUDY 9.10   THE RELATIONSHIP WHICH WENT WRONG

Philippe had been working for several years in a large corporation. His first manager had been fine, but the second, a section head, was much more difficult

'He interfered in the details of our work, but at the same time was very indecisive. He worked long hours behind his computer, and often looked very tired, but he didn't work at all effectively. It was immensely frustrating, and after a time it began to affect the work of the team because we were suffering from delays. We evolved a way of getting round him in order to get things done, by building good relations with colleagues in other teams. It wasn't a very satisfactory situation, but I thought we were managing.

Then came appraisal time, and it was my turn to go into his office. To my astonishment he accused me of not meeting my deadlines. I was furious—I told him that the delays were also due to his indecisiveness. His response was to throw me out of the office.

From then on he completely ignored me. I went to his manager to explain what had happened during my appraisal, and he was quite understanding. Shortly afterwards the section head and I were both transferred to different locations. Just recently I saw him again in our head office. I was quite prepared to put the past behind us and to be civil, but he walked straight past me.'

Philippe was particularly unlucky. This was the first really difficult manager he had worked for, so he was understandably reluctant to confront the person directly and preferred to work round him. The section head's criticism of Philippe's performance was entirely unexpected, and when Philippe then confronted him with his mistakes he reacted very aggressively. Since the section head was tired and probably worried about his own performance, it was logical for him to interpret Philippe's indignant response as a personal attack. In retrospect, perhaps one of the older colleagues on the team should have talked the team problems over with the section head at an earlier and less sensitive stage on the project, when there was still time to resolve the situation. Typically, the section head's manager was prepared to be sympathetic to Philippe, but did not intervene with his subordinate directly. Philippe took the full brunt of the section head's anger.

Timely action, while the problems are still manageable, is often preferable to the 'wait and see' approach. If you do decide to wait, keep monitoring the situation carefully to ensure that the relationship is stable. In Philippe's case, the situation was deteriorating faster than he realized.

Sorting out the problems with your stakeholder
Any kind of confrontation with your manager or client is always risky, particularly if it entails criticism of the person's behaviour. Some people tell of cases where a frank and open exchange of views, unplanned and spontaneous, has cleared the air and improved the relationship. However, for every case where this has worked there are probably another four or five which turn out very rapidly to be career-limiting moves.

Class 2 relationships suffer frequently from poor communication, particularly if for some reason you have not done the consolidation and reconnaissance recommended in the previous section. You may not have a clear idea of how your stakeholder feels about you and your performance. Such relationships can easily slide into vicious circles— neither party quite trusts the other, so neither party is open with the other, so trust decreases and so on. You have to be prepared to break the vicious circle by making the first move and expressing your own worries, even if this may leave you feeling exposed.

Three basic options exist for sorting out problems. You can:

- Address the problem with the stakeholder directly
- Change your own behaviour to elicit changes in the other person's behaviour
- Ask others in your network to intervene diplomatically on your behalf.

Combinations of these options also work very successfully.

CASE STUDY 9.11   BOB AND THE MANAGER WHO BY-PASSED HIM

Bob had been getting increasingly fed up. He was a marketing manager responsible for a new product launch. This was his first big project, and initially he had been very excited about it. However, his relationship with Lawrence, his manager, had not worked out as he had hoped. Twice now Lawrence had talked direct to Bob's staff about the progress they were making, rather than asking Bob. Bob felt humiliated—'I'm being by-passed,' he told his wife over dinner.

Bob knew he was not too good at conflict handling, so he went to an older and experienced colleague. She listened sympathetically, and with her help he planned his approach. He asked Lawrence for a meeting the next day.

Bob explained in the meeting that he wanted to discuss how they were working together. He said that Lawrence had set very clear objectives for him, and that he had found that helpful. However, when Lawrence had contacted his staff directly to check progress on the launch, rather than talking to him, Bob had felt by-passed. Lawrence frowned. Bob went on, 'I really don't understand why you couldn't ask me about the project. Am I doing something wrong? If so, what should I be doing differently?'

Lawrence admitted that he did not feel entirely confident that Bob was in control of the project. Bob's first reaction was to feel angry, but he quelled his indignation. 'What would you need from me in order to feel that I am in control?' he asked. The two men discussed the style of Bob's reporting. Bob suggested they could try a different approach—he would follow up after his report to check if Lawrence needed any more information. They finished the meeting by confirming the action points.

Leaving the meeting, Bob thought Lawrence had been a bit unfair—if he had explained initially what he had needed in the reports, Bob could have given him the information. However, once Bob had explained how he was monitoring the progress of the team, Lawrence did seem more convinced, and the action plan they'd agreed looked promising. The next few weeks saw an improvement in their relationship.

Guidelines for constructive confrontation

- *Avoid personal attacks and blame.* It is very tempting to attack your manager, saying something like 'You didn't tell me what information you wanted—how can you expect me to provide it?' Personal attacks provoke a response in kind. Blaming others is often used as an excuse to make no effort in a relationship which is going wrong. If you can convince yourself that the problems are all the other person's fault, why should you change any of your own behaviour? Blame can feel good at the time, because it offers a temporary stress release. In the long term it prevents you from developing a constructive approach to solving conflicts.
- *If in doubt, get advice from your allies.* Conflicts by their nature can leave you confused and upset. Talking the problem through with a trusted friend or ally enables you to take a more objective view. Moral support from your network is essential to help you persevere in difficult situations.
- *Say what is going well.* Your stakeholders will be sensitive about feedback—it is a risk area in the relationship. Giving praise before you give the criticism encourages you to keep a sense of proportion. Bob says that Lawrence had set clear objectives, and that he had found that helpful.
- *Focus on behaviour.* Bob described the problem in terms which were as neutral as possible. He also explained how he felt about Lawrence's behaviour. 'When you contacted my staff direct, I felt by-passed.'
- *He intervened early as soon as he noticed the problem recurring.* This sort of problem is like a leaky roof—if you leave it, it gets worse not better.
- *Explore what you may be doing wrong.* Bob asks Lawrence what he could do differently. Being open to criticism is particularly difficult when you feel angry with the other person, but it is a key step in making progress. The fault is very rarely only with one party and by being open to feedback you can avoid the blame trap. Change your own behaviour in order to elicit changes from others. Here is a story from a manager who learned the value of this approach early in her career.

'I FAILED TO ASK FOR FEEDBACK—AND LOST THE BATTLE'

'Years ago I got into a conflict with another colleague in my team, and this escalated into a conflict with Nathalie, our manager. It happened very suddenly—previously I had got on with her very well. She was someone who wanted to have warm relationships with everyone, and when she was confronted with the argument she just dithered. In the end she chose the path of least resistance, and the decision she took failed to meet anybody's needs satisfactorily—including mine. Our relationship quickly deteriorated.

In retrospect I can see where I went wrong. At the time I was very angry with the other team member, and disappointed with the lack of support and decisiveness from Nathalie. I saw the problem as everybody else's fault. I still feel I was let down, but that happens at work—I now take it much more philosophically. I could have unblocked the stalemate if I'd asked Nathalie what I was doing wrong. It would have choked me to do it, but I would have uncovered those elements of my own performance which—I now realize—caused her to have doubts about me. If I'd been more prepared to make changes myself, she might have been more prepared to support my proposed solution.

I learned from the mistake. If I get into problems now, I ask for honest criticism. If you can take it constructively, you can sort out problems very fast. And oddly enough, people respect you more, not less.'

You run a risk that your stakeholder may exploit your goodwill and dump all the blame on you—but failing to take any action is risky also. Be prepared to pay the cost for both of you, at least for the time being.

After a meeting like this you may experience some awkwardness in the relationship, and you may even regret having taken action. The situation usually recovers once you both see some results. After that point some relationships improve dramatically, because you have increased the degree of openness between you. You take one step back in order to make two steps forward.

The next case comes from an experienced internal consultant, who decided to take direct action with Hal, a senior manager and an important client. Hal was charming, but he was also accustomed to getting his way. In meetings he tended to overrule those who disagreed with him. The consultant was determined to make some changes.

DEALING DIRECTLY WITH A DOMINATING CLIENT

'We were in the middle of some very important meetings about organizational changes. Hal had strong views about the reorganization, and he was used to pushing his ideas very forcefully. I knew that in the meetings we were planning, his usual steamrollering tactics wouldn't work—his colleagues were too canny and too experienced to put up with them.

A lot of my job consisted of helping Hal to become more aware of his own weaknesses. He needed to become more open to other people's ideas and more prepared to have a genuine debate. I had to confront Hal for his own sake and for mine—if I was seen during the meeting as his lackey, both he and I would have lost credibility with our colleagues in the section. I wasn't sure how Hal would react to criticism, and he came from a culture where managers could blow you out of the water if you confronted them.

I enlisted the help of my colleagues who were also internal consultants, and we produced a list of procedures to help Hal run the meetings more effectively. We tried to persuade him that the more he pushed, the more opposition he'd get. We also tried to get other people whom he respected to give him the same feedback, so he'd hear the same message from different sources.

The first meeting we were planning was intended to agree a course of action. There were two strategies being discussed—Hal supported one, and Fred, one of his more powerful colleagues, supported the other. At the start of the meeting, we got everybody present, including Hal, to agree a set of ground rules, as follows. First we would look at the pros and cons of both options, and everybody would have the opportunity to present their views without interruptions. All information would be logged on flipcharts, and from the information we would draw out the next steps. A small working party would then be set up to cycle once more through the information, before moving on— with everyone's approval—to the next step.

I had agreed with Hal in advance that if he tried to twist or break the rules, I would confront him in the meeting. Sure enough, several times I had to say "Let them talk, Hal" or "Don't attack." Inevitably he tried to influence the drafting of the information, and I stopped him and pointed his behaviour out. To his credit, he then backed off.

I had also discussed with Hal in advance how he would deal with Fred, who supported the other plan of attack. I told him that he must let Fred have his say in the meeting—and be seen to be letting Fred have his say. I told Hal that Fred would accept Hal's views as long as Fred felt there had been a fair debate.

At the start of the meeting the staff were quite negative—they'd been exposed to Hal's tricks before, and were sceptical of any real discussion. We followed up personally with all of them to find out what they thought. They were all more positive after the meeting—and Hal admitted that the changes had been worth the effort.'

Learning points

- *The consultant focused on behaviours* with his client—both in the preparation phase and during the meeting itself. He was very specific about which of the client's behaviours were helpful and which were unhelpful. Hal had a clear idea of what he needed to change.
- *He was consistent in confronting Hal* when needed during the meeting. This confrontation in public was potentially very risky, but because Hal trusted the consultant and agreed to this approach

beforehand, it served as a powerful reinforcement. It also demonstrated to the other colleagues present that Hal was genuinely prepared to listen to their views—and that the consultant was not 'Hal's lackey'.

■ *The consultant used his colleagues in his network* to help draw up the ground rules and to work with him in the meeting. He also enlisted the support of other senior staff to get the message across to Hal that he had to work differently. Teamwork is often more effective than individual intervention with managers who have deeply embedded habits which you want to change.

Taking direct action of any kind requires courage and a commitment to your own values, as well as a genuine concern for the values of others. If both parties in the relationship have a basic respect for the other person, as was the case between Hal and the internal consultant, then you can often make real progress.

Asking others to intervene for you

Occasionally you may respect your stakeholder, but the respect is not reciprocated. This is a humiliating experience, and one where you will have to pay the cost for both parties if the situation is to be improved. Your initial interventions may be rejected out of hand, or the other person may simply make it very clear to you that he is not interested in your views. Failure to act also costs a price, in terms of your own self-respect and your ability to be true to your own values. One way of handling this difficult situation is to ask another contact inside your organization for help.

Working through a third party is a useful way forward if your stakeholder is very sensitive to criticism and loss of face. Be careful not to complain overtly about the person causing you problems, however, because you may put other senior managers in a position where they feel obliged to defend their colleague. Find a tactful way of expressing the problem, and ask for advice.

CASE STUDY 9.14   JEAN-LOUIS ASKS FOR HELP

Jean-Louis was a department head in a large corporation. He was getting increasingly depressed working for his director. The only reason he could keep going, he said, was that he liked and respected the staff reporting to him. He had also invested long years of loyal service in the organization, and was unsure whether he could get a similar post elsewhere.

The director had moved to this post two years ago. He changed the division from a friendly, relatively informal organization to a stiff and formal hierarchy. He had introduced new layers and rivalries, and used a 'divide and rule' policy to break down the co-operation which had been such a strength of the division. Everybody was demoralized.

Confronting the director, no matter how constructively, was out of the question. His formal style ruled out any form of feedback. But Jean-Louis was not prepared to give up on the relationship yet—he thought if he did so he would be abandoning his staff. Also, the division was due to be reorganized over the next few months, so the timing was favourable.

Jean-Louis went to Charles, another director of a different division for whom he had worked previously. Charles was an older man with a lot of influence. Jean-Louis raised the issue very diplomatically, saying that his division was under heavy work pressure and that he was concerned about the level of service he could provide. He had to restrict himself to some hints about the problems with the additional levels and the rivalries. He also offered some constructive suggestions and asked Charles if he could put in a word with his director if a suitable occasion arose.

The outcome of the reorganization wasn't quite what Jean-Louis had hoped for—but it was better than some of the scenarios that he had feared. The director removed part of the hierarchy following, Jean-Louis suspected, some quiet advice from Charles. This enabled a little of the previous collaboration gradually to return. Jean-Louis knew that in another couple of years the director would retire, and the small improvement was enough to enable him to settle down and wait for the director's departure. Good enough, he thought.

This was a Grade E relationship, where Jean-Louis was not yet prepared to abandon hope. Tactful consultation of the other director eased the tension and provided some progress.

Class 3 relationships: the need for alternative strategies

Class 3 relationships are characterized by an increasing feeling of frustration and powerlessness. These are the relationships where you have given up any hope of recovering the situation, and you are left with the choice of putting up with it or of looking for an alternative job inside or outside your organization. 'It's the uncertainty that makes it all so difficult,' said one manager with a particularly unpleasant boss. 'In our organization the situation can suddenly change—he may disappear from one day to the next. Or they might decide to leave him here until he retires.'

In Class 3 relationships, the biggest danger is the feeling of despair. Many people describe a feeling of being trapped—'I felt a prisoner to my mortgage,' as one manager put it. Over the long term people can feel tired and depressed, and this creates stress also for their staff and family. One internal consultant described his experience with a team of seven senior managers, who were directly affected by a major reorganization of the large plant where they were working. They were in the midst of a bitter conflict with the director to whom they reported. 'When I arrived on the scene, I discovered that three of the seven were off work with "nervous exhaustion". Two managers were in the middle of marital breakdowns. In the end six of the seven left through early retirement. It was a very damaging process for all concerned.'

The more tired people feel, the harder it is for them to find the energy to take any positive action. Performance also drops, so the managers suffering inside a Class 3 relationship become more vulnerable inside their organization.

The key priority is to identify some alternative strategies for yourself as soon as you cross over the threshold between Class 2 and Class 3. It is often much easier to tolerate a difficult relationship if you are working in parallel on some escape routes. If you start planning early, you are less likely to make impulsive decisions which you may later regret.

Identifying alternatives also enables you to preserve your self-respect. Many of the tensions in Class 3 relationships result from a feeling of being bullied or manipulated by a person with more power. The manager in the following case thought carefully in advance about what he was—and was not—prepared to tolerate. Careful use of sanctions can enable you to maintain your sense of worth.

CASE STUDY 9.15   CAREFUL USE OF SANCTIONS WITH A DIFFICULT MANAGER

The situation

'I had decided to leave the department of the large corporation where I was currently working, and to transfer to a new subsidiary starting up in Eastern Europe. There was no hurry with the transfer, so I'd been asked to stay in my current post for one more year. My manager, Greg, was a very able man but not well liked. He had a tendency when he knew people were leaving his team, for whatever reason, to take it very personally. I'd watched several cases where he'd been really unpleasant to staff during the last months they were working in his department. I had always got on well enough with him, so I hoped he'd behave himself with me.

As soon as he knew I was leaving, his behaviour towards me started to deteriorate. I had decided in advance that I would say something. We still got on well at the task level, so I was quite friendly when I talked to him. "Look, Greg," I said, "I will not have my last year made a misery. I'm telling you now that if you try anything, I'll go straight to Ted (Greg's manager)." "You wouldn't dare!" said Greg. "Just you try me," I said.

The conflict emerges

We seemed OK for a while, but then an incident occurred where Greg had a perfect opportunity to pick on me. I had a consultant, Walter, working for me at the time. Walter was highly talented, but unbelievably disorganized. Getting his expenses sorted out was always a nightmare. That month he was really unlucky (or maybe he was lucky!) because his bag was stolen from his car with all his expense forms and receipts in it. I had to work out what to do next.

I proposed to pay Walter on the basis of the average of the last seven quarters—that seemed reasonable. But I needed Greg's approval. He exploded—"I can't accept that! How do I know I can trust you?" It all got very personal and very official. I pointed out that if I was going to embezzle the organization I'd try something more ambitious than Walter's expenses. The argument escalated—this was a typical example of Greg's aggression.

Applying the sanctions

So I went to Ted, and pointed out that Greg was accusing me of trying to defraud the company. Ted knew me well. He went straight to Greg and told him to behave himself. Two minutes later, Greg summoned me. "I never want to see you again in my office until you leave," he said. That was fine with me—and that was how it was.'

This manager had worked out that there was a limit to the real influence that Greg could exert over him. He had a good relationship with Greg's manager, and has continued to work successfully for the corporation for some years. Of course, Class 3 relationships are by their nature very risky, so the situation could have turned out quite differently. Suppose you have no positional power—what then? There are a number of 'holding actions' which you can consider while you are weighing up your choices.

Use your network

Now is the time to get moral support from your allies, practical help from your other stakeholders so your performance does not drop, and advice from your personal contacts. If you have invested in others in the past, they will help you.

Update your curriculum vitae

Find out the possibilities for alternative jobs either inside or outside your organization. If you are feeling more adventurous, you may like to consult some of the literature on making more dramatic career changes (see the chapter notes).

Avoid 'badmouthing' the opposition

Resist the temptation to mount a mutiny. You may feel like putting a one-page advertisement in a national paper to attack your enemy and protest your innocence, but the truth is that in organizations senior people are rarely prepared to take sides. Feel free to let off steam with trusted allies, but criticizing your boss in public, for instance, is unlikely to promote your case and your own credibility could suffer. A stoically constructive approach will probably win you more sympathy and respect.

Set a fixed time frame

Job moves always entail risks of their own. You lose your existing network, and may need to learn from scratch about a new technical area. Sometimes the change provides welcome stimulation, but you may prefer not to rush into the unknown. Agree with yourself how long you are prepared to tolerate the existing situation, in the hope that one of you might be moved. In the meantime, continue to explore your other options.

Look after yourself

You will be going through a period of strain, and should look after yourself. Diet, exercise, good holidays, contact with people whom you really like, developing outside interests—these may sound irrelevant, but they help you to keep the problem in perspective. Careful self-management makes the difference between surviving a difficult time with dignity and falling prey to sickness and stress.

Maintain your standards

Stress can cascade down a department, making work miserable for everyone. If the relationship with the difficult stakeholder is your prime responsibility, you must try to act as a buffer to restrict any negative effect on other people to a minimum. Your staff and colleagues will know there is a problem, of course, but the standard of support you offer to your staff should not drop. Similarly, the standard of service you offer to your internal and external clients must be maintained.

Plan some sensible damage limitation. Your responsibilities can weigh heavy when you are tired and depressed, but if you neglect them then the pressure you experience will increase. The solution is to monitor your management systems as soon as you anticipate that your relationship is seriously deteriorating. Check the way in which you have organized your team. Are you delegating clearly and adequately? Are objectives and priorities clear to staff, so they can manage their own time and resources effectively? Are you still giving feedback, organizing training and coaching, running performance appraisals, so that staff do not feel neglected? Monitor these organizational aspects carefully so that the performance of your unit is not affected and morale is maintained as far as is realistic.

Difficult times with difficult stakeholders often offer opportunities in retrospect which you might never have anticipated. You may discover you have more friends and allies than you had thought. You may make a job transfer that initially looks like a step backwards but which turns out to be a very positive move. Even the nightmare scenario where you are fired may turn out not to be as bad as you had feared. One manager who was made redundant said that 'the experience has opened new doors for me. I hated that job—the last year was the worst I'd ever known. I have got some part-time projects now which I'm enjoying, and a number of other contacts which look promising. I'm genuinely relieved that I left.'

Summary of Class 1, Class 2 and Class 3 relationships with your stakeholder

Class 1 relationships need reconnaissance and consolidation if they are to fulfil their potential. Identify your stakeholder's agenda, expectations and preferred working style. Look for areas of common interest and synergy. Watch out for sensitive areas like trust, loyalty and handling disagreements.

Class 2 relationships require some sort of intervention on your part in order to resolve the problems you are experiencing. Be prepared to pay the cost—you stand to gain, or lose, a great deal. Use one or more of the following approaches:

- Raise the issue directly with the person concerned.
- Change your own behaviour in order to elicit changes in the other person.
- Ask for help from others in your organization.

Avoid blame, focus on behaviour, be open to feedback yourself.

Class 3 relationships can be damaging to your self-esteem. Look for alternative strategies before you get too tired. Use your network, look for other jobs, set a time frame for yourself. Manage your stress level carefully, and ensure that stress does not cascade down to your staff. When you are over the worst, try to leave feelings of bitterness behind and to draw the learning from the experience. The cost to you of Class 3 relationships will always be high, so if you are hesitating whether or not to give up on a Class 2 relationship, you may want to make one more attempt to salvage it.

Working with stakeholders from other cultures

As organizations become increasingly multinational, managers are increasingly expected to form constructive working relationships with colleagues and staff from other cultures. Many people enjoy this aspect of their work. It offers opportunities for travel, increased job variety, and a chance to gain insights into the very different ways in which people across the world approach work and life outside work.

Other cultures offer their own challenges, however. Sometimes the hidden assumptions and beliefs create a different set of tripwires. You find yourself facing misunderstandings and a whole range of responses which appear very puzzling. Cross-cultural communication is a huge and complex area, and you can find references for specialized literature in the chapter notes. Here is a brief description of what we mean by culture, together with examples of the problems you may encounter and suggestions for working successfully with stakeholders whose background may be very different from yours.

What we mean by culture

You can think of culture as a shared set of values and beliefs. There are national cultures, regional cultures, corporate cultures and so on. Each culture represents what Geert Hofstede called 'the collective programming of the mind'. When you visit other countries, some of the cultural variations are immediately obvious. You may note differences in the buildings around you, in the clothes that people wear in the office, and in the way in which your colleagues run meetings. Other differences are more subtle and become apparent only after you have worked in the country for some time.

Generalizations about other cultures offer useful starting points, but they can be misleading. No two people from any one culture are entirely alike. There are aspects of each of us which make us unique. At the same time, we each have values and beliefs which we share with most people from our own culture. And further, we share certain core values which are common to almost everyone in the world.

You can think of culture as a series of levels, built up over the lifetime of an individual (Fig. 9.4). Level 1 represents assumptions and beliefs which are partly or wholly unconscious. At Level 1 we find it difficult to imagine the existence of assumptions other than ours, and we may confuse our assumptions with the truth. Level 2 represents the values we have internalized as a result of our family upbringing and our experiences at school, at college and generally in the community in which we grew up.

Level 3 represents our views and values as an individual. These make

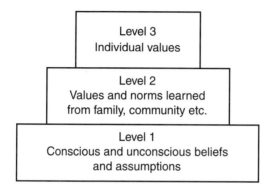

Fig. 9.4 Individual culture as a number of levels built up over time

you unique. You might choose to adopt certain individual values which differ quite dramatically from those of your culture of origin. One manager who had been born in Indonesia, for instance, said that 'In my home culture the expression of feelings is unheard of. After I moved as a small child to Holland, I was exposed to a culture where people are quite prepared to say what they think. I like this in the Dutch—I admire the way in which they can have a fierce argument in a meeting, then go off and have lunch together and laugh and relax. I have adopted the same kind of openness myself.' For this manager, many of the cultural differences which he noticed at Levels 1 and 2 were more than mitigated for him in Holland by the 'meeting of minds' at Level 3.

When you work with colleagues from other cultures you embark on a voyage of discovery. You may have anticipated certain significant differences, but find when you get to know your colleagues better that the major contrasts are actually in areas quite other than those you had expected, as the following story shows.

CASE STUDY 9.16   'YOU DON'T KNOW WHAT YOU DON'T KNOW'

'I was working at the time in West Africa, and my boss was on leave. We'd had a tip-off that one of our senior staff was involved in a fraud. After the investigation and his departure, we had to decide on his replacement and the chain of moves which followed. I sat at my desk and tackled the problem with the best of my European logic, coupled with my limited understanding of local culture.

I was in the office on a Sunday morning, admiring my new departmental organization, when fortunately a trusted Gabonese colleague came in and started talking. I realized slowly from what he was saying that I had been about to make a serious mistake. The staff I had been putting in my plan were from different local tribes—a factor which I'd failed to take sufficiently into account. My solution looked good to an expatriate. However, I had a whole cluster of staff from one tribal grouping in one area, and another cluster working in another, related, area. The department relied on co-operation between the two sections, and my plan was unworkable—so it was back to the drawing board with my new piece of knowledge. When you're working in other cultures, you always have blind spots—you don't know what you don't know.'

The manager in this story had a good relationship with the Gabonese colleague who opened his eyes to the possible consequences of his action. It is extremely important to find for yourself a 'cultural guide', ideally someone who understands your native culture and the one in which you are working, and who supports your personal and organizational agenda. Attending courses on cross-cultural working, reading the literature, talking to colleagues who have worked abroad are all ways of preparing yourself—but inevitably you will only become aware of some of your blind spots when you are actually living and working in the culture itself.

Most managers will expect to suffer some 'cultural shock' as they move far from home. Hidden pitfalls can also be just as deep and dangerous nearer home, however. Ruth Ann Lake, an American consultant who has been living and working in Italy for many years, tells this story.

CASE STUDY 9.17   'SENIOR STATUS' IN ITALY:
MISUNDERSTANDING CULTURAL DIFFERENCES
'An international company with its European headquarters in northern Europe had established an office in Milan. The office had operated successfully for some years under the leadership of an Italian general manager. Problems started when a new general manager was appointed. Because the Italian operation was now growing fast, head office decided to appoint one of their top managers, a Dutchman, who had an excellent track record in business development. The Dutchman had children already settled at school, so he left his family behind and worked very long hours from Monday to Thursday, leaving on Thursday evening with a bulging briefcase of documents.

The staff in the organization fell into two groups. There was a number of younger consultants who were under 40 and spoke very reasonable English. There was also a number of older consultants ranging from 45 to 60, who were very experienced but whose English was poor—as is often the case in Italy. The Dutchman was so busy analysing the business prospects that although he started with Italian lessons, he soon abandoned any attempt to speak Italian at work and ran all his meetings in English. This gave the younger consultants an enormous advantage, and increased their influence considerably. As time went by, they found themselves placed on all the major projects. Their older colleagues felt more and more excluded. A rift emerged in the organization.'

The mistake

For a time the company's performance continued to be positive, but suddenly the bubble burst. Many of the older established organizations, which had been supplying this organization with its major contracts over many years, were traditional, hierarchical family businesses. The owners of these businesses were used to a certain amount of formal ritual. One of the most important of these rituals was the contract-signing meeting, often followed by a business lunch in an excellent restaurant. The Dutch general manager, who was extremely busy, was impatient with all this formality. "Why should I waste my time?" he said. "Send Gianni, one of our best young managers—he can take my place."

This was a bad mistake. When news reached the client that the general manager had "refused" to come in person, and had nominated a much younger man to replace him, the "padre padrone" of the family business felt deeply insulted. Word spread fast among the community—the general manager's action was perceived as a major affront.

When he was told this, the general manager grudgingly agreed to come to the signing meeting in person, but it was a tense affair. Taking Gianni with him didn't help. The client did not want the younger man to hear his halting English (the Italians refer to this as "bruta figura"—looking a fool), nor was he keen to have Gianni serving as interpreter. In any case, the Dutchman left the lunch early. Two months later, he heard that the client had refused to award the major follow-on contract which the Dutchman had assumed would go to his organization.

The consequences

The loss of the contract was a clear lesson, but the organization had also lost ground in the community in other subtler ways. The older staff had large established networks of contacts, which previously had supplied invaluable information about clients and their needs. As the older consultants had lost face, much of this information had not been used, and the organization was in danger of losing touch with its client base. Turnover, which had risen at the start of the Dutchman's posting, began inevitably to fall. Some of the older consultants left the organization, setting up competitive businesses and taking some of the clients with them.

By now, however, the Dutchman had come to the end of his allotted time in Italy, and he moved on to a posting in the Far East. He was replaced by a more experienced and more flexible Belgian, who came over with his wife, already spoke fluent Italian and was a great admirer of Italian culture. Coming himself from a country where age and status are recognized as important, he quickly settled down and was accepted by the community. Clients and staff alike breathed a sigh of relief.'

Guidelines for working with colleagues from other cultures

- *Expect the unexpected.* Remember that your values at Level 1 are largely unconscious. You will become aware of them only when you are confronted with some unexpected consequence of your actions.

- *Try to stay open-minded.* When you are faced with an unwanted reaction, it is easy to jump to negative conclusions about the other culture. Such conclusions are often based on misunderstandings and on false assumptions. Your first step should be to try to understand the positive intentions and some of the positive consequences of a particular cultural value.

- *Explore the thinking behind the different cultural values.* If you are willing to step back and compare different norms and values, some interesting insights emerge. The Italian story, for instance, shows how different cultures attribute status. Most managers in the UK and in the USA will expect status to be accorded on the basis of a person's performance—this is what researchers Charles Hampden-Turner and Fons Trompenaars call 'achieved status'. The Italian clients accorded status on the basis of experience and age, and this is 'attributed status.'

CASE STUDY 9.18   AN EXAMPLE OF EXPLORING DIFFERENT VALUES: ACHIEVED VERSUS ATTRIBUTED STATUS

People who come from cultures where achieved status is the norm will often dismiss the concept of attributed status as encouraging nepotism, complacency, 'dead wood' and discrimination against younger, more competent colleagues. Hampden-Turner and Trompenaars point out that it also has a number of advantages, however. First, everyone ages, so attributing status according to age is not necessarily unfair. Second, the system tends to work as a self-fulfilling prophecy. Because older people are automatically treated with respect, they often perform better. Third, because these older managers feel secure they make better coaches and mentors. They have much to gain and little to lose by helping the 'juniors'.

Their colleagues of the same age in achievement cultures will often feel threatened by younger staff and see them as dangerous rivals. The motivation to pass on knowledge, network contacts and expertise is much smaller.

Achieved status can promote high standards and encourage everyone in a corporation to achieve his or her maximum potential. However, ascribing status by achievement is fraught with its own problems. If you have to conduct performance appraisals for your staff you will know how difficult it is to assess individual performance fairly and accurately. How can you tell if the results— good or bad—from one unit are primarily due to the efforts of the manager? She may have an excellent team who have contributed much more than she has. If the link between performance and reward is weak, many of the advantages of the achieved status system are lost. The two ways of according status— ascription and achievement—each have their own strengths and weaknesses.

- *Respect others' values, even if you do not agree with them.* Before we judge other cultures too harshly we should look at our own values objectively and critically. Taking the trouble to explore the pros and cons of both sets of values helps us to understand why the other culture has adopted its own system. We may still feel that our system is right, but at least we can respect what the other culture has to offer—and that means that we will treat our colleagues from the other culture with more respect also.

■ *Be prepared (within reason) to adjust.* Fons Trompenaars points out that respect must lead to some kind of reconciliation. The manager in Gabon changed his system once he realized it was unworkable. The Dutch manager in Italy failed because of his inflexibility. Once you understand the intentions behind the 'alien' set of cultural values, you should work out a solution which can meet the different cultural needs.

■ *Be honest with yourself about your prejudices.* Recognizing your own cultural stereotypes and prejudices is essential if you are to work successfully with colleagues from other cultures. One manager who had worked in a number of different countries across the world offered the following advice.

CASE STUDY 9.19 DEALING WITH YOUR OWN PREJUDICES

'You find race prejudice in all directions and from people from all sorts of cultures—you can't pretend it doesn't exist. You have to do your best to consciously correct your own negative stereotypes. A trick I found useful when I was working outside Europe was to try to imagine what my approach would be if I were sitting opposite a negotiator from a nation that I instinctively hold in high esteem, and where I have a positive stereotype (for me that could be a German or a Scandinavian). This would set the basic orientation for my approach to the person coming from a different country. I would vary my tactics, to meet cultural expectations, but the basic ingredient of a good working relationship—the respect—would be in place.'

Pitfalls with the language—and what to do about them

Language is a major problem area for managers working outside their home culture. Managers from countries such as Holland and Switzerland have been brought up to be competent linguists. British managers are notorious for their reluctance to speak other languages, though some younger managers working abroad are proving to be the exceptions to the rule. The following suggestions are intended to make you aware of some of the major pitfalls associated with the use of language. You may not have the time to master a foreign language, but you can at least make life a little easier for colleagues of other nationalities who are having to meet your communication needs.

Learning the local language is important—even if you can only speak it a little. One manager working in Prague has made considerable efforts to master the complexities of the local language. With the help of his secretary and a lot of practice, he recently gave a 20-minute talk to his staff in Czech. They really appreciated the effort he made. Knowing even a few of the most used expressions can give you an insight into some of the core values that underpin the local culture. If you make no attempt even to acquire a minimum, passive understanding of the local language, you will be isolated from your staff and your community.

Do not consult only the staff who speak your language. Robin Pedler of the European Centre for Public Affairs points out that 'British managers, for instance, have a strong tendency to consult only the English speakers in their organization, and to think that's enough. However, the staff who speak English, and who are happy to talk to you, may have a positive bias towards a British manager. Their enthusiasm may not be shared by the non-English-speaking staff. If you cannot speak the local language, you cannot work on their worries. You may think you have built support for an idea, only to find that your coalition was nowhere near as solid as you had hoped.' If you cannot speak the local language, ask trusted local colleagues to sound out the views of a broader cross-section of staff.

A closely related mistake is to underestimate and ignore colleagues who do not speak English. The Dutch manager in the Italian story expected the consultants to speak English, and when he discovered this was not the case he excluded them in effect from all important decisions. Ignoring their experience on this basis was shortsighted.

Native speakers of other major languages may make similar mistakes. One French manager was posted to Madrid to set up a start-up operation. He failed to learn Spanish because he assumed that his staff and clients would speak French. This was not the case, and the start-up operation duly collapsed.

If you must speak English, use the offshore version. Offshore English is adjusted to make it easier for non-native speakers to understand. Native English speakers should strip out colloquial phrases, simplify the sentence structure and emphasize the key points. There's an excellent section on offshore English at the back of Vincent Guy and John Mattock's book *The New International Manager* (see chapter notes).

Listen, summarize and clarify. Phrases such as 'Do I understand correctly that..?' and 'Could I just summarize what we've covered so far?' are extremely useful. You should use them judiciously, however— they can be interpreted as a patronizing response to the other party's command of your language. Beware of any potential loss of face.

Two general reminders

- *Be realistic about just how much influence you have if you are working abroad.* Andy Johns, a manager who has worked extensively abroad, points out that 'As a Westerner working in Asian countries, for instance, you have less influence than you might think you should have. You need to define and agree a realistic target for your influence level—this is vital for sorting out daily, tactical problems.'
- *Lobby individuals from different cultures before they attend larger meetings.* Behaviour which may impress a stakeholder from one culture could irritate a colleague from a different country. Andy Johns suggests that if you have to deal with stakeholders with different cultural expectations, you may need to do the groundwork with the individuals in one-to-one meetings first, so you can adjust your behaviour accordingly. Call the plenary meeting only when you think that the positions of all the important parties are reasonably close. During the plenary meeting you will have to use 'middle of the road' behaviours, and this will preclude any real influencing. If you have done the real work beforehand, your role during the meeting will be mainly to clarify and summarize progress.

Keep an open mind to similarities, as well as differences

The guidelines so far have been intended to help you cope with cultural differences. To close the chapter, here is an example of the opposite perspective—when cultural differences are not so great nor as complex as you had been led to believe.

CASE STUDY 9.20 WORKING WITH MANAGERS FROM EASTERN EUROPE—WHAT ARE THE DIFFERENCES?

Gill Cottray regularly trains managers from Eastern Europe. 'When I started, I was given lots of advice about the different nationalities and their potential incompatibilities. I listened attentively and planned how I could avoid any unnecessary conflicts. It sounded very complicated.

When I gave my first course for Eastern Europeans, I found the reality was quite different. In practice there seemed to be far more of a difference between the generations than between the nationalities. The younger managers were enthusiastic about the recent changes in the economic climate, whereas their older colleagues tended to stick to the authoritarianism of their traditions. It made my job a lot easier than I had anticipated—as long as I was aware of the generation gap, I could allocate syndicate groups successfully. I have worked with a number of groups since and found the pattern to be quite consistent.'

Gill's experience has been partly confirmed by recent research findings comparing younger managers in the private sector with their older counterparts in state-owned companies. A group of younger managers from Latvia, Poland, Russia and the Czech Republic agreed that the affinities between them (their Level 3 individual values) far outweighed the differences.

CASE STUDY 9.21   'WE HAVE A GREAT DEAL IN COMMON'

'We are the new generation of Eastern European managers. Many chief execs in our countries are now under 35. It's the young managers who are now in leading positions, particularly in international companies like ours.

We work hard, and—within reason—we earn good money as a result of our efforts. Of course, the link between performance and pay is a very new concept in the East. And it's our support for this system that we have in common, although we come from quite different countries. It really affects the way you work. The old system has always operated on a pay per grade basis, not according to pay for performance. Our parents—liberal though they may be—find the new system hard to understand. Whether you're a Latvian or a Russian, this is something all the younger managers experience.

The result is that we have far more in common with other young people, regardless of which part of Eastern Europe they come from, than with the older generation of our country of origin.'

It pays to keep an open mind when you work with different cultures, particularly when you work with people from countries which are in the midst of dramatic changes.

Summary of working with stakeholders from different cultures

- *Culture is a shared set of beliefs*. Think of it as a series of levels, built up over time.
- *Watch out for hidden pitfalls*—'You don't know what you don't know.' Find a 'cultural guide' to help.
- *Stay open-minded*, and explore the thinking behind the 'alien' set of values. Be prepared to adjust—respect should lead to some sort of reconciliation.
- *Be honest with yourself about your own prejudices*. Correct your mindset so that you treat all your stakeholders with the necessary respect.
- *Watch for pitfalls with language*. Try to learn at least a few phrases of the local language as a minimum. Do not consult only

the staff who speak your language. If you must speak English, use
the offshore version.

- *Look for similarities as well as differences.* Sometimes potential
cultural conflicts will be outweighed by affinities at Level 3—
individual values.

Notes

Figure 9.1 is based with permission on work from Dr David Cormack's *Change
Directions—new ways forward for your life, church and business*, Monarch,
1995. David's comments on paying the cost for repairing relationships are
based on his book on conflict-handling, *Peacing Together—from conflict to
reconciliation*, Marc, 1989.

Some of the material on reconnaissance and consolidation has been based on
the famous article by J. Gabarro and J. Kotter, 'Managing your boss' reprinted
in 'People: Managing your most important asset,' *Harvard Business Review*,
1992.

The material on different preferences is based on the work of Isabel Briggs
Myers and Carl Jung (see Myers, 1990) or call Oxford Psychologists Press (Tel
44 1865 510203) for details of training courses and further literature. You
could read more about the difference between the power, achievement and
affiliation drives in David McClelland's academic work, *Human Motivation*,
Cambridge University Press, 1987.

If you are interested in becoming a top-class manager/leader, you might like
to read the inspiring *On becoming a Leader* by Warren Bennis, Addison-
Wesley, 1989.

For more on conflict handling with stakeholders read *Coping with Difficult
Bosses* by Robert Bramson, Nicholas Brealey, 1992. A good general book on
conflict handling is John Crawley's *Constructive Conflict Management—
managing to make a difference*, Nicholas Brealey, 1992. See also Ken and Kate
Back (1982), Paddy O'Brien (1992), and *People and Project management for IT*
by Sue Craig and Hadi Jassim, McGraw-Hill, 1995.

Managers who work under consistent pressure may be interested in *Life and
Death in the Executive Fast Lane—essays on irrational organizations and their
leaders* by Manfred F. R. Kets de Vries, Jossey-Bass, 1995. For more on stress
management, see *Thriving on Stress* by Jane Cranwell-Ward, Routledge, 1990.
There are a number of good books an career changes, including *Changing
Course—a positive approach to a new job or lifestyle* by Maggie Smith,
Mercury, 1992.

Internal and external consultants might enjoy reading the unusual *Rules for
Rulers—the politics of advice* by Arnold J. Metsner, Temple University, 1990.

For literature on culture, see Trompenaars (1993), Guy and Mattock (1993)
and *Culture's Consequences* by Geert Hofstede, Sage 1994. The comments on
ascriptive versus achievement status are drawn from *The Seven Cultures of
Capitalism* by Charles Hampden-Turner and Alfons Trompenaars, Currency
Doubleday, 1993.

Moving groups forward and managing change

Many organizations are currently in the midst of major change initiatives, and these pose particular challenges for the managers expected to implement the changes. Organizations are also expecting staff to adjust to continuous change, often in the name of continuous quality improvement. Any change triggers anxiety and resistance in varying degrees, as people are understandably reluctant to let go of the past—at least until they have had a chance to assess what the future holds for them.

This chapter addresses the dilemmas and pitfalls of managing any dramatic change, such as improving major business processes, or moving to a new corporate culture. We will also address changes which are smaller in scale but nonetheless necessary, such as smoothing out interfunctional conflicts and encouraging staff to take responsibility for improved co-operation with their colleagues. You can read about a range of techniques and approaches which have been used effectively by senior managers with very different personal styles. Managing any change successfully depends not only on your understanding of the change process but also on the ongoing application of the principles of good management which underlie all effective team work. The chapter closes with a description of how one leader/manager has ensured continuously high levels of performance and a constant quest for new ideas in her organization.

Involve key stakeholders throughout the change process

The key principle of the BUILD approach to change is to involve your key members of staff at every stage in a change project, in order to increase commitment. This sounds fine on paper, but it is not an easy principle to follow if the change you are proposing has major repercussions for the people whom you are consulting, and if the success of the change project is entirely dependent on those individuals' full support. The potential for resistance is then huge, and many such initiatives fail.

Here is the story of a senior human resources manager who facilitated just such a change, and who enabled a group of senior managers to make some tough decisions about the way in which they were running their business. You will notice that he involves his senior colleagues at every step—from the initial problem definition, right the way through to action planning. His organization manufactures and distributes a range of highly specialized products worldwide. The recommendations described at the end of this case have now been fully implemented, and the HR manager is working on a new series of change initiatives.

CASE STUDY 10.1   HELPING SENIOR MANAGERS TO MAKE SOME TOUGH DECISIONS

Identifying a potential area for improvement

'I've always recommended making major changes during times of organizational growth, when people won't be so worried about heads rolling. Our organization had a strong market leadership position for our products, so this was an ideal time to improve our services. We had started to review the way in which we treated our customers, and we wanted to audit the effectiveness of our support systems, particularly our European customer-related processes. I had the feeling that parts of our structure were out of date.

I'm a great believer in the use of benchmarking procedures to challenge the status quo, and when we ran the tests we could see that indeed our delivery process was too slow. When I showed the results to our senior managers, there was a range of reactions. A senior logistics manager said that we had too much inventory around. The head of manufacturing of the European centre said that we could speed up the delivery process by closing down some of our warehouses and using his warehouse to service the rest of Europe. Other factors emerged that were contributing to our slower responses—our technical support staff needed to be reorganized, for instance, and the deployment of the sales force was empirical and lacked focus.

The birth of the change project

When I talked this through with the new chief executive, my manager, he set up a project to review all our customer-related processes. We were to address production scheduling, sales administration and technical support. The project team included the regional sales manager, the marketing manager, and the logistics manager. They were all brilliant, young and aggressive—fiercely and understandably protective of their part of the business. They were not going to make concessions easily.

The project leader was a young technical manager. He was apprehensive but enthusiastic about his role, because this challenging project would give him the opportunity to show his leadership skills, and he hoped eventually to move out of his technical position into a broader managerial role.

Using project management principles

My job was to act as facilitator for this clever but volatile team, and to support the project leader. We worked full-time on the project and the other team members were asked to spend between 20 and 30 per cent of their time on the project. I wanted to ensure that the team followed sound project management techniques, to enable us to work steadily together towards our goal. I had a lot of experience in project management and in using business process re-engineering. I knew all the team from my work on senior management courses, and we had a lot of respect for each other.

I suggested to the project leader that we should start by checking that our project was properly planned and conducted. We started by specifying our objectives and the business justification for our project. We defined the scope, and made a project plan and a work-breakdown structure. We then scheduled all our team meetings nine months in advance.

Our choice and use of methodology was going to be key to the success of the project. I wanted us to be able to set our direction, agree how we were going to get there, and measure our progress at each step. The project leader and I had to fight a constant battle to get the team to stop jumping to solutions, without analysing the problem first. This frustrated some of the more impatient members of the team, but I knew that we needed a stepwise approach, with agreement after every step, if we were to reach full consensus on the final conclusions and recommendations emerging from the project. We used a combination of sound project management and a business process redesign approach to discuss together the impact of the different organizational processes, and their value for the business.

Dealing with the tensions

Some of the discussions got highly emotive. Much of my work as a facilitator was to calm down the nervous guys, and make space for the quieter, more creative team members to speak. At the end of the afternoon people might be feeling tense and frustrated, but I'd always suggest that the team meet again at eight in the evening for an apéritif. Over drinks the hostility would dissipate. It was important to normalize any tension—to explain that we were only fighting because we were tired.

Other classic facilitation techniques which I used were to:

- Intervene directly if anyone was shouting
- Get each person to respect his colleagues' positions
- Extract from their statements their real, legitimate concerns
- Emphasize continually that we were all working towards a reconciliation of view points—that was the logical way forward.

Making progress—and confronting some difficult decisions

We realized that a major part of the solution to the slow delivery lay in closing down some of our warehouses in different parts of the organization. This was going to affect potentially the territories of the managers present in the room.

We needed a sound basis of agreement on how to decide whether or not to keep a current warehouse.

I pushed for a logical process for reviewing the current situation, getting the group to work on questions such as "What's the logic for keeping a particular warehouse? What are the conditions for keeping it?"

During this debate, I emphasized that by agreeing criteria, the managers were not excluding the possibility that they could later disagree with any particular decision. This didn't commit them—yet—to a particular course of action.

The breakthrough

Our definition of criteria led us to ask some key questions: "Where are our main customers based? Who are they? What are their service expectations?" Once we made a map of our customers we discovered that some of our warehouses were actually very well placed. And it became obvious, logically, which of our warehouses had to go. The really intensive work was behind us.

The final recommendations made by the team were supported by all members. The warehouse staff would be redeployed or relocated. We made some other additional changes—I would have liked us to have been more radical in some areas, but realized that my senior colleagues didn't want to go further, and when that's the case you have to let go of some of your proposals. The project leader was promoted, as were some of the other team members. The project was pronounced overall a success.'

Learning points

- *Get full support from the team at every stage.* The HR manager ensured that he had full agreement from the team at every step in the change process. He also had the full support of his chief executive. The final recommendations then emerged (after a lot of hard work!) as a logical conclusion supported by everyone.
- *Use appropriate procedures.* The careful use of procedures drawn from project management and business process redesign provided the team with the reassurance that they were following a path with proven value. The HR manager's known expertise in these two areas gave him the credibility he needed to support and direct the team.
- *Be realistic.* The HR manager was realistic about what he could and could not achieve. When he saw that some of his suggestions would not get full backing from his colleagues, he dropped them.
- *Deal with the emotions.* He anticipated and accepted that there would be fights, but he made it quite clear that these were normal reactions to the stress of devising a major change. By introducing the custom of evening drinks together, he got the team used to the idea that harmony would be restored.

Dealing with changes that have been directed by senior management

What if you are leading a team that has to implement changes dictated by senior management, where you have had no direct say in the changes yourself? This is inevitably the case in large corporations, where it is impossible practically to involve everyone in the early stages of determining the change. In this situation you would notice a range of reactions from your team. Some staff would disagree with the need for change. Others might resent the fact that they had not been consulted, or fear the consequences of a leap into the unknown. In this section we will consider the process of adjusting to change in more detail, in order to outline some of the priorities for you as a manager if you have to lead your group when they are feeling uncertain and resistant.

Change versus transition—the crucial difference

The American author William Bridges has highlighted the difference between change and transition. Change is a rational, logical process. When senior management decide that change is necessary, they put forward a change plan with a time schedule. The change has a beginning, a middle and an end, and the end date is the deadline by which the change is to be completed. If we take a simple example, suppose that your organization is moving office from a major city to a rural area. Senior management will assume that the change has been completed by the time that staff and equipment are installed and functioning. The deadline could be the end of the calendar year.

Transition is very different from change. Transition is the process by which an individual gradually adjusts to the change. In order to manage change effectively, you must first manage the individual transitions of your staff. Transition does not start with a Beginning—it starts with an Ending. When your staff hear that they have to move office, they will think of all that they are going to lose. If they move into the country, they will miss their house, their neighbours, their family, their children's schools and all the elements of daily routine that people value. Their partners and children will probably be upset. Office moves are usually coupled with some sort of reorganization, and this means that your staff may also have to adjust to a loss of colleagues, status, familiar routine and so on. It is a lot to give up—and it takes each individual a different period of time to come to terms with the upheaval. Senior management may stress the joys of country living, but most of your staff, and probably you yourself, will notice and experience the losses first.

The next phase, as staff slowly come to accept the losses, is what

Bridges calls the Neutral Zone. It is not, as managers hope, the time when staff will fully embrace the change. Instead it is a period of confusion and fatigue, where people feel suspended between the old system and the new. They will appear to get on with their work as usual, but they will be spending a lot of time talking to colleagues, or staring into space at their desk, trying to make sense of the change and their own reaction to it. The Neutral Zone can last for months or even years if managers fail to help their staff cope with the uncertainties of change. The managers responsible for implementing the change may themselves be in the Neutral Zone, so in periods of transition you can sometimes see a number of tired, confused managers struggling to lead their tired, confused teams. Motivation and performance suffer as a result.

If, however, the first two phases of the transition are managed effectively and sympathetically, and if people genuinely believe that the new system offers advantages for themselves and for the business, they will finally come to full acceptance of the change. This is what Bridges calls the Beginning, where people plan their new roles and really get to grips with the new challenges.

People do not move smoothly out of one phase in their transition and into the next—the phases overlap. Suppose we think of four months in the transition of one person adjusting to a change. In the first month she is feeling primarily sad and fed up about what she is losing. In the second month she is beginning to come to terms with the losses, but now she is also showing the fatigue and confusion typical of the Neutral Zone. In month 3 she still experiences some pangs of regret for what she has left behind, and she is still tired and confused, but she is also starting to appreciate some of the advantages the new system can offer her. By month 4 the regrets are fading, and although she still spends time in the Neutral Zone her feelings of optimism about the change are increasing.

To complicate matters further, your staff will each progress through these different phases at different rates. Suppose your senior management have announced that a number of levels will be removed from your part of the organization, and that everyone will be working in a new, flatter structure. You have been placed in charge of a team of thirty people. Three months after the announcement, five members of your team are still sceptical and depressed—they are taking longer to work through the Endings phase. Seven other members are getting impatient—they are in the Beginnings phase, and want to get going with the changes. The rest of your team are doing their best to carry on with their daily tasks, but they are not yet enthusiastic about the new structure. They are in the Neutral Zone.

This situation demands considerable flexibility and skill on your part

You cannot rush your staff who are in the Endings or the Neutral Zone, because if you do so they may get stuck in these initial phases. At the same time you must find some challenges for those who have already adjusted to the change. The solution is to:

- Anticipate problems realistically
- Keep communicating—give as much information as you can
- Be prepared to spend time with individuals who need more attention—especially if they are important members of your team
- Put in place a number of measures which will help individuals to adjust to the change as smoothly as possible.

Anticipate problems realistically

Ignoring the feelings of loss associated with the Endings phase is a mistake that many managers make. When senior managers initially present an organizational change to staff, they often overemphasize the benefits. In the case of the office move, a senior manager may talk about the lack of pollution, the better housing and so on. This is understandable from his perspective, but as a message it is grossly inappropriate if the majority of his audience are listening with sinking hearts as they realize what they will have to give up. The senior manager will be criticized after the presentation for being 'out of touch with the staff' and his credibility will suffer. The change initiative will get off to a shaky start.

A better solution is to explain very clearly the reasons for the change, and then give an overview of how the organization plans to support people during the transition period. What practical measures will be introduced to help people plan their move? What information will be available? What visits have been organized to the new site? Whom can people contact if they want to talk through their worries? Once these issues have been addressed, the senior manager can touch briefly on the benefits of the move, so that those who are already in favour of the change can hear more about what they and the organization stand to gain. The people in the audience who are worrying about losses will probably not be listening at this point, but at least they can reflect on the practical measures which the manager has outlined.

Managers often spend a lot of time searching for some magic formula by which they can make difficult messages more palatable. If you are realistic, you can see that staff will not be positive initially about the move—they must have time to adjust. The best way forward is to structure the presentation to meet the needs of your staff as accurately as possible at this initial stage in the transition process.

Once you have presented the initial information realistically, how can you help your staff to move through the Endings phase? In his book on transitions Bridges makes a number of useful suggestions, but two points are particularly important. You should communicate your message clearly, several times over. You must also expect staff to be unsettled and upset, so you should make time available for them to talk to you.

Communicate the message in different ways—share what you know

People will not fully understand the message about a major change the first time that they hear it. In a presentation, for instance, they switch off at intervals to process the information they have received, and they then miss the next part of the story. They need to hear about the change several times, and through different media, if the message is to sink in. Point out also any elements of the work context which will not change— any procedures, structures or people which will remain in place. The presentation could be backed up by a letter or memo and by an article in the company magazine, so that people have time to read and reflect, and by smaller meetings where staff have a chance to discuss the changes.

The principle behind good communication is to share as much as you can as soon as you can. Managers are often reluctant to talk to staff at an early stage in the change process, because of the inevitable gaps and uncertainties in the information available. The danger is that rumours will soon fill the information vacuum. If staff hear of a change via the newspaper and not via you they will lose confidence in management. Instead, tell staff what you do know and explain that some aspects of the change have not yet been decided. Some certainty is better than none, and most people are sensible enough to realize that you will not be able to give them all the answers. Give an indication of when you think the remaining information should be available.

Make time to talk to staff individually

'How will this affect ME?' is the question uppermost in everyone's mind in times of change. People always worry about the impact on themselves. While your staff are fretting about their future, they will not be able to concentrate fully on their work.

Organize individual interviews as soon as possible after the change has been announced. Again, your staff will understand that you will not be able to answer all their questions, but answers are not the point of the exercise at this stage. What your staff want is your undivided attention, at least for a short time, together with your confirmation that you have understood and noted their main concerns and that you will get back to them as soon as you know more.

Failure to listen to your staff will inevitably delay their adjustment to the change. Managers who place priority on the task before the relationship often find this difficult to believe. Their tendency is to wait until they have all the relevant information at hand, but in reality they will never have all the answers available in a tidy package. Another frequently made mistake is to confuse these short personal interviews with counselling, and to jump to the conclusion that these talks should therefore be delegated to colleagues in human resources, or to outside consultants. If the change is likely to distress some people, then it is sensible to offer counselling to those who would appreciate additional help. If you do not feel confident about your counselling skills than it is also reasonable to get assistance from people with relevant expertise. The talks described here, however, are more a form of orientation—an opportunity for people to ask the questions and raise the points that are most important to them. For many people, it is enough to know that their manager has taken them seriously, and they will then get on with their job. Listening to them, and sharing the information that you have available, is the least you can do for them.

A common protest from managers is that they have no time to talk to their staff individually. You will, of course, be particularly busy during times of change, but helping your staff to make a smooth transition and to remain as motivated as possible must be one of your priorities.

CASE STUDY 10.2   FINDING THE TIME TO SUPPORT YOUR STAFF

One senior manager described how he had helped his department of nearly ninety staff adjust to a major change. In the first three weeks after the announcement of the change, he scheduled talks with every member of his department. He decided against delegating the interviews to his team leaders because he knew staff would prefer to talk to him personally. During those weeks he had a heavy workload of his own, so he was staying long hours at the office. He backed up the talks with a small information office operated full-time by an administrative assistant, and by a help-line for partners and families. In retrospect, he said, the talks were well worth the effort, because his staff adjusted to the change noticeably faster than their colleagues in other departments, where the managers had not made time for them. 'Your staff need some personal attention at this stage,' he said. 'It's as simple as that.'

Helping staff through the Neutral Zone—the value of temporary systems

Once people move into the Neutral Zone, their needs begin to change. Sensitive relation-oriented managers often continue offering emotional support, but in reality the most useful help you can provide is to set up some clear, well-organized management structures. Bridges recommends the use of temporary systems, specially designed to help people cope with the uncertainties around them. Delegate tasks with shorter time frames and well-defined goals, so that people can move forwards one step at a time. Put in as much clarity as you can manage, so that even if staff are worrying about major areas of ambiguity which you can do nothing about—an impending merger, for instance—then at least inside the unit, in the short term, there is a degree of order and predictability. Celebrate even small successes. Think of your role as helping people to settle back successfully into work after a period of illness which has left them tired—they will need clearer goal setting, careful monitoring, sensitive coaching and feedback. If you are tired yourself during this period, make sure you get at least the minimum number of breaks and the necessary support from your friends and network to keep yourself going. Consult Bridges' book on transitions (see chapter notes) if you would like more suggestions for dealing with any of the three phases.

Into the Beginnings

The Beginnings phase is primarily a planning period, where you and your team agree who will do what. If you are managing a large group and you know you have staff who are already in the Beginnings phase while other colleagues are struggling in the Neutral Zone, ask those who are ready for the change to head up the transition teams which will plan the change process. Delegate to them some of the management tasks which are needed to help the rest of the team to keep performing at an adequate level. In this way you can make the most of their energy and enthusiasm while the rest of the group is catching up, and you will have some of your planning already in place when the whole group is up to speed.

The following case shows how one manager coped successfully with his team when some of the group were in the Beginnings phase, and some were still in the Neutral Zone. A major reorganization had been announced three months earlier in the multinational organization where Chris was working. The reorganization had important implications for Chris's team both in the short and medium terms, with the prospect of further major changes to come.

CASE STUDY 10.3   LEADING A GROUP THROUGH A TRANSITION

The organizational change

Chris had recently been appointed manager of a team of nineteen following a major reorganization. The new post was a challenge—two departments had been merged, so that staff from the process research department were now working alongside people with a manufacturing background like himself. A number of levels had been removed, so that, in principle, laboratory assistants, for instance, could take on the same responsibilities as their graduate colleagues. These and other changes were intended to make the organization more flexible, more competitive and more responsive to customer needs.

The problem for Chris was that, almost simultaneously with the announcement of the change, he had been given a high-priority project to manage at a different location. This meant that Chris had had little opportunity to set up the friendly and effective relationships he wanted with all his staff. Some of them hardly knew him. And he was also working with new colleagues at his own level, and with a new boss.

Consulting members of the team

The team had continued to work conscientiously in his absence, but Chris knew that there were some complaints and that the announcement had left many of them feeling uncertain. When he finally had a couple of days in his own office, he consulted two of his staff—a bright, young graduate, and an older, experienced lab assistant. He heard how people were indeed responding differently to the change. Some were getting impatient—they had heard about the new way of working, but as far as they could tell, nothing in the department had really changed. Others were worried—the lab assistants, for instance, were feeling very overworked, with no prospect of relief on the horizon.

Chris decided to take the team out for a day to review the state of affairs and to plan the way forward. He enlisted the help of a consultant to facilitate the day, so that he could participate fully in the discussions with his staff. In order to promote co-operation and openness right from the start, he invited his new boss to attend the meeting. He also invited his colleagues from two other departments which were his customers. He asked the graduate and the lab assistant to draft the objectives and the agenda for the programme, and to brief the consultant, and he also consulted a senior member of his team to check that the programme made sense.

The workshop day

The day began with an overview of the objectives, followed by a very brief reminder from Chris's boss of the reasons behind the reorganization. Then the group got down to the more difficult issues. The first group exercise was an invitation to look at what had changed, and what had not, and how people felt about the situation. As frustrations were surfaced, the groups were also asked to put forward a number of priority issues for discussion—these were to form the more detailed agenda for the day. Chris was working in a small group with the other senior managers at the time, so that staff in the other group would feel no inhibitions in raising problems. He noted that the list of priorities from his group was very similar to the lists from the other groups—a good sign that he was in touch at least with the main areas of concern. 'Now we've got to do something about them,' he said with a wry smile.

Progress was steady from this point, as the group, including the managers, was very keen to get some decisions agreed. A number of sub-groups were asked to address the different issues and to come up with action plans. Some issues proved easier to address than others. The lab assistants had flagged problems of communication between the different sites, and proposed a number of site visits and exchanges. They were visibly pleased when Chris agreed on the spot and told them to go ahead and organize the trips. Sorting out roles and responsibilities, and addressing the uneven workloads, were much harder problems to tackle, because of all the interdependencies involved. Nonetheless, the sub-groups made a good start, and their suggestions provoked some lively and fruitful discussions in the group.

By three in the afternoon, the atmosphere in the room was noticeably different, compared with the rather hesitant, watchful expressions of the group at the start of the day. There was a growing sense of confidence that they were getting somewhere. One request to Chris from the group was for personal interviews, so each person could discuss his or her future. Chris had embarked on a programme of interviews, but they had been interrupted by his project work. He agreed to pick up the process again. For the complex organizational issues, a number of task forces were set up, each with a sponsor. In line with the flatter organization, the sponsors consisted of one senior member of the team, two graduates and one lab assistant—a good cross-section.

The group concluded the day with a careful review of the action plans, together with the names of those responsible for the actions and the deadlines for completion. The team were careful to take Chris's outside commitments into account, so they restricted his action points to those they considered essential, and they agreed that the work of drafting proposals and recommendations would take place largely without him. It was a realistic plan, and they felt confident they could meet it. As the group set off for a meal together, Chris stayed in the room for a few minutes, clearing up and collecting his thoughts. His colleagues and his manager had worked as hard as he had, supporting and facilitating the groups. It had been a good day. The next step was to follow up on the action plans and keep momentum going.

Learning points

- *Consult staff early.* Chris talked to a representative cross-section of his team and asked for their help in organizing the workshop.
- *Repeat key messages.* Chris's manager reminded the team briefly of the reasons for the change at the start of the day. Even at this stage in the transition process, repetition of the new vision for the organization is important.
- *Use staff who have made the transition to guide others.* A good example is the use of sponsors to run the task forces and drive the change processes. The sponsors volunteered to take on this responsibility.
- *Invite staff to take responsibility for implementing the changes.* The task forces showed maturity in restricting Chris's involvement to a realistic minimum.

- *Tackle complex issues one step at a time, to demonstrate progress.* This is particularly reassuring for people in the Neutral Zone—they can see where they are going. Staff who have more or less completed the transition will be pleased to achieve results.
- *Set up temporary systems,* in this case in the form of the task forces. Task forces exist for as long as they are needed, and offer a flexible means of solving problems.
- *Organize personal interviews.* The need for interviews was raised during the day.
- *Small successes are important.* The lab assistants, for instance, were pleased with the approval for the site visits.

Culture changes—vision, creativity and modelling of new behaviours

Major change can be initiated in a number of ways. In the previous case, it came via restructuring. In the next case, a high-priority project was used as a vehicle for change. Hadi Jassim was one of two senior managers responsible for running the Decibel project, which introduced the ten-digit telephone number plan in Holland. The project was a huge technical and communication operation involving the whole of the Dutch PTT organization and its clients and over 500 dedicated staff. It was highly successful—all milestones and quality tests were achieved according to plan.

The success was all the more remarkable because the senior managers had to make major changes in the culture of what was a very traditional organization. Here are some examples of the way in which Hadi and his colleagues managed to alter the mindsets of their staff in order to meet the technical and organizational challenges of the project. The senior management team created a clear vision, used creativity techniques to break down barriers, and modelled new behaviours themselves in order to promote change.

CASE STUDY 10.4   A VERY CLEAR VISION TO BOND OUR TEAM—THE POWER OF 10

'From the first day of the project we "locked in" to some of the powerful associations with the number 10. In Holland where we work, a 10 is the highest mark you can get on your school report, and so for many adults it is associated with success. To mobilize the huge numbers of people working on our project (almost 1000 full-time and part-time staff at its peak) we needed a powerful linking vision that would bond them together, and set them firmly on the path to achieving our goals. We played with the number 10 in a variety of ways to keep the vision fresh in their minds:

- We used the name of the project: DeciBel
- Our key deadline was 10–10–1995
- Our first major milestone came on 4 June (4 + 6)
- We had 73 people in the project team
- We held stocktaking sessions each month on the 10th
- We started the project on 10 January.

After a while the staff started playing with the number 10 as well, spreading the 10–10 message internally through our huge project:

- They competed in the car park to take parking slot number 10
- They booked rooms in hotels which included the number 10
- They'd fill up their cars with petrol at pump number 10
- They'd send in holiday postcards with pictures including a 10.

To keep momentum going, we engaged a rap singer who made up a rap song with the "10,10, DeciBel" message as the refrain. He went round the different districts rapping away, and soon we'd bump into colleagues in bars and shopping centres who'd greet us with "10,10 DeciBel" and the characteristic hand gesture which accompanied it. Our message was certainly getting across. All our team members knew that the 10–10 deadline *had* to be met.

Creative solutions to improve lateral communication
We'd created an identity, but we soon found ourselves struggling with a problem that identity in itself couldn't solve. Our organization had its roots in traditional, vertical departments, where staff were unused to communicating and working together. We were fighting a "silo mentality".

Creativity was a fast route to breaking down the barriers. Our quarterly review meetings formed the starting point of the change. We began the meetings conventionally enough with a serious review of milestones and the usual careful consideration of activities and risks. But after the formal review we'd make a shift to a more light-hearted approach, encouraging our teams to play a number of games. In each review the game would be different, but each game had the same goal: to encourage cross-fertilization, communication and co-operation between the different teams.

Teams would present each other in a humorous way. The technical team had to present the communications team, the communications team had to present the roll-out team and so on. Or teams had to play a crazy version of the guessing game "Who am I?" representing not people but the activities on the project. Teams played versions of the game *Pictionary* to represent themselves or their colleagues. And all these entertainments required the key quality we were promoting: intelligent, lively curiosity in what the other teams were doing.

The next challenge—encouraging coaching
Along with the "silo mentality" we inherited another common problem—that of the "little black book". Our staff were often reluctant to share their knowledge and expertise for fear of losing status and security in the

organization. Like the pilots who guided ships in the seventeenth century across uncharted waters, some of our team members guarded their own versions of the "little black book" very jealously. With such a defensive attitude they would never support the drive for cross-fertilization of ideas that was so important for our project. Our "silo mentality" was coupled with a "knowledge monopoly".

We tried another metaphor—that of the team as "super-organism". Our pool of 73 staff was like a super-organism that was approximately two and a half thousand years old. Think what a wise old creature this super-organism must be! We hammered the theme that together we had access to more than 500 years of experience. If we all thought of ourselves as one organism, rather than as lots of individuals, the potential synergy was huge.

We reassured our staff. 'There's nothing like coaching a colleague for making you clearer about the ideas yourself,' we said. Coaching makes you more of an expert—not less of one. We used a coaching model to give staff a structure to get going and to use their time as effectively as possible. We did lots of coaching ourselves, to model the method and to show that senior staff were happy to share their knowledge. We were also grateful recipients of coaching from our staff.

The concept of 'problem ownership'

The concept of "problem ownership" was quite new to the people on the project. Everybody wanted to achieve—but they didn't realize that they had to take the initiative to check that things really got done. For instance, they thought that if they sent out a memo to their colleagues from their computer about something, that they had fulfilled their responsibility. We had to explain to them that the memo was only a beginning—it was just a reminder to themselves that an action had been started, and that now they had to follow that action up until they were certain that it had been completed. We had to inculcate the "problem ownership" mentality if we were to achieve the tight time scales for the project.

First we introduced them to the term and kept repeating it with everyone we met in all our meetings together. It was like chipping away at a piece of wood. We also talked about "results paths", and offered examples all the time—like the memo story—to illustrate the concept. Whenever possible we actively looked for opportunities to coach our staff, and to model the behaviour. Slowly people started to take the concept on board, and it's really rewarding when they begin using the term and you hear it reflected back to you—that's when you start to see results. These are just some of the ways in which we managed to change the culture and help our staff to prove their full potential.'

Learning points

- *For a clear, bonding vision, use simple messages.* The more simply a message is expressed, as in 'the power of 10', the easier it is for people to remember.
- *Be creative.* The senior management team used games and a sense of fun to reinforce the key behaviours they wanted to promote.

- *Coach and model new behaviours.* It is not enough just to tell people what to do—you have to back the message up with demonstrations and examples.

Exploiting opportunities for change—coming in as a new manager

A good opportunity for implementing change in your team is when you first start in a new managerial post. Your arrival enables you to look at problems with a fresh eye, and to get moving quickly on the solutions. The next case describes how a manager used a workshop event as a vehicle for tackling a common problem experienced by many managers—that of interfunctional communication. Active co-operation between functions is essential for high-performing teams, but the reality in most organizations is very different. Lack of co-operation can take many forms, ranging from open hostility to the quiet sabotage underlying apparent compliance. History also plays an important role—people often have long memories for previous instances of poor service, and this can lead to a mistrust which is passed on to new joiners. Even in friendly cross-functional teams, as in the following case, there may be hidden criticisms and misunderstandings which impede smooth communication and prevent the team from achieving its full potential.

Alan, the manager in the following story, worked with Peter Callender of Balance Consulting Group in a 2-hour session, using some simple but effective procedures to surface potential areas of friction and to draw up an action plan which would enable the team to sort out problems and build on its existing strengths.

CASE STUDY 10.5   IMPROVING CROSS-FUNCTIONAL CO-OPERATION

Alan was responsible for a team of four managers and their staff, working for a major corporation in the fast-moving consumer goods business. Overall performance was good, but the team was interested to find out how they could make it even better.

Peter, the consultant, split the group into the four functional groups represented in the team: logistics, sales, marketing and public relations. Each group sat in a different location, and was given two stacks of coloured slips of paper. They were asked to send messages to the other groups about the services provided by them. Messages of appreciation—'What you do that I find helpful'—were to be written on the green slips. Messages of criticism—'What you do that I don't find helpful' were to be written on the pink slips. Each group was asked to ensure that they wrote roughly an equal number of green and pink messages, but they were free to write as many messages to each other as they wanted.

As they wrote, Peter picked up the messages and delivered them to the different groups. Their reactions were interesting—there was a lot of laughter, but also some disappointments, some indignation and some thoughtful silences. The messages became noticeably more candid (and more humorous) as the 30-minute message session progressed.

The next 30 minutes were spent on processing the messages. Each group was given flipchart paper on which to order and stick the messages. They were asked to select one example of a positive message, from any of the other three groups, which they particularly appreciated. Similarly, they were asked to select a piece of criticism which they felt was particularly significant, and to agree among themselves what action they could take to redress the situation and deal with the complaint. The output from this session was a 5-minute presentation of their reactions and action plan, which they would present to the whole group.

The presentations and ensuing discussion took the next hour. Some important underlying misunderstandings had been surfaced, together with some sensible ideas for resolving the problems. There had been messages of praise which had been much appreciated, but even in this basically harmonious team, the number of complaints outweighed the compliments. Here are some examples of the actions taken by the team.

The marketing group's action plan

Emma, the spokesperson, showed a green message: 'We really appreciate it when you involve us early in the marketing process.' Her team had been particularly pleased because they had been making an active effort to invite colleagues from other functions to key meetings, and this was confirmation that they should carry on with this approach.

The pink message read 'We give you an events plan, but we don't receive any updates from you—we have no idea what's going on.' There were related complaints of sudden changes which had occurred, with no explanation for the other functions. The marketing team proposed to give regular updates in the regular group meetings. 'We will also initiate discussions internally in our team to find ways of better anticipating these changes—we've got some ideas which we can share with you later,' Emma concluded.

The need for better information between the functions

The need for more information emerged from all the presentations which followed. Julie was the public relations manager. One complaint from another team had been 'Why does one part of the business [a particular product was named] get more press coverage than ours?' Julie realized that she needed to explain the target reader groups for the different publications, and the policy behind her press coverage strategy. 'I also need to show you what we can and cannot realistically achieve.' She agreed to visit the different functions over the next three months with a presentation for them.

Pippa, the logistics manager, realized that she needed to explain some of the internal constraints and processes she had to deal with, and gave a quick on-the-spot overview of some of the potential blockages. This was in response to a pink message that said 'We give you timely forecasts but still you have problems with stock.' She added that her department was now working with a new spreadsheet which would give them more up-to-date information and enable them to offer a faster service.

Toffael, the representative of the sales group, had been told 'Your team doesn't confirm promotions to us as far in advance as we'd like.' Again, he committed to sharing more information about the promotion process, and to involving his colleagues from other services earlier in the sequence of events leading to a promotion.

The session closed with a recap of action points together with the name of the person responsible and a deadline for completion of each action. The team agreed that the session had been very useful, and that they should complete a similar review inside the team in three months' time.

Learning points

- *Address problems early*—the longer you wait, the worse they get.
- *Balance criticism with praise*—it encourages teams to keep a sense of perspective about their colleagues, and also makes it easier for each team to accept the negative messages. It is also important for each group to start their presentation with a key compliment they have received, before addressing the complaints.
- *Move on briskly from the feedback session to the action planning*—your aim is to get commitment to change. By focusing on corrective action for one key piece of criticism, you are more likely to get practical results.

Taking it further—dealing with more serious problems

This section gives some ideas for running a longer session if you suspect that the intergroup problems are more serious.

If you are working with managers from other functions, you will need to ensure that they are all fully committed to the need for change. You must feel fully confident that this is the case before you organize the session, otherwise you could lose credibility. During the session itself you can debate among yourselves and your teams about the details of implementation, but each manager must make explicit his or her full support for the purpose of the session.

You could start by asking each group to draw up a matrix on a flipchart of their strengths and weaknesses as perceived by themselves and as perceived by the other functions. This would encourage openness and debate across the group. You could then move on to the green and pink slips exercise.

Ask each group to give explicit examples of problem areas, to back up their comments on the slips. Examples will prevent the negative feedback from becoming too personal. Insist that each group maintains a reasonable balance between praise and criticism.

To stimulate the action planning phase further, you could ask each group to give three suggestions for specific actions that the other functions could take in order to improve their service.

In a one-day session, aim to surface the problems in the morning and to work on resolving the problems in the afternoon. Check you do not get bogged down with complaints in the morning, however—it could make the atmosphere over lunch rather strained! One way of avoiding this problem is to share the initial suggestions for improvement in the last session before lunch, so that people could sit in mixed groups and discuss the options informally.

Consider mixing the groups cross-functionally in one of the afternoon sessions where the different options are being discussed, then using functional groups again for the final action plan discussions and presentations.

If you are nervous about safeguarding the atmosphere in the group as well as organizing the action points, you may find it helpful to work with an internal or external consultant who will manage this part of the process for you. In groups where the friction is not so intense, you could manage the day yourself. Some discomfort is inevitable if you are to make a real change, but you want the day to end on an optimistic and confident note.

Be realistic about the progress you can make. Any commitment to change, no matter how small, should be acknowledged and affirmed. People will be very concerned in meetings like these that 'our function shouldn't be making all the effort'. You may be better off with a small number of agreed actions from each group, rather than a very ambitious master plan, in order to set a firm foundation for improved co-operation in the future. You can always set a date for another meeting in which you continue working on problems and solutions.

Maintaining high performance in your team

So far we have considered a number of ways in which you can promote effective change. The last case in this chapter is a reminder of some of the principles of good management which should underpin any change. These principles provide the continuity that staff need as a backdrop to innovation and continuous improvement. Leadership styles vary widely according to personal preferences, but the clarity of vision and the friendly atmosphere described in the next story is one example of a winning formula.

CASE STUDY 10.6   'COLLEGIAL BUT COMPETITIVE'—
SYLVIA TÓTH AND CONTENT NV

Sylvia Tóth is chairperson of the management board of Content Beheer NV in Holland, which consists of over 76 temporary employment agencies and 1300 staff. Sylvia has been with Content since 1972, when she started by working as a 'temp' herself. She thinks that much of management has been overcomplicated by theory, and she has a very clear vision of how a large business should be run. Her philosophy for managing people, which she explained to me during a visit to her office, is a simple one: stress the need for high performance, and back it up with a warm atmosphere.

The emphasis on performance

■ *Content is very clear about its house rules*—'The clearer, the better,' Sylvia said. She pulled out a small brochure, outlining eight 'key points' which were clearly and simply expressed. If you were running a Content office, you would know exactly where you stood. Beyond the eight key points, staff are expected to take their own initiative, and decision-making has been delegated to the lowest level. Training is provided for newcomers, with video feedback sessions in the first few months to consolidate high standards. Staff get appraisals twice-yearly, and an interview in which their potential and future prospects are assessed once a year.

■ *The link between performance and reward is strong.* Content has a profit-sharing system, calculated per area and awarded every three months. Staff are initially recruited in a one-year contract—if they do not perform within that time, they have to leave.

■ *Sylvia has always been tough on performance.* In the 1970s, when the organization was very young, some of the staff in offices kept pets. As soon as Sylvia became a manager, she went round the offices to halt the practice. 'It's tempting to let the high-performers get away with bending the rules but you mustn't do it. They set the tone and the standard— they're the role models.'

■ *To promote high standards, teams are encouraged to compete against each other.* Sylvia showed an invitation to a company sports day, shortly to be held. The invitation announced that awards would be given for the Content bureau of the year. Teamwork is promoted above individual excellence. There was a Grand Finale, for instance, to be held in a secret location. The text in the brochure was 'We know that some people would like to practise in secret for this event in the Ardennes, that's why we've not given the location. Brains and humour are as important as muscle power, so this is a last chance to go for gold with your team!'

■ *Staff are kept on their toes.* 'There's no room for complacency. We're in a highly competitive business. We observe other organizations in the marketplace to find the one point where they may be stronger than we are. That's our clue for what to improve.' Sylvia expects fast reactions. 'I encourage my people to feed through their ideas—they're my eyes and ears. One out of ten ideas will be a winner. That's how we got into computer training in the mid-1980s, for instance, because someone noticed the growing need for people who were able to work with word processors. We've made a lot of money from these and other suggestions.'

A friendly atmosphere

Sylvia feels strongly that a focus on performance should be backed up by an emphasis on a warm and friendly atmosphere. 'Staff need money *and* attention.' She demonstrates this belief in a number of ways:

- *She is generous with compliments.* 'If a person's basic performance is up to scratch, you should work on people's strengths, not nag them about their weaknesses.' She gives compliments at the top of the organization, so that her senior staff—her 'culture role models' will do the same and the practice will filter down to the bottom of the organization. She makes it very clear that she is not using praise as a way of winning personal loyalty from her senior staff, but in order to set the example of the management style she wants to promote.
- *She believes firmly in the personal touch.* Sylvia's the kind of person who can happily do at least three activities at once, so she was working while I was interviewing her. At one point she interrupted the interview with an apology and rushed out of the room to order flowers for someone who had helped her with a favour that afternoon. 'You must show them you've noticed,' she said.
- *She is realistic about people's strengths and weaknesses*—including her own. 'You have to work round people's blind spots. I'm impatient—the organization has to work round that. If someone's good at sales, but bad at the financial preparation of bids, make them sales manager and give them financial support.' Contrast this with the 'blame culture' that so many people in the private and public sectors have to endure.
- *She treats her staff like her clients.* She invests a lot in the quality of her internal publications, for instance. 'Why should we design fine brochures for our external clients, and expect our own staff to be content with a photocopied sheet of A4?' She showed me a copy of the internal magazine—colourful and lively—and the invitation to the sports day mentioned earlier, which was on high-quality paper with cartoon illustrations and amusing text. It looked the kind of event that you really would not want to miss.

A place where people want to work hard

Sylvia has set up a culture which is challenging but also supportive—'It's a happy place to work in,' she said. 'People apply every day. Staff bring their friends and former colleagues into the organization. Women who have worked for us come back after they've had babies.'

After my interview, I realized I had forgotten to pick up an annual review from the head office in The Hague. Waiting for the traffic lights to turn at a cross-roads I spotted what must have been the nearest Content branch office on the opposite corner. I double-parked and rushed in with a rather confused request—conscious that I was late for my next appointment. The young man and woman were instantly helpful, and handed over a copy with a smile. It was a nice demonstration of the corporate culture which Sylvia had been describing—'fast, friendly and flexible'. Clearly her philosophy works.

Summary of moving groups forward and managing change

- *Involve key stakeholders* right from the start. Get their agreement at each stage of the change process. Check you have support of senior management.
- *Use procedures*, such as benchmarking to prove the need for change, and project management to tackle problems stepwise.
- *Remember that transition starts with an Ending.* Expect your staff to feel unhappy and unsettled, and use sensitive, realistic management approaches to help them adjust. Communicate over and over again, and give people time to talk to you.
- *Use temporary systems in the Neutral Zone.* Ask staff who have already adjusted to the change to take on organizational tasks and to help lead the change in your unit. Aim for small, fast successes.
- *A clear vision, creativity and careful modelling* by senior management can promote changes in the mindsets of your staff.
- *Use the window of opportunity when you are new to a job to implement changes.* Encourage your staff to set up their own action plans for improvements.
- *All change initiatives are easier for staff to accept if they take place in the context of consistently good management.*

Notes

The material on transitions is drawn from William Bridges (1991). See also Cormack (1995), Kanter (1983), Kotter, (1985), and Pfeffer (1994). I have stressed the point about personal interviews based on my own experience as a consultant.

Hadi Jassim's story is an extract from the article 'Project Management: A powerful tool for leading change' by H. Jassim and S. Craig, which appeared in the December 1996 version of the *Handboek Bestuurlijke Informatiekunde*. Reproduced with the permission of the publisher, Samsom BedrijfsInformatie bv.

The green and pink slips exercise is a classic organization development approach. There is a good demonstration of a more sophisticated version in the sixth video from the series *Transformation* with Richard T. Pascale, entitled *Conflict: The fuel of transformation*, available from BBC Executive Video Seminars, Woodlands, 80 Wood Lane, London W12 0TT.

Index